EURODOLLARS AND INTERNATIONAL BANKING

This volume is concerned with the nature of the Eurodollar market. It examines the historical evolution of Eurobanks and Eurodollars and offers an economic analysis of the Eurodollar market, a policy analysis of issues surrounding the Eurodollar and finally discusses the impact of international banking facilities.

The broader Eurocurrency market represents the most astonishing phenomenon in the modern world of finance because Eurocurrencies consist of bank deposits located in jurisdictions outside that of the currency of denomination. The Eurodollar market emerged in 1957 with transactions dominated mainly in dollars. By 1981 the volume of deposits had reached an estimated $1.6 trillion. The Eurodollar market will undoubtedly continue to play a major part in the equilibrium and disequilibrium of the financial world in years to come.

This collection draws on the practical knowledge of international bankers, the experience of prominent central bank officials and the analytical tools of academic observers of the market. Economists, as well as public policy-makers, share the view that banking systems, due to potential bank failures and the monetary role that banks play, deserve special regulation and the intervention of the monetary authorities. This book will be an important step towards understanding where the Euromarket came from, how it really operates now and where it will all end.

EURODOLLARS AND INTERNATIONAL BANKING

Edited by

Paolo Savona and
George Sutija

M
MACMILLAN

in association with
International Banking Center
Florida International University

First published 1985

Published by
MACMILLAN PUBLISHERS LTD
(Journals Division)
and distributed by
Globe Book Services Ltd
Brunel Road, Houndmills
Basingstoke, Hampshire RG21 2XS
and England

Filmset by Latimer Trend & Company Ltd, Plymouth

Printed in Hong Kong

British Library Cataloguing in Publication Data
Eurodollars and international banking.
1. Euro-dollar market
I. Savona, Paolo II. Sutija, George
III. Florida International University.
International Banking Center
332.4′5 HG3897
ISBN 0–333–36553–4

Contents

Preface vii
Notes on contributors ix

Introduction 1
Paolo Savona and George Sutija

Part I

1 Eurobanks, Eurodollars and International Debt 15
René P. Higonnet

Comment 52
Jane Sneddon Little
Rainer S. Masera
Helmut W. Mayer

Part II

2 Eurodollars: An Economic Analysis 77
Robert Z. Aliber

Comment 98
Peter M. Oppenheimer
Paolo Savona

3 The Interbank Market 111
Richard J. Herring

4 Eurocurrency Arbitrage 123
Ian H. Giddy

Part III

5 Eurodollars: Policy Analysis 139
Guido Carli

Comment 161
Charles A. E. Goodhart
Alexander K. Swoboda
Richard C. Williams

Part IV

6 International Banking Facilities and the Eurodollar Market 183
Henry S. Terrell and Rodney H. Mills, Jr

Comment 206
Patrick H. P. O'Sullivan
R. Roderick Porter
Jeffrey R. Shafer
George Sutija
Atsushi Watanabe

Note on the Permanent Advisory Committee on Eurodollars (PACE) 220

Name Index 221
Subject Index 223

Preface

The International Banking Center at Florida International University was created by the Board of Regents of the State University System as a 'centre of excellence' to promote international banking in the state of Florida. Among other activities the Center serves as a forum for discussion of international financial problems. In February, 1983 a conference on Eurodollars was held in Miami organised by the Center and sponsored by local banks under the chairmanship of Paolo Savona and George Sutija, editors of this volume.

The editors would like to express their gratitude to the authorities of Florida International University, President Gregory B. Wolfe and Provost Steven Altman as well as to the Director of the International Banking Center John M. Porges for the support received in the organisation of the conferences and the preparation of the manuscript.

The editors are particularly grateful to Dr Anna Maria del Prete from the Italian Ministry of Budget and Planning for advice and counsel and Mrs Rosa L. Padron from the International Banking Center for the enthusiasm, dedication and goodwill she always demonstrated in her work. Mr Juan Mario Sutija, student at Florida International University and Mr Davor Peter Sutija, student at the University of Pennsylvania did yeoman's work during the conference. Mr Robert Allan Schwarzreich, student at Florida International University assisted the editors in the preparation of the manuscript with his knowledge of international economics and editorial skills. Miss Francesca Ferrini typed the manuscript with great sense of humour and devotion.

The editors would also like to acknowledge their appreciation to the sponsors of the conference, namely, Bank America International, Bank of Tokyo, Chemical Bank International, Credit Suisse, Flagship Banks, Lloyds Bank International, Southeast Banking Corporation and Florida International Bankers Association and also, to the participants who have come from many parts of the world. To our colleagues, speakers at the conference and the authors of this volume, the editors express their deep sense of friendship and desire for future meetings and collaboration.

PAULO SAVONA
GEORGE SUTIJA

Notes on the Contributors

Robert Z. Aliber is Professor of International Finance at the University of Chicago. He was formerly Senior Economic Advisor to the Department of State, and a staff economist for the Committee for Economic Development and the Commission of Money and Credit. He has written extensively on exchange rates, gold and international financial relations. His publications include *The International Money Game, Monetary Reform and Inflation, National Monetary Policies and the International Financial System* and *Corporate Profits and Exchange Risk*.

Guido Carli is President of the European Confederation of Industries (UNICE) and serves as a senator in the Italian Parliament. He was formerly Governor of the Bank of Italy and the Minister of Foreign Trade. He was a member of the Board of Directors of the International Monetary Fund and held several other important positions. He has published extensively on problems of international economics, banking and trade.

Charles A. E. Goodhart is a chief adviser at the Bank of England. He taught at Cambridge University and at the London School of Economics in the field of monetary economics. He was, briefly, an Economic Adviser in the Department of Economic Affairs in London. He is the author of *Money, Information and Uncertainty*, and other books and articles, mostly on monetary economics and monetary history. He is widely known for his pioneering study on the relationship between macroeconomic developments and political popularity and he is the famous author of the 'Goodhart Law': any statistical regularity, notably in the monetary area, will break down when pressure is placed upon it for control purposes.

Ian H. Giddy is Associate Professor at Columbia University's Graduate School of Business. He served formerly as a financial economist at the Comptroller of the Currency and the Board of Governors of the

Federal Reserve System. He has written many articles on international banking, foreign markets and corporate international finance. Most recently he has co-edited the *International Money Market* and the *International Finance Handbook*.

Richard J. Herring is Associate Professor of Finance and Director of the Wharton Program in International Banking and Finance at the Wharton School of the University of Pennsylvania. He has also served as consultant for the US Department of the Treasury, the Council of Economic Advisors and the Bankers Trust Training Program. He has published several articles on international banking, balance of payments problems, capital controls, international influences on interest rates, and the foreign exchange and Eurocurrency markets. With Richard C. Marston, he has written a book entitled *National Monetary Policies and International Financial Markets*, and he has recently edited two books of essays commissioned in honour of the Wharton centenary, *Managing International Risk* and *Managing Foreign Exchange Risk*.

René P. Higonnet is Professor of Economics at the International University of Japan. He was formerly Director of the International Banking Center at Florida International University, and was an economist with the International Monetary Fund and the European Economic Commission. He has taught economics in France and the United States, and is the author of many articles on the problems of international monetary and banking relations.

Jane S. Little is an economist at the Federal Reserve Bank of Boston. She has been associated with the Bank for the last sixteen years. She is the author of the book *Eurodollars: The Money Market Gypsies*, as well as many articles on international finance and foreign direct investment.

Rainer S. Masera is head of the Research Department of the Bank of Italy, and a member of the G-10 Group of Deputies. He was formerly an economist with the Bank for International Settlements, and taught at the Universities of Bergamo and Rome. He was co-chairman (with Robert Triffin) of the Monetary Policy Group of the Center for European Policy Studies. He is the author of three books, *The Term Structure of Interest Rates, Government Deficit and Budget Constraint* and *Monetary Unification and the European Monetary System*, as well as numerous articles and essays on domestic and international monetary and financial economics.

Helmut W. Mayer is Assistant Manager with the Bank for International Settlements. He has been associated with the Bank for the last twenty years, working on international monetary relations, with special emphasis on international banking. He has served on various central-bank committees concerned with the Euro-Market, international banking statistics and the international co-ordination of banking supervision. In addition, he is the author of numerous publications in the field of international banking and exchange markets.

Rodney H. Mills Jr is a senior economist in the Division of International Finance at the Board of Governors of the Federal Reserve System. He has worked for the former Chase National Bank. He has published a number of articles on international finance.

Peter M. Oppenheimer is a Fellow in Economics at Christ Church, Oxford University. He was formerly on the staff of the Bank for International Settlements, and was visiting Professor at the London School of Business Studies. He serves on the Council of the Trade Policy Research Centre, London, and is a director of two investment trusts. He is a consultant to international organisations and business firms and has published extensively in the field of international economics and public policy.

Patrick H. P. O'Sullivan is North America Division Chief Financial Officer for the Bank of America in Los Angeles. He was formerly Vice-President of both the Bank's Miami and London branches. He was also head of the Bank's Airlines/Aerospace Group for its Europe, Middle East and Africa Divison.

R. Roderick Porter is a senior vice-president and manager of the Chemical Bank in New York City. He is responsible for domestic liability management, money market trading, international banking facilities and other North American Treasury operations. He was formerly the general manager of the Chemical Bank offices in Tokyo and later in London, and was the head of the Bank's North European regional office.

Paolo Savona is President of the Economic Council for Planning at the Ministry of the Budget and Economic Planning, and Head of the Italian Delegation at the OECD Economic Policy Committee. He is also President of Credito Industriale Sardo (a development bank in

Sardinia) and Professor of Economics and Finance at the Free University of Rome. He was formerly with the Central Bank of Italy, and was Director General of the Confederation of the Italian Private Industry. He has published two books, *International Liquidity* and *Monetary Sovereignty*, as well as numerous articles and essays on domestic and international monetary and financial economics.

Jeffrey R. Shafer is Vice-President for Research and Statistics at the Federal Reserve Bank of New York. He has been associated with the Federal Reserve System for the last twelve years. He taught economics at the Carnegie-Mellon, and Yale University and has published extensively in the field of international finance, particularly on exchange rates.

George Sutija is Associate Director of the International Banking Center and an Associate Professor of International Business and Banking at Florida International University. He was also Associate Dean and Chairman of the Department of Public Administration in the College of Business. He was formerly a Representative and Program Officer for the Ford Foundation in Latin America. He has published in the field of international management.

Alexander K. Swoboda is Professor of International Economics at the Graduate Institute of International Studies, Geneva, Professor of Economics at the University of Geneva, and the Director of the International Center for Monetary and Banking Studies. He has also taught at the University of Chicago, Johns Hopkins, the London School of Economics and at Harvard University. He is a leading authority in the field of international finance and has published numerous articles and edited several books. He is a regular participant in major international monetary and financial conferences.

Henry S. Terrell is the Chief of the International Banking Section, Division of International Finance at the Board of Governors of the Federal Reserve System. He has been associated with the Board for the last fifteen years. He has published extensively in the field of international finance and international banking.

Richard C. Williams is the Assistant Director in charge of International Capital Markets for the International Monetary Fund. He has headed missions to major financial market countries, and prepared reports on conditions and prospects in international capital markets. He worked formerly with the US Departments of the Treasury and State and has published several monographs, papers and articles on the problems of international finance.

Atsushi Watanabe is in charge of the Money Market Desk of the Funds and Investment Department of the Bank of Tokyo in New York City. He is responsible for funding activities of the New York Agency and its International Banking Facilities. He worked formerly with the Bank in Tokyo.

Introduction

PAOLO SAVONA and GEORGE SUTIJA

This volume is concerned with the nature of the Eurodollar market. The broader Eurocurrency market represents the most astonishing phenomenon in the modern world of finance because Eurocurrencies consist of bank deposits located in jurisdictions outside that of the currency of denomination. Economists, as well as public policy-makers, share the view that banking systems, due to potential bank failures and the monetary role that banks play, deserve special regulation and the intervention of the monetary authorities.

The Eurocurrency market is not a banking system in itself but rather an extension of the major countries' domestic banking systems. The major banks participating in the domestic and the offshore wholesale banking markets are the same, the currency is the same and the depositors and borrowers are largely the same. It is, therefore, not surprising that the ability of this market to avoid certain regulations has aroused the concern of the world's monetary and banking authorities. It is not so much the size of the market which makes it important, but rather the innovation it has brought, such as Eurodeposits, Euroloans and a host of other monetary transactions. The market is also important for its effects on domestic banking systems, on domestic monetary policies, and perhaps on inflation, interest rates and the distribution of credit.

The Eurodollar market emerged some time in 1957 with transactions denominated mainly in dollars, and by 1981 the volume of deposits had reached an estimated $1.6 trillion. The Eurodollar market will undoubtedly continue to play a major part in the equilibrium and disequilibrium of the financial world in years to come. In this collection of papers we draw on the practical knowledge of international bankers, on the experience of prominent central bank officials, and on the analytical tools of academic observers of the market. They examine the historical evolution of Eurobanks and Eurodollars and offer an economic analysis of the Eurodollar market, a policy analysis of issues surrounding the Eurodollar, and finally discuss the impact of international banking facilities.

The first paper by René Higonnet 'Eurobanks, Eurodollars and International Debt' follows an essentially eclectic historical approach indicating problems, both past and present. Higonnet sees lack of accurate information on Eurodollars, relaxation of strict banking practices and imprudent and unsound banking policies as major reasons for the current crisis. While Higonnet believes that there is little cause for surprise in the behaviour of commercial banks in the Eurodollar market, it is another matter to explain why central banks have been so kind to this market. He cites episodes that show clearly that when the volume of international liquidity is vast and growing without controls, central banks find it increasingly difficult to control the liquidity of their respective banks and economies, as well as the rate of growth of the national money supplies. He argues that the Euromarket has made monetary management far more difficult at the national and international level. Higonnet suggests reform and states that there are three major points to be addressed. First, better accounting practices, and elimination of fictitious banking profits through realistic loan-loss provisions. Second, regulation of foreign lending, especially to countries with a history of default. Third, adequate supervision of all offshore banking centres. Finally, Higonnet raises the point that since the largely unsupervised foreign banking in the Euromarket has resulted in some degree of crisis, why not adopt measures that are so readily available?

The reaction by the three discussants Jane Little, Rainer Masera and Helmut Mayer was one of strong disagreement with several points made by Higonnet. Little indicates that although Eurobanks are relatively free from regulations, it does not mean that they are unsupervised. Further, that progress towards a co-ordinated and co-operative approach to surveillance of the international banking system is being made. She questions Higonnet's optimism regarding the ease with which non-distorting control could be placed on the Eurodollar market, given the significantly different approaches towards banking regulation held in various countries. Rainer Masera criticises Higonnet's suggestion on the need to check the growth of the Euromarkets by setting reserve requirements at an identical level for all Eurobanks irrespective of currency denomination. He does so on two grounds. First, the abolition of competitive advantage would also require the integration of internal methods and tools of control in all the major countries, and second, Higonnet's plan would, in fact, place different burdens on each of the currencies, depending on the existing spreads on interest rates. Masera suggests that the explanation of the growth of the Eurodollar market may be found in a general equilibrium worldwide portfolio model of financial intermediation. These are the relevance and interactions of inherent competitive advantages and the efficiency of Eurobanks themselves in spurring financial innovation and that the net demand for Eurocurrency deposits has been primarily related to world trade and worldwide payments imbalances. Although not laying the blame on imprudent policies of commercial banks for the current state of affairs, he, in any case, concludes by saying that we are now moving along a narrow and dangerous path. Helmut Mayer finds a balanced overall view of international banking and its past development missing in Higonnet's essay. He indicates that three general features emerge. They are: a heterogeneous set of influences which have been responsible for the rapid growth of the Euromarket, the highly polyvalent character of the market; and finally, the use of the Euromarket by the official sector as a source of balance of payments and development finance. As did Jane Little, he questions Higonnet's optimism in regard to implementation of banking control mechanisms and further states on the microeconomic level such controls are already in place or in the process of being put into place. However, on the macroeconomic level, the extension of domestic instruments to the banks' international business would be more difficult. In conclusion, he believes, in sharp contrast to Higonnet, that international bank lending will continue to have an important role to play in balance of payments and development finance, although on a somewhat more modest scale and in a more co-ordinated way than in the past.

Robert Aliber's paper 'Eurodollars: an Economic Analysis' focuses on the institutional basis for the development of the offshore market as well as the impacts of the growth of the offshore market on various economic factors. He indicates that the major institutional feature that explains the growth of Euromarkets in bank deposits is differential regulation of financial transactions. Further, that the difference in reserve requirements mean that costs of 'producing' deposits are lower in offshore banking centres than in domestic banking centres. In discussing the expansion of the Eurodollar system and competition within the banking industry, Aliber notes that although the US banking industry was not deregulated until 1980, none the less the expansion of US banks represents informal and partial approach to deregulation. This informal approach to deregulation permits banks with 'excess capital' to expand more rapidly, much as if deregulation had taken place domestically. This, in turn, results in increased competition among banks for deposits denominated in the major currencies. He analyses the monetary implications of offshore deposits and states that from the viewpoint of monetary analysis, the location of offshore banks is irrelevant; the only relevant phenomena is that they are subject to a lower level of required reserves. Therefore, the effective reserve requirements in the dollar area is lower. Another factor presenting difficulties for monetary control is that the evidence suggests that the growth of offshore deposits is not predictable and is also quite large. The growth of the Eurodollar system has been associated with a significant increase in money and credit, with the multiplier in the dollar credit system higher than might be inferred from the required reserve ratio for domestic deposits. Aliber concludes with the three observations. First, the probable impact of the growth of offshore deposits on the foreign exchange value of the dollar is modest because any increase in offshore deposits in any period is small relative to the total stock of dollars. Second, there exists no offshore banking system as a system, rather there are offshore extensions of several national banking systems. Third, assuming the growth of offshore deposits is primarily a result of differential regulation, then the regulatory implications are that incentives for shifting from domestic deposits to offshore deposits should be reduced or eliminated.

The discussants, Peter Oppenheimer and Paolo Savona, are in general agreement with much of what Aliber expressed. In particular, Oppenheimer accepts three central contentions of the Aliber paper; however, two factors which are equally important are under-emphasised. They are the significance of the interbank market in transmitting information and thus lowering transaction costs, and the specifically international nature of much of the market's activity. Thus, in the interbank network, international bankers have found a highly effective device for increasing the fluidity of global credit flows. Oppenheimer objects to Aliber's multiplier approach not on the grounds that it is wrong, so much as it is unhelpful. In concluding Oppenheimer notes that regulation in some form is necessary for stability, yet in a market system paradoxically regulation tends to spawn deregulated centres. Paolo Savona proposes five major points he considers vital for consensus analysis of decisions in the field of Eurobusiness. One, understanding the offshore monetary transaction is possible only within a framework of a general equilibrium or disequilibrium portfolio model. Two, many different active forces determine the volume of offshore business in the framework of a general equilibrium portfolio model. Three, the world money multiplier is higher in the presence of an offshore market than in its absence. Four, although the influence of the offshore market on exchange rates is modest in the long run, it is relevant in the short run. Fifth, the influence on inflation due to offshore markets is yet to be understood; none the less, it is clear that offshore credit activities affect the world supply schedule of real goods. Savona objects to Aliber's views which limit the explanation of offshore markets to institutional features, rather he includes the autonomous need for international money which results from the needs of world trade, and the need for higher levels of financial information. The Euromarket is the response to these needs, not merely the result of institutional factors. In addition, Savona objects to the idea contained within Aliber's paper that the creation of domestic reserve base is influenced by the existing offshore markets. Rather, his analytical position on this issue is that the discrepancy between savings and investment schedules is influenced by offshore markets which, in turn influence the supply schedule of real goods. In concluding, Savona emphasises that the concept of international monetary base is very useful in forecasting the likely future development of the Eurodollar market and in giving a theoretical explanation out of 'adhockeries'.

Richard Herring's paper 'The Interbank Market' stresses the importance of this market, pointing out that the Euromoney market is fundamentally an interbank market. Further, he questions the prevalence of the practice of netting out interbank activity in most economic analysis and indicates that this market serves several economic functions. The first and fundamental function of the market is to redistribute liquidity on a global basis between economic units having surpluses and those having deficits. The question of how or why these liquidity adjustments take place in the interbank market is explained in the paper. First, in general, some banks will have an advantage in soliciting deposits from non-banks. Second, other banks may have a special advantage in making loans to non-banks. Third, the interbank market is a very efficient mechanism for economising on transaction costs. Fourth, credit transformation, currency transformation and maturity transformation will probably take place in varying degrees along the interbank chain. This interbank chaining of deposits permits different banks to specialise in different functions and transformations and as a consequence may permit the intermediation between non-banks to take place more efficiently. It is this increase in efficiency of intermediation which is the primary contribution of the interbank market to the world economy. The second major function of the interbank market is to facilitate the management of foreign exchange and maturity positions. Essentially, the interbank market provides an efficient means for managing both the foreign exchange and interest rate risks. The third major function of the interbank market is in facilitating the avoidance of taxes, constraints and other frictions in the domestic money markets, a point well emphasised by Aliber. An essential feature of these arbitrage transactions is that domestic transactions are channelled through foreign offices in order to avoid domestic regulations. Herring raises some policy concerns arising from interbank activity, namely; the erosion of the national regulatory and fiscal policies that the market facilitates; that in times of stress the same channels that so efficiently transmit funds from surplus to deficit units can also transmit shocks; and the possibility of contagion demands that each country take an interest in the quality of supervision and the availability of the lender of last resort facilities in other countries.

Ian Giddy's paper 'Eurocurrency Arbitrage' argues that an understanding of arbitrage between the domestic and offshore markets and among the different segments of the Eurocurrency market, would go a long way towards eliminating incorrect models of the Eurocurrency market. And as a result, inappropriate policy prescriptions would be eliminated. In particular he suggests that analysis of the Eurocurrency market must focus on two sets of relationships: one, the link between a rational credit market and its external segment; and two, the connection between two or more segments of the Eurocurrency markets denominated in different currencies. He further indicates that the Eurodollar market is an integral segment of the total market for dollar credit, with interest rates in all segments determined simultaneously, while the different currency segments of the Euromarket are perfectly integrated due to the forward exchange market. The tensions created by these two sets of influences may be reconciled in one of two ways: one, through integration of the international money market; and two, through segmentation of the international money market, for instance, by imposing capital controls that insulate the money market. There are essentially two strands of thinking among those who believe that arbitrage determines the relation between domestic and offshore interest rates. The first point of view is that of the market-price-of-risk, which holds that the Eurodollar deposit rate should lie above the domestic rate by a level given by the risk premium demanded by depositors. The alternative view is the cost of regulation theory, that the Eurodollar premium is solely determined by regulatory costs, for example, taxes and reserve requirements. Giddy, in contrast to the above approach seeks to impose the true arbitrage condition, which makes no assumption about the existence of loan portfolios whose funding could be rearranged. In developing a model Giddy adopted Kreicher's 'arbitrage tunnel' for an examination of arbitrage incentives. In concluding, Giddy makes several important points. First, he states that domestic and Euromarket interest rates in the same currency are linked in a fairly mechanical way through the relative cost of regulations faced by banks issuing deposits in the two sets of markets of which the logical implication is that change in risk perception and other factors will not influence the Eurodollar premium. Second, as the US money market expands so will the Euromarket, thus, if perceived risks of the Eurodollar relative to domestic deposits diminish, there will be a rightward shift of depositors' supply curve and the market will grow proportionately. Third, the Eurodollar market has expanded more rapidly than the domestic market not because of some magic multiplier, but because of greater familiarity and declining perceived risk on the part of depositors.

Guido Carli's 'Eurodollars: Policy Analysis' offers us a wide ranging and rather comprehensive paper on the Eurodollar market. He discusses the historical development of policy issues, problems in regulation and supervision, problems in lending of last resort, the question of an international standard and finally current difficulties in international lending. In examining the history of policy decisions, Carli indicates that it is clear that the issues of regulation at the national level and supervision at the international level have dominated the debate on the Eurodollar market on the part of the authorities. Furthermore, any sort of global indirect regulation of the Eurodollar problems was totally lacking. He suggests that at least three factors underlie the inability of the authorities to implement a system of regulation and supervision of the Eurocurrency market. First, the persistence of the ideas of the 'banking school' at the international level with their view that growth in the credit system is a self-regulating process. The second factor is the practice of monetary sovereignty at the national level and third, the confusion in the theory of international money and its excessive compliance with vested interests. Taking a look at current thinking on lending of last resort, Carli notes that the choices of the monetary authorities are influenced by the idea that either the market or the national authorities have to deal with this problem, as there is no such thing as an international banking system. He indicates the desirability for some international rules regarding lender of last resort. However, the three previously mentioned constraints which prevented systematic regulation also hinder prompt and effective lending of last resort. Carli indicates that the real risk exists when a debtor country reduces current imports to repay its debt because imports are essential to the development of both the exporting and the importing country. The banking risk, which is the possibility of insolvency of the debtor country, is often treated independently of the real risk. This insolvency risk of a country is two-pronged. The extremely rapid real adjustment imposed by the United States and the laxity of credit by international banks to LDCs. He suggests that once the size of the real problem has become apparent, its solution can only lie in the recovery of international trade that will prevent insolvency. He remarks that the lack of an explicit set of rules to control the international standard led to the conditions of a tight domestic control of the money supply, and then to a strong dollar on the international markets. It is, therefore, necessary to go back to the original concept behind the Bretton Woods Agreement, but not necessarily to its implementation.

The three discussants, Charles Goodhart, Alexander Swoboda and Richard Williams invariably found Carli's paper to be comprehensive in scope and rich in analytic insight. None the less, they each found areas in which they had differences with him. Charles Goodhart begins by questioning Carli's belief that the current absence and present need of a lender of last resort in the Euromarket is almost self-evident. As an illustration of his view, he points to the Banco Ambrosiano case where the need to sort out and establish responsibility would remain at least as important and as complicated even if there was some international central banking or stabilisation body. In addition, he questions Carli's suggestion in regard to regulation of monetary base because the practical problems of imposing monetary base control within a system in which funds can be deposited not only in any market but any currency, would be severe. Indeed, before considering whether the Euromarkets need any additional regulation Goodhart indicates that it would be helpful to analyse shortcomings of which they are accused. In regard to Euromarkets being an independent source of more rapid world monetary growth and being partly responsible for bringing about the current indebtedness problem, he finds both these claims to be exaggerated. In conclusion, he notes that supervision and regulation are not exactly the same thing, and that on the supervisory front much progress has been made. Further, that although establishing yet another supra-national official body would not necessarily make international agreements on banking practice easier to obtain, this, however, does not mean that central banks should not try to come to some agreement on what does represent good banking practice in international markets. Swoboda in discussing regulation of Eurocurrency markets states some standard arguments. First, he suggests that there is no good reason why the market should be regulated on the grounds of efficiency. Second, the Eurocurrency markets are viewed as interfering with domestic monetary control, and creating liquidity and solvency problems that threaten the stability of the world banking and financial system as a whole. In spite of this Swoboda does not think that regulation is the solution to these problems. He strongly agrees with Carli that lack of a clearly defined international standard is, indeed, at the root of many current problems of the world economy. However, on the question of the desirable exchange rate regime is where he takes issue with Carli's views on international monetary organisation. He indicates that there is some attempt of going back to a form of the 'stable but adjustable parities' system which cannot, on a realistic basis, be achieved in the long run. He then focuses attention on threats to the stability of the international financial system arising from the sharp rise in the volume of non-performing loans held by a large number of banks. He indicates that changes in the economic environment, at least in the late 1970s, were largely unexpected and are undoubtedly responsible for turning some good loans *ex ante* into bad assets *ex post*. However, their effect has been compounded by a number of other factors. First, the concentration of lending to a few large sovereign borrowers is a new element. Second, the prevalence of syndicated loans in banks' portfolios makes it difficult to price risk efficiently. Third, the perceived riskiness of loans to banks was lowered by implicit or explicit guarantees. This third factor has also created some important distortions in the flow of international lending. Swoboda concludes with some policy implications. In regard to the efficient transfer of resources from surplus to deficit areas he remarks that markets are ideally suited and that distortionary incentives should be removed on both efficiency and stability grounds. Finally, the soundness of the international banking system should be the purview of supervisory authorities. They would, however, be greatly helped in this direction by stronger market discipline, correct pricing of risk and the removal of distorting incentives. Richard Williams in discussing Carli's paper touches on but one theme, namely, that the system has given rise to a serious misallocation of private capital and a possibly inescapable debt trap for the developing world, with potentially very serious systematic effects. Despite the extent of serious strains in the world economy, the evidence suggests that the problem can be overcome by a co-operative effort of all involved. In the case of debt servicing problems, co-ordinated action among the International Monetary Fund, the monetary authorities of creditor countries and commercial banks can play a major role. The important thing is that the difficult situations which arise be worked out effectively and on a timely basis. Sometimes this has required that the banks involved be willing to continue to increase their exposure and that their central banks do not impede this process. In conclusion, he remarks that it is important that the bank supervisory authorities do not over-react and introduce new constraints in an abrupt manner.

In their paper 'International Banking Facilities and the Eurodollar Market', Henry Terrell and Rodney Mills integrate IBFs into the analysis of the Eurodollar market. They raise several questions: Has a greater proportion of international banking activity been shifted to the United States? Have IBFs improved the competitive position of US banks? Have IBFs resulted in observable change in interest rate relationships? Terrell and Mills found that banks located in the United States in December 1982 held 21 per cent of total international banking assets, while just fourteen months prior, that is, before the inception of IBF facilities, they held 15 per cent of these external bank assets. On the basis of this, they conclude that the establishment of IBFs has resulted in an increase in the share of international bank intermediation conducted in the United States. While the establishment of IBFs has extended the geographical scope of the Eurocurrency markets, this should not necessarily be expected to increase the global volume of combined international and domestic banking activity. However, the expanded opportunities for unregulated international banking transactions may induce a shift from the domestic to the international sphere. Terrell and Mills designed a simple statistical test of that hypothesis and concluded that, to date, IBFs have not stimulated the growth of external banking assets. To induce foreign customers to shift deposits from regulated domestic accounts to IBFs, banks must pay slightly higher rates on IBF deposits than are paid on deposits at non-IBF domestic offices. Clearly banks will have the leeway to pay higher rates on deposits at IBFs because these deposits do not bear the costs of reserve requirements and FDIC insurance. The authors indicate that the empirical evidence of the impact of IBFs on interest rate differentials is inconclusive, and, in fact, other factors seem to have had a much more important impact on the differentials. In conclusion, Terrell and Mills indicate that IBFs have not altered the international banking scene to any significant extent, except by drawing a larger slice of international financial intermediation to the United States. And that in fact IBFs are probably best viewed as a small step in the general deregulation of banking.

While all the discussants are in agreement with Terrell and Mills that IBFs have not changed international banking in the first year of their existence, they approach the topic from markedly different perspectives. Patrick O'Sullivan offers us in his own explanation of why IBFs have not yet had their anticipated impact. He states that although New York IBFs have over $100 billion of deposits, the only real switch has been from one set of books to another. And since neither a different cost structure nor availability would be attached to these loanable funds, new borrowers would not be attracted into the market. Furthermore, the Federal Reserve System imposed restraints on IBFs to prevent them from domestic borrowing, lending and investing. The author indicates that, in their present form, IBFs offer only a different sovereign risk for depositors and that there is no other reason for other offshore depositors to move into IBFs. In a very brief set of remarks, Roderick Porter states that although IBFs have marginally improved the competitive position of several major cities in the US as international banking centres, in time, that should create a halo effect which in turn should improve the competitive position of US banks. Jeffrey Shafer approaches the issue of IBFs from the broader perspective of current trends in international banking and in international bank regulations. The introduction of IBFs means that a growing share of banking activity in the US is devoted to servicing the needs of non-residents. This cross-border banking is due to regulatory distortions. However, trends in the direction of cross-border banking like the IBFs should not be of major concern. What is of far greater concern are the potential problems for the conduct of monetary policy both domestically and internationally, as central banks have less control over money and money-like liabilities relevant to price stability in their economy. Shafer indicates that banking regulation could move either in the direction of greater regulation of international banking or domestic regulation could be reduced. He sees the optimum path as embracing both directions, for he is convinced that we will always have a need for some regulation for monetary control, however, this is not meant to justify all current regulations. Shafer indicates two general principles that could serve as guides to central banks' decision-making concerning regulation in the years ahead. First, a central bank should not establish regulations affecting its banks that favour business conducted in other currencies over its own currency of issue. Second, a central bank should not establish regulations for its banks that favour business conducted with non-residents over business conducted with residents. Although IBFs regulations are not in accord with the latter of these principles, they are, none the less, consistent with the longer run movement towards greater consistency. Finally, Shafer states that a stable situation will only be reached when there is greater consistency in the rules applying to domestic and IBF deposits, and when foreign central banks have moved towards less discriminatory regulatory structures. George Sutija examines recent developments of international banking in the state of Florida, particularly in the city of Miami which has become a fast growing international financial centre. He cites the reasons for the drastic increase of foreign bank deposits, legal and illegal, and international banking activities due to trade, travel, tourism, educational and health facilities, and investments in real estate, industry and commerce. Most of these activities are related to Latin American economic developments, particularly in some countries like Venezuela. He describes the level of activity of IBFs in local banks during the period of time that they have been permitted to operate. Atsushi Watanabe primarily limits his remarks to IBFs and Japanese banks. He indicates that the inter-IBF market continues to be a primarily Japanese bank market. In addition, he states that IBFs should be authorised to compete without constraints with the Euromarket in order to serve as a catalyst for increased participation and activity. He suggests that the establishment of a Japanese IBF should be considered within a framework of general deregulation and should continue to develop at a moderate pace.

Part I

1 Eurobanks, Eurodollars and International Debt

RENÉ P. HIGONNET[1]

INTRODUCTION: PRESENT PROBLEMS

The present paper is a companion piece to my 'Latin American Debt: More Rescheduling?', an essay prepared for the conference organised by Florida International University (February 1982) on 'Foreign Debt and Latin American Economic Development'.[2]

That paper, which included a short history of Latin American debt, announced, correctly as it turned out, that Latin America would default in the near future on its external debt, and tried to explain why. Latin America always has been a graveyard for bankers.[3] In the early 1980s, Latin American countries, as well as several developing countries in other parts of the world, were, by any conceivable criteria (ratio of debt to GNP, exports, etc.) heavily and dangerously over-indebted. Irving S. Friedman describes the reluctance to see things as they are:

> Unfortunately, until lenders reduce lending to a borrowing country, warning signs can be pushed aside and neglected. Lending itself ameliorates the situation and makes an otherwise unacceptable situation tolerable. This, however, cannot last, unless the reasons for the warning signals disappear. When lenders reduce or stop lending, crises result. Crises seem to come unexpectedly. They usually do not. There are warning signs.[4]

Friedman's observation, based on a long and rich experience of analysing foreign debt, is also true of the generalised default of 1982. This was not an unforeseeable event, sometimes called a 'systemic' event. It was preceded by numerous warning signals pushed aside and neglected. These were especially numerous and strong in the case of Mexico, a country whose default in mid-year 1982 started the chain of defaults and which, as an important producer of oil, certainly did not suffer from deteriorating terms of trade brought about by the restrictive economic policies of the industrialised countries. They had appeared on an almost daily basis in the financial press for several years before default: failure of exports other than oil products, poor results in the tourism industry, substantial expenditure by Mexicans abroad, vast capital exports, etc. ... The difficulties of Argentina and Brazil – to name but the largest debtor countries – and their causes, had also been notorious for a long time.

The OECD Annual Review of the United States, dated November 1979, shows that over the period 1971–9, the US *ex-post* real savings deposit rate was, on the average, below zero.[5] This is an extraordinary figure, and it is a surprise that negative rates did, in fact, last so long. This failure of the US authorities to raise real interest rates to positive values allowed for the progress of inflation and the degradation of the dollar exchange rate. There was hardly any possibility that the United States would have everlasting negative real rates of interest. When these interest rates, as well as those of the Eurodollar market, would some day become positive, possibly at a high level, the foreign debt would become unbearable as: (a) the real burden of the debt rises substantially, (b) the volume and prices of the debtor countries' exports, primarily basic commodities, are usually adversely affected. Their terms of trade deteriorate.

The only question was when would interest rates rise, by how much would they go up, and for how long would the monetary stringency last. But, when foreign indebtedness has, in countries with a record of systematic default, risen by leaps and bounds to hitherto unheard of levels, even a mild and short-lived monetary stringency may be enough to bring about generalised default. This is particularly so when lax inflationary policies, together with unrealistic fixed rates of exchange, can and do bring about external deficits of virtually unlimited size.

In such circumstances, many banks which have consistently underestimated the sovereign risk in lending to LDC countries (which never disappear), and over-estimated the ability and willingness of their respective monetary authorities to bail them out, are then left with a significant proportion of dubious assets. The rescue operations of the IMF, if and where successful, will perhaps bail them out in time, that is, when the payments position of debtor countries improves. However, at the present time they are rather bailed in as they are forced to contract further loans. This, in some cases, may turn out to be sending good money after bad. There are countries which, after accepting the IMF medicine, cannot, or will not, carry out the policy changes agreed upon.

Yet few of the larger banks, in the United States and the United Kingdom, have created substantial loan-loss reserves. Banks known to be in a delicate position announce hefty increases in profits and increase dividends.[6] Indeed, the larger the volume of non-performing loans which must be rescheduled, at a substantially higher spread over Libor, the higher the accounting profits. Pride of place should perhaps go to Citicorp. The following is from the *Financial Times* of 16 March 1983:

> Brazil has long been Citicorp's most profitable overseas operation, but, in 1982, the group's local operations excelled themselves ... Citicorp's Brazilian ... income before taxes and securities transactions rose 54 per cent to 287 million dollars ... Citicorp's average assets in Brazil grew by 11.3 per cent to 5.6 billion dollars, and its return on assets rose by a quarter to 2.74 per cent. Based on this measure, Brazil is five times as profitable as the rest of Citicorp's operations.[7]

The British clearing banks have adopted the same stance. The following is from the *Economist*, 19–25 March 1983:

> The big four British clearing banks have satisfied themselves that there is no real risk of a Latin American country defaulting. So they have set aside next to nothing from their 1982 profits against such a possibility. All their results are bizarre ... Despite tax guidelines earlier this year, which opened up the possibility that provisions against sovereign loans could be specific and, therefore, tax-deductible, the banks are believed not to be making specific provisions against Latin American sovereign debts.[8]

All four banks have decided to increase dividends. Although banks shy away from the disclosure of relevant statistical comparisons, the *Financial Times* has published some estimates[9] of overseas problem loans (Table 1.1).

Loss making via poor risks becomes a profit centre of a sort: the more a bank manager must reschedule, the more he is found wanting, the more, however paradoxically, he appears as a financial genius who should remain in office. Whereas those bank managers who do not have to reschedule under duress should, by such standards, be

TABLE 1.1 *Problem exposures overseas year-end 1982*

Bank	*As per cent of total assets*	*As per cent of group equity*
Citicorp	7.5	204
Bank America	5.6	148
Chase Manhattan	7.1	177
Barclays	n/a	n/a
Midland	7–8	218–244
Lloyds	n/a	n/a

dismissed for failure to bring in these 'profits'. During this time of deteriorating asset values, the banks need, in the words of Mr Peter Cooke, the Bank of England's chief regulator, 'to consider the appropriateness of the maximum possible retention of profit to reinforce capital resources, if necessary at the expense of liberal distribution policies'.[10]

Possibly the banks in several countries have little incentive to increase loan-loss reserves because of the tax system. In the United States loan-loss reserves are presently deductible only up to 1 per cent of 'eligible' loans, as against 2.4 per cent during the 1930s, and most banks are close to their permissible maximum.[11] In Japan, the ministry of finance denies to the banks tax relief on provisions against possible loan-losses overseas with respect to some twenty foreign borrowers. In other words, the banks are to make these provisions out of after-tax profits. According to a Japanese commentator, 5 per cent reserves on such bad debts would horrify Japanese banks because they are at a level tending to wipe out net profits of 1981–2.[12]

Although representatives of central banks have pointed out that banking supervision has of late been strengthened substantially, and there is no reason to doubt this, yet this is some distance away from reports recently published in the financial press.[13] It would appear that:

(1) Some international banks are still largely unsupervised. Bank secrecy laws in some offshore centres prevent domestic banking supervisors from gaining access to complete information about banks' operations in those places.
(2) The ability of bank supervisors to monitor the affairs of banks on a global basis by looking at consolidated accounts differs widely from country to country.
(3) A growing number of banks operating in the international markets

are headquartered in developing countries where supervisory standards are often more lax than in industrialised countries. Over 100 of the world's top 500 banks come from non-OECD countries. Furthermore, bank supervisors have no common approach on definitions, methods, standards, limitations and rules.

Mr Lamberto Dini, director general of the Bank of Italy, is well aware of this situation:

> The soundness of the international banking system . . . requires more uniform and effective supervisory action in the various financial centres, and more far-reaching cooperation among the responsible authorities. For the time being, one useful instrument consists of authorizations that would allow banks to expand in centres that provide adequate supervision and are willing to cooperate internationally.[14]

The simple device of denying to banks the permission to expand where supervision is inadequate could and should have been adopted long ago.

These problems and difficulties have substantially changed our view of the Eurocurrency markets. Only a year ago, the main concern expressed in the literature was the extent to which an uncontrolled monetary creation contributed to world inflation. What we are facing today is the possibility, though not the certainty, of an international banking crisis, through the default of some Eurobanks. Whether this crisis will take place or not depends on such factors as economic recovery in the US, changes in the price of energy, the rate of growth of international trade, and the promptness of the monetary authorities in preventing incipient panics, if any. We must face the consequences of bankers' imprudence during a surprisingly long period of negative real rates of interest in the dollar region, as well as in other regions. A realistic assessment is that of Dr Masera, of the Bank of Italy, formulated in 1980:

> The prudential aspect of the Euromarkets is the one that deserves more attention and more immediate consideration: the combination of maturity transformation and sovereign risk in a world payments system characterized by sizeable and lasting imbalances, and by the large inherited debt positions of many countries, suggests that risks incurred by the Eurobanks may be high and their position vulnerable.[15]

There has taken place a relaxation of discipline in the behaviour of many commercial banks, too often unchecked by the supervising monetary authorities. Of course, the banks had been under pressure from industrial exporters, anxious to see them finance their exports, and from governments, anxious to limit their financial contributions to LDC countries. Governor Guido Carli reminded us that, at the Venice summit, the heads of state of the seven most industrialised countries did assign to commercial banks a major role in the recycling process. This is true, but is no excuse. The banks alone must bear the responsibility of their own lending decisions.

The reluctance of the banking profession everywhere to provide systematic, thorough and periodic information on its stocks and flows, its activities and position, has always been notorious. Monetary authorities often show a similar reluctance to divulge some types of information, such as the extent of their intervention in the exchange markets. By way of explanation for their silence they offer the lame excuse that they must not feed panics and must maintain freedom of action. What is needed is not only more detailed information, such as a detailed breakdown of assets and liabilities according to maturity, geographical areas, lines of business, etc. . . . but also guidance concerning the treatment and analysis of this information. For example, should a management or participation fee be immediately included in profit when collected, or should it be spread over the life of the loan?[16]

An institute has been recently created in Washington by several large banks in order to improve the information available to banks on economic and financial developments in debtor countries. This is no doubt a worthwhile function, but another one would be to supply more information to the public about the banks.

The lack of accurate information is most remarkable in the case of Eurodollars. No one really knows the volume of outstanding Eurodollars, an eye opener to the fact that supervision of Eurobanks is of an unsatisfactory nature. If the same degree of supervision existed on Eurobanks in offshore centres as exists at home in say, France or the United Kingdom, then there would be fairly reliable data available, which, in point of fact, do not exist now.

Net Eurodollars at the end of June 1982 were estimated by the BIS at 965 billion dollars.[17] This is to be understood as net of interbank transactions, which are very large, and deserve considerable attention. Eurodollars are here understood as Eurocurrency, that is, not only dollars in the strict sense, but including, in a more limited volume,

Eurocurrency in denomination other than dollars. But (and this again shows how defective our knowledge of Eurodollars is) Governor Henry C. Wallich has produced, from what he knows to be incomplete data, interesting and substantially lower estimates for 1978.[18] According to him, some 85 per cent of the so-called gross size is accounted for by interbank liabilities. This is in notable contrast with the lower percentages used by other writers. Governor Wallich points out that the BIS estimates net out only interbank liabilities to banks within the reporting area, i.e. still include interbank liabilities to the commercial and central banks outside the reporting area. When these liabilities are also deducted, the ultimate monetary liabilities to nonbanks turn out to be about 160 to 170 billion dollars. Furthermore, some 55 billion dollars of this is already included in national monetary statistics (of which 52 billion dollars is in US data) so that, at the end of 1978, only 100 to 120 billion dollars are to be regarded as 'stateless money', unaccounted for in national monetary statistics. Whilst 100 billion dollars is a substantial amount of purchasing power, it is not large enough, on a worldwide basis, to support the view, sometimes expressed, that the Eurodollar market is a monstrous engine of inflation. From a purely American point of view, the growth of net Eurodollars in the strict sense (dollar denomination only) could only mean that when the intent of the Federal Reserve authorities was to check the growth of the total quantity of dollars, they had to try a little harder.

For the same year end, 1978, net Eurocurrency was 375 billion dollars according to the BIS, with a dollar component of 340 billion, and 485 billion dollars according to Morgan Guaranty.[19]

Central bankers could and should have long ago put their respective commercial banks under more pressure to supply exhaustive standardised data on a regular basis, with separate information concerning their offshore branches, one by one, and communicate aggregate figures to the BIS. The information so supplied is more trustworthy if followed by frequent and thorough examination of the books, with hefty fines in cases of misrepresentation or dissimulation.

Unless there exists adequate information, a not very sound borrower can easily conceal from each of his lenders that he also borrows substantially from others. That has happened in the past and is happening now. In the late 1920s, German banks had borrowed short-term in London sums far in excess of what was commonly believed, and were able to do so because each British bank did not know what the other ones were doing. The Bank of England did not know, and did not care to know. British banks had themselves borrowed these funds, on a short term basis, from French banks, and found, when the French banks pulled their money back, that their German assets were frozen. This is well described by Paul Einzig:

> Since the foreign banks which arranged the acceptance credits were of first rate standing, London banks refrained from expecting borrowers to provide documentary evidence of the genuine character of the transactions which were supposed to be financed by the bills. During the late 'twenties the originally valuable safeguards of the transactions degenerated into meaningless pretence. Credit lines were for large round amounts and the individual bills sent to the London banks for acceptance were for relatively small broken amounts; but sometimes by a miraculous 'coincidence' their total was exactly the large round amount of the credit line. When a lie is obviously a lie and deceives nobody by its obviousness, it ceases to be a lie. The London banks and acceptance houses were fully aware that a large part of the credits were used, not for the self-liquidating short term transactions which the bills were supposed to represent, but for credits granted by the foreign banks to their clients for longer periods. These finance bills – which in fact they were in spite of pretending to be genuine commercial bills – were renewed every three months, though in order to keep up the pretence the foreign banks kept changing the respective amounts of individual bills drawn on the credit.[20]

This reference to the unsound interbank practices of the late 1920s is not out of place, since at the end of February 1983, Mr Willard Butcher, the Chairman of Chase Manhattan Bank, accused a number of banks of having 'misused' the interbank deposit system, the condition of which he described as 'unhealthy'. The interbank market was 'very easy to enter'. It was therefore easily abused by debtor countries as a device to finance balance of payments deficits. It would appear that in 1982 debtor countries, such as Mexico and Brazil, allowed the foreign branches of their banks to push the interbank markets in New York and London as hard as they could, obtaining as many deposits as possible. Such short-term deposits, perhaps naively hitherto regarded as sacrosanct, are now considered so risky that the usual 0.25 per cent margin over Libor is completely out of date for what can become, under duress, a medium term loan, often carrying a 2.5 per cent margin over Libor and possibly threatened with perpetual rescheduling. Indeed those bankers who recently were lending massively to countries with a long record of systematic default on foreign debt and of financial and monetary laxity, are now running for cover, trying to withdraw vital credit lines from struggling debtor nations. Computers are said to work overtime to expose the black sheep. The reluctance of Eurobanks to face greater exposure in high risk situations is understandable. None the less, it is a paradox that a police action of a sort should be necessary to force them to maintain funds in those countries, when a real effort is being made with the guidance and help of the IMF to implement sound, promising policies, as only recently these same banks were vying with each other to offer more loans, when unsound, hopeless disequilibrium policies ruled the day.

Wherever and whenever there is no adequate information and inspection, there is more opportunity for imprudent and/or unsound banking practices. These are all the more to be feared as the Eurodollar world is not the relatively safe one of short-term self-liquidating loans, or iron clad guarantees, or substantial collateral. It is a world of short-term deposits to famous banking names and of medium-term loans fraught with 'sovereign risks'. The smaller banks, using mostly interbank funds, have simply followed the lead of the major banks, leaving to them the dealings with the non-bank clients. Buying a share of the loans thus managed appears to have been conducive to a decline in the critical assessment of the credit-worthiness of the non-bank clients. The smaller banks, acting according to some herd instinct, placed their trust in the major banks participating in 'balance of payments' loans, when they should have devoted attention to the credit-worthiness of countries and the economic viability of projects to be financed. The major banks reduced in this way their exposure on each loan, collected attractive fees that were promptly labelled profits, and cultivated the goodwill of the authorities of the borrowing countries with a leverage effect corresponding to the volume of funds brought by them, yet supplied by others. A race took place for maximum amount rather than optimum amount of loans. The study of country risks must have been limited in view of the banks' surprise in learning, time and again, during rescheduling negotiations, of a substantial unpublicised debt.[21] Most of the smaller lending banks probably did not engage in the study of country risks. They are now trying to get out of the sovereign risk business.

Illusions and delusions may also have distorted the bankers' expectations of eventual assistance from their respective monetary authorities, their lenders of last resort. The view has often been expressed that, in order to avoid panics, the monetary authorities would have to intervene, whatever they may have previously said they would do or would not do. The Basle communique of September 1974 assured the international financial community that means were available for the purpose of providing *temporary liquidity* in the Euromarkets and would be used if and when necessary. This is a restrictive but reasonable stance, as central banks cannot be expected to commit themselves in advance to automatic and unlimited support of imprudent lending. Yet several large banks may require help over a long period. No matter how irresponsible the business of a bank may have been, it may be in the general interest not to permit it to collapse. The classical example is offered by British financial history, when the Bank of England declined, with some justification, to help Overend and Gurney: the panic of 1866 has remained famous in the financial history of London. In 1890, the Baring crisis was really no crisis in the sense that the Bank of England, to avoid havoc among the discount houses, formed a syndicate of banks to guarantee the liabilities of Baring before the public had heard of any difficulty.[22] Conversely, a central bank might decline to provide assistance to a small bank because its fall is not considered likely to generate a panic. One of the characteristics of our time is that small firms in difficulty are abandoned to the harshness of the law and of the market, whereas large firms are bailed out, even when in much worse shape.

According to William Hall, the Basle Concordat of 1974, which is supposed to determine who is responsible for supervising what and was described by Mr Peter Cooke as ‘a most important cornerstone of international supervisory co-operation’, is now seen by many bankers as an unnecessarily woolly document, with no real teeth. It has not prevented some banks from escaping the supervisory net and has fudged the issue of responsibility for the overseas subsidiaries and joint ventures of international banks. This issue is easily the hottest of the year, as the unpaid creditors of the Luxemburg subsidiary of an important European bank have brought the matter to court.[23] According to the Basle Concordat, in the case of foreign subsidiaries, the primary responsibility rests with the host authorities, but parent authorities must take account of the exposure of their domestic banks’ foreign subsidiaries and joint ventures because of those parent banks’ moral commitments to those foreign establishments. Has the concept of moral responsibility any practical significance? The real meaning of this text would seem to be that no one assumes any real responsibility at all. The central bank, if any, of the host country, say the Cayman Islands, will certainly not pay the creditors who are also unlikely to recoup lost funds from whoever has 'moral responsibility'. What of a subsidiary carrying the name of a famous bank which would also own nearly one hundred per cent of the capital stock? Should legal appearance rather than economic reality be the criterion of responsibility? It is not even quite clear what parental responsibility precisely means. When the central bank unhappily involved in the Luxemburg subsidiary referred to above insists that it is not committed by the Basle Concordat, it is technically correct, but that merely demonstrates the emptiness of the Basle document and the limitations of central bank co-operation. If the creditors of the Luxemburg subsidiary get paid, it will be either because they have a strong legal case, or because the central bank involved is so upset by the criticism and the loss of international confidence in its banking system, that it prefers to pay up or to put pressure on others to pay.

The second element of danger mentioned above was the extensive practice of maturity transformation. P. A. Wellons writes:

> Bankers Trust Company has claimed responsibility for first transforming, in 1968, a portion of what is essentially an international short-term capital market into one of longer maturities. The transformation generally is accomplished by use of an interest rate adjusted at regular intervals ... Often part of a syndicate of international banks, each lender funds its portion of the medium-term loan by borrowing on the short-term eurodollar market for successive three, six or twelve months periods throughout the life of the loan.[24]

This roll-over technique was initially acclaimed as a path-breaking innovation, the ideal solution for both borrowers and lenders. New loans of this kind went from 5 billion dollars in 1970 to 133 billion dollars in 1981. Only recently has it been more generally perceived that the roll-over technique can be unsound banking.[25] Except during periods of monetary stringency, the long term interest rate is above the short term rate; this pattern of rates is sometimes called the 'usual' term structure of interest rates. Time intermediation, then, makes it possible to pay a generally lower rate of interest to depositors with respect to the situation which would prevail if assets and liabilities were perfectly matched. The price to pay for this benefit is a higher degree of risk, not only in terms of higher interest rates in the event of a monetary stringency, but in terms of ultimate solvency. The interest rate risk is somewhat reduced by the revision of the interest rate charged to borrowers, but the ultimate solvency risk is not. Banks which wish to impress their stockholders and the public with the prudence of their management insist, in their annual reports, on their efforts to match the maturities of assets and liabilities. There was no such prudence in the growth of international banking operations at the unhealthy rate of 25 per cent per annum during the 1970s, a rate of growth higher than that of any other economic magnitude. In the words of Mr Lamberto Dini, director general of the Bank of Italy:

> The general adoption of liability financing instead of asset settlement for external imbalances reveals the relaxation of discipline that took place. The growth of international banking was accompanied by an erosion of the ratio of own funds to assets, an increase in maturity transformation and greater concentration of risks . . . Banks appear to have acted on the implicit assumption that central banks would intervene to get them out of trouble. In this connection it needs to be emphasized that banks are individually and totally responsible for their decisions regarding creditworthiness and that they have to shoulder the consequences of their decisions. The task of central banks is to protect the confidence and the stability of the system, not to make good the losses of badly run individual banks.[26]

Karl Otto Pohl, the president of the Bundesbank, notes that the monetary problem cannot be dissociated from the trade problem, for those who receive no credit cannot import.[27] In the same way, Mr Dini is concerned with the possibility that the developing countries debt should set off a deflationary spiral leading to new reductions in activity and greater financial disequilibria. Keynes made exactly that point 53 years ago when he urged central bankers to make every effort to revive the international market for long-term loans, which would revive enterprise and activity everywhere.[28]

What seems likely is that, whatever the intensity of the banking crisis ahead, the taxpayer may be called upon to foot part of the bill. The American taxpayer learned through the press that some of the loans extended to Poland had received guarantees from the Federal Government. The increase in the resources of the IMF, somewhat overdue, is financed by the taxpayers of the member countries. Mr Dini is convinced that the industrial countries will necessarily have to shoulder a part of the real cost of the excessive accumulation of foreign debts by developing countries over the last ten years. That could turn out to be expensive.[29] As Keynes said long ago, it does not pay to be good. Those countries which have borrowed most recklessly would get the greatest free financing from the taxpayers of the industrial countries; those which have behaved with responsibility would get very little such financing.

At a time when banks with large sovereign loans to Latin American and other countries announce higher profits and declare higher dividends, the well known banker, Felix Rohatyn, does not share their optimism. He advocates the creation of a new international agency which would issue to banks long-term low interest bonds in exchange for dubious loans. Mr Rohatyn is aware of the prospect of an outcry against bailing out the banks, but suggest that some kind of a scheme is vital in order to ensure a strong and healthy banking system.[30]

BIRTH AND EARLY GROWTH OF THE EURODOLLAR MARKET

According to Adam Smith (not the Adam Smith of the *Wealth of Nations*, but the author of the *Money Game*) Dregasovitch of the USSR invented the Eurodollar in 1957, or the people under him did, and he just took all the credit. Dregasovitch, then, in fear of a possible freeze of Soviet funds by the American authorities (or so say all the books, which may well copy each other) moved the Russian balances from New York to a Russian bank with a British charter, the Moscow Narodny Bank and, to a lesser extent, to a Paris Soviet owned bank, the Banque Commerciale pour l'Europe du Nord whose telex was 'Eurbank'. This, perhaps, is why before such dollars were called Eurodollars they were for a while Eurbank dollars, or Continental dollars, or foreign market dollars. According to Smith, the first Eurodollar business was an $800 000 loan issued on 28 February 1957 by Moscow Narodny Bank, through a London merchant bank. That amount was borrowed and repaid in dollars outside the American banking system, without any interference from any monetary authority. Perhaps Dregasovitch had made a previous call on some Bank of England official to ascertain the attitude of the monetary authority. It is, in any case, no accident that the funds were sent to London, one of the most important and efficient banking places in the world. The funds would not have been sent to a country such as Germany where foreign banks do not enjoy as much freedom as they do in London, since, in Germany, exactly the same regulations, including reserve requirements, apply to all deposits and loans irrespective of whether their denomination is or is not that of the home currency. Moving dollars from New York to London did not change the currency risk (e.g. devaluation) but modified or reduced the political risk by changing the country of jurisdiction, or we might say, got rid of all jurisdictions. It is not clear, however, that Soviet funds in the US were more exposed to a freeze in 1957 than during the Korean war. There may well have been other reasons, the most obvious one being the low rate of interest paid by banks in the US. Also, because of a ban in the United States at that time on lending to communist countries, there were no prospects of banking developments or eventual borrowing there, whereas it was conceivable to create in London and Paris good banking ties, first through lending, and next through borrowing. Anyway, if it had not been done by the Russians, it would have been done by somebody else, and the subsequent development of the market would have been much the same.

Thus, in 1957, a new and original, international money market in short-term dollars and other currencies emerged in London. New and original? In economic theory or business practice, it is always difficult to establish novelty: several writers have brought attention to similar transactions that have been seen before, such as transactions in sterling deposits in non-sterling countries before the First World War. During the 1920s, there was a business in sterling and dollar deposits in Berlin and Vienna, and again in the 1950s, borrowings of Italian banks from French banks. Reference has even been made to the medieval practice of drawing bills payable at the quarterly fairs denominated in foreign currencies other than those of the country of payment. As these practices, however, were unsystematic, desultory, ahead of the times, or disapproved of by the authorities, they never resulted in a growing, durable, organised international short-term money market. The Eurodollar market of the late 1950s, then, must be regarded as a financial innovation and a momentous one at that. It is momentous because of its extraordinary growth rates, as well as due to the size it has reached, even net of interbank transactions. Additionally it is important because money markets, until then essentially national, are now connected through large money flows and a modified pattern of interest rates which is basically the result of international forces, even though the influence of the United States is predominant. It is also important because of its influence on world trade and prices. Short-term dollars? Perhaps so, but just as to what is short-term, may, in point of fact, turn out to be long-term, so can the long-term turn out to be short-term. A common clause enables a depositor to withdraw his deposit or a borrower to repay prematurely, upon payment of a stated penalty.

London based banks, that is first class banks, not newly formed banks or fly by night banks, accepted deposits denominated in foreign currencies, for two purposes:

(1) To relend at once in the same currency denomination, to other banks, mainly Canadian, French and Italian banks, an activity somewhat similar to that observed in the US Federal funds market, though without a central bank.
(2) To buy British Treasury bills, or to lend to non-bank institutions, in effect to British local authorities, hire purchase finance houses or similar borrowers; but, in this case, with appropriate cover to eliminate the exchange risk.

These deposits denominated in foreign currencies were usually for one month, and received an interest appreciably higher than that offered on equivalent term in New York. When, in July 1959, the London *Economist* first took note of foreign currency deposits with London banks (the Radcliffe report mentions them, but does not use the word Eurodollar) these were offering 3 to 3.25 per cent for large deposits, whereas New York banks were offering only 2.5 per cent and charging 4 per cent for loans. Eurobanks were charging less for loans, even though they were paying more for deposits. It is difficult, however, to compare US with non-US rates, and, therefore, US and non-US banking spreads, because of the American banking practice of requiring a compensating balance which may vary from borrower to borrower and according to business conditions. Various writers have ascribed this larger American spread to the monopoly and oligopoly elements in American banking. The American banking structure is a rather complicated one, with several lobbies, which have successfully manoeuvred legislators into the adoption of laws stifling competition. The most remarkable example is the US legal prohibition of interest payments on deposits of less than thirty days. This restriction was a perennial request of bank lobbies and systematically turned down until adopted during the Roosevelt administration. In the 1930s, short-term interest rates were so low that it did not matter much; from the 1950s on, it did matter, as attractive interest rates could be secured from banks outside of the United States. But the difference between the American spread and the London Eurodollar spread was also due to other reasons, such as cost differences, since free banking is less costly than regulated banking. London based banks engaged in successful intermediation because the Bank of England made it both nice and easy for them to do so. The Bank of England could easily have prevented or tightly controlled these transactions on various grounds, as many of the lenders or borrowers were British firms or subjects or as the transactions took place in the United Kingdom. It would have been sufficient to impose on all money market transactions an identical, non discriminatory set of regulations, irrespective of the currency denomination. The market would then perhaps have grown elsewhere. In effect, the Bank of England has created this market in London by its quiet policy of discrimination in favour of this type of transactions. Very shortly after the birth of the Eurodollar market, the major European countries declared their currencies freely convertible into dollars. This removed an obstacle to the growth of the Euromarket. So it was by mid-1959 that the London *Economist* pointing out the danger of counting the same Eurodollars again and again, mentioned a rough estimate of $500 million, of which the major part was made up of dollars lent and relent by London banks. Foreign currency deposits converted into sterling and covered by forward exchange operations were then estimated at between 100 and 200 million dollars. One year later, by mid-1960, Alan R. Holmes and Fred H. Klopstock wrote that any estimate of the market volume rested on tenuous grounds, but that the total was believed to exceed one billion dollars.[31]

CHARACTERISTICS OF THE EURODOLLAR MARKET

From this early period, the fundamental aspects of the Eurocurrency market were clearly noticeable.

(1) It is an interbank market with typically large transactions. In other words, it is a wholesale market for a small number of operators, commercial banks, central banks, other financial non-bank institutions, large firms especially transnational companies, and some very wealthy individuals. All, or almost all transactions are interbank; non-bank operators normally deal through banks. But a reduction of Eurodollar transactions brought about by a tightening of exchange control may give rise to non-bank operations, legal and illegal.

(2) The market is largely unregulated. Commercial banks are not limited by reserve requirements, which set a ceiling to the expansion of loans and are expensive. Taxes, if any, are soft, business is secret, and

therefore, the statistical coverage poor. If bank examiners in an offshore centre question the soundness of loans, the adequacy of the capital base, or the ethics of some transactions, it is possible to shift some or all of the business to another offshore centre where banks examiners are less inquisitive. Offshore banking has pleasant aspects, even though intense competition among banks forces them to pass on to depositors most of the cost advantages in the form of higher interest rates on deposits.

(3) Although some statements might create the belief that a new breed of banks was born, banks called Eurobanks or offshore banks, there is perhaps not a single new bank in this business. With large transactions decided upon very promptly and communicated by telephone and telex on the basis of reputation, it is essential, because of the risk aspect, to carry a first class name in order to collect deposits. Thus branches of large American banks abroad, very tightly controlled from the head office, were reported able to secure deposits below the going market rate where lesser known names had to pay more, borrowing from the larger banks. Indeed, it is believed that some branches of large banks have little contact with final non-bank users, relending to these other banks. For example, relending one billion dollars with a spread of one-fourth of 1 per cent brings in 2.5 million dollars per annum at a modest marginal cost. Not only is the volume of interbank deposits very large, but it is apt to change upon modification of the perception of risk. The tighter the inspection and control of banks by a national monetary authority, the greater their ability to collect deposits in the Eurodollar market: virtue at home makes it easier to sin abroad – if one wants to![32]

(4) The deposits accepted by the Eurobanks are usually dated, although there are escape clauses, 24 hours, seven days, two months, etc. They are typically not above three months. In principle, then, Eurobanks should not find it difficult to match, at a cost in terms of foregone opportunities, the maturities of their liabilities and those of their assets, in order to reduce the risk associated with unforeseen changes in the level and structure of interest rates. But they often engage, on a large scale, in deliberate time intermediation, also called time arbitrage, i.e. borrowing short and lending long. Whoever behaves in this way is vulnerable to sudden and unexpected withdrawals of deposits. It is perhaps not so much that the banks are anxious to take such risks, but rather that they are strongly induced to do so when depositors insist on short-term, whereas the borrowers are keen on much longer terms. Indeed, time arbitrage is considered to be one of the

important functions of the Eurodollar market. Business firms can be found to be simultaneously on both sides of the market. They may find it worthwhile to borrow at a term, of say, six months and deposit on a seven day basis. Given the usual term structure of interest rates, this is likely to result in a cost considered as more than offset by the extra convenience and security.

(5) The Eurodollar market receives funds from everywhere for the purpose of making loans to everywhere. Some restrictions may be imposed by some central banks which, for instance, deny access to the market to certain types of firms. Deficits in foreign payments are of importance to the growth of the Eurocurrency market, although there need not be a simple cause and effect relationship, a point very often made by American authors in the 1960s when the United States experienced a protracted deficit.[33] Countries with deficits in foreign payments are generally net borrowers from countries in surplus, which is no surprise. Some theoretical studies have made a sharp distinction between dollars held by US *residents and non-residents.* In practice, however, the distinction is not all that clear. Thus Oscar Altman noted that some of the funds in the Eurodollar market, deposits owned by US corporations and individuals were nevertheless reported by US banks as liabilities to foreigners. Substantial funds have moved from the US mainly from New York, to the head offices of Canadian banks, much to the displeasure of US officials, and these Canadian banks then relent to New York. Other funds, much more modest in volume, have been brought across the border in suitcases. Canadian banks, although they do not solicit such funds, nevertheless welcome them, clearly a lovely distinction. Are such funds American or Canadian? If the US depositor, say a large American firm, gives to a Canadian bank the address, in Panama, of a Panamanian subsidiary specifically set up for this purpose, they might be called Panamanian. Why should a bank care, and why should a monetary authority assist in the enforcement of controls of another monetary authority? If data on movements and ownership of Eurofunds are not reliable, then the Eurodollar system is a vehicle for large, hard to ascertain transfers of resources among countries, and the source of important gains and losses in foreign exchange transactions. The very large item 'errors and omissions' in balance of payment tables reminds us of how little we know about short-term capital movements.[34] The willingness to assume uncovered exchange risk has been an important characteristic of the system. Some banks have deliberately assumed exchange risks, but that is not common banking behaviour, whereas 'roll-over' risk has been much

more common. Others have suffered losses on foreign exchange transactions because of the unauthorised initiative of subordinate officials. Uncovered positions in future foreign exchange transactions are not rare with business firms. Reasons for this include choosing deliberately to assume risks with which they are familiar, inadequate cover facilities and finally failure to fully appreciate the degree of risk. Some central banks have lost heavily because they have extended cover to their commercial banks and/or could not, for political reasons, dump an unwanted accumulation of a specific currency. Robert Triffin wrote recently:

> A second reason for the Europeans' growing dissatisfaction was the huge losses entailed by their accumulation of depreciating dollars . . . As far as central banks are concerned, the use of the dollar as the main component of international reserve accumulation entailed enormous bookkeeping losses. Those reported by the Bundesbank, for example, totaled 43 billion Deutsche marks in an eight year period (1971–78). At the December 31, 1978 dollar-mark exchange rate (1.828 marks per dollar) this would translate into a $23.6 billion loss, more than three times the total international reserves of Germany at the end of 1969.[35]

(6) Banks heavily involved in the Eurodollar market usually present it, in their publications, in the best possible light. When an illustration is given, it is that of a short-term self-liquidating financing of a transaction in international trade. From such an example, one of the world's largest banks has argued, in a way which reminds one of an argument of the 19th Century Banking School, or of the real bills theory, that the inflationary impact of Eurodollars is nil since every loan is eventually repaid! In point of fact, however, not only has the Eurodollar market a wide variety of sources, it also shows an 'immense variety of uses to which these dollars are put, whether in international finance and commerce arbitrage of every kind, or speculation'.[36] Thus, among the borrowers in the early development of the Eurodollar market, we find the Belgian Treasury, because of the Belgian National Bank's reluctance to make more advances to the Belgian government, and the governments or state banks of communist countries. Vast amounts have been borrowed for purposes such as financing a general credit expansion, or a balance of payments deficit, or to circumvent a credit squeeze. This is altogether different from the idyllic self-liquidating, bona fide, international financing of exports or imports.

The lending bank may have no idea of the use to which its loan will be put; it merely wishes to be satisfied that the borrower is a good banking name, or a good business name, so that the risk of non-repayment appears very small.

In short, to do offshore to attract short-term deposits and make loans was initially a privilege of large banks, allowing them to go abroad, with the explicit or tacit assent of the central bank, what that same central bank prohibits to all banks at home.[37] The French have an expression for this sort of thing: putting on a false nose.

THE CENTRAL BANKS IN THE EURODOLLAR MARKET[38]

There is little cause for surprise in the behaviour of commercial banks in the Eurocurrency market; it is pretty well explained by the profit motive. It is, however, more delicate to explain why the central banks have been so kind to this market, why in 1962, for instance, they owned, according to Oscar Altman, more than two-thirds of all Eurodollars. A cynic once said that in order to ascertain the true motives of a central bank, one must subtract the list of official motives from the list of all possible motives. Let us, then, see what the possible motives are for central bank transactions in the Eurocurrency market.

(1) *The yield motive.* Central banks deposits in the Eurocurrency market will bring more attractive returns than gold (zero) or US Treasury bills. This was more important to the central banks of the poorer, less developed countries, than to the central banks of high income countries.

(2) *The secrecy motive.* During the 1960s, unsound American financial, monetary and exchange rate policies resulted in a large and untractable balance of payments deficit. This led the US government to apply substantial pressure on other governments in order to induce them to accumulate dollar claims rather than gold. Through swaps with their commercial banks, the central banks could try to sell dollars as quietly as possible, or engage in various transactions in foreign exchange and gold.

(3) *The liquidity motive.* If the central bank wishes the commercial banks to expand credit, yet is afraid of subsequent losses of official reserves, it may simply encourage them to borrow on the Eurocurrency market. The central bank will get the dollars and issue to the banks the additional reserves which make possible the expansion of loans. The

reverse policy would bring about a contraction of credit, unless thwarted by the ingeniousness of banks and non-banks.

(4) *The interest rate motive.* This is closely associated with the liquidity motive. If, for instance, a central bank dislikes the prospect of an increase in interest rates in the Eurodollar market, it may try to influence the interest rate there by supplying dollars.

(5) *The exchange rate motive.* A central bank may, for instance, dislike the prospect of an increase in the exchange rate of the dollar and supply dollars to the Eurocurrency market. It may have what it regards as an excessive amount of dollars, and avail itself of every opportunity to sell them. In other circumstances, in a different period, it may have a totally different behaviour.

Three points should be considered when discussing the behaviour of central banks in the Eurocurrency market:

(1) In most cases central banks have intervened in the market, in an isolated way, but they have sometimes engaged in a concerted move, generally through the BIS (for instance at the end of 1966), when Eurodollar interest rates went up sharply. On the whole, it has been a story of '*Bellum onium contra omnes.*', with more selfishness than co-operation.
(2) Central banks have differed among each other in the latitude given to non-bank operators to act in the Eurocurrency market, and, over time, have changed their attitudes *vis-à-vis* their own nationals.
(3) Because of the weight of the United States in the world economy, and because the bulk of Eurocurrencies has, in fact, been made up of dollars, far more weight must be attached to the policies, active and passive, of the Federal Reserve System, than to those of any other central bank.

The Eurodollar market has, on occasion, given more latitude for central banks to pursue unsound policies.[39] One such example which will be offered here, is that of the United Kingdom. In the late 1920s, Montagu Norman, trying to manage a disequilibrium system with an overvalued pound, was borrowing abroad on short-term and selling dollars forward. The collapse of sterling in 1931 was the result. The Bank of England was doing the same thing in the mid-1960s, with the same result. The difference, however, was that the Eurocurrency market at first made it possible for the British authorities to secure large resources, but then subsequently contributed to the difficulties of the pound. Indeed, one writer, Jean Denizet, has accused the Euromarket of having brought about the sterling crises of 1966 and 1967, and the devaluation of the pound. His argument is that when Eurodollar rates went up close to those of British local authorities, holders of such British paper dumped it massively to invest in Eurodollars, bringing about a drain on British gold and dollar reserves, which were themselves mortgaged by forward operations.[40] Of course, sterling was in fundamental disequilibrium, but the phenomenon described by Denizet is real. Thus, Leland B. Yeager, describing the difficulties of sterling, writes: 'Funds attracted earlier by high interest rates in London were now moving out again as rates rose in New York, on the Continent, and in the Eurodollar market'.[41] As Governor Otmar Emminger was to note, the development of the Eurocurrency market has given a new magnitude to destabilising short-term capital movements.[42] Central banks have initially given more attention to the (temporary) ease with which these short-term funds can be imported, enabling them, for a time, to pursue expansionary policies without much concern for reserves, balance of payments, etc., rather than to the ease with which these funds may leave. This, then, confronts them with a dilemma: either have an exchange rate crisis, or push up internal rates of interest through a severe credit squeeze with consequences on output and employment. It is a question whether the benevolent stance of the Bank of England on the Eurodollar market has paid off.

Several central banks have experienced disappointments with the Eurocurrency market, which has not always been as tame as was hoped for. A case in point is that of Italy. There is little doubt that, initially, the Bank of Italy thought that increases and decreases in the recourse to the Eurodollar market could be profitably used, as one of several policy tools, in the implementation of monetary policy. The Bank of Italy felt it had enough power over Italian commercial banks to induce them, or force them, to borrow or to reimburse in the Eurodollar market, and underestimated future non-bank capital movements. For several years, the Bank of Italy gave forward cover to Italian commercial banks, at no cost to them, which by any standard is a very nice gift. Its behaviour is thus described by Alberto Ferrari, director general of the Banca Nazionale del Lavoro:

> In the early sixties and during the period of inflation from 1959 to 1963, Italian banks were encouraged to import liquidities from the Eurodollar market. Since, at that time, the interest rate was higher in Italy than on the Eurodollar market some banks fully availed themselves of the possibility offered by the government and

> borrowed massively . . . It was because of this policy that the Bank of Italy was able to finance the deficit of external payments without loss of official gold and dollar reserves.[43]

In the language of bankers and economists, this is called favouring liability financing over asset settlement. In plain language, it is postponing the adoption of necessary financial measures to correct a growing foreign payments imbalance.

This lack of timely action by the central bank is unfortunate, because it almost always guarantees the growth of the foreign payments imbalance, so that correcting it at a later stage is far more difficult and painful. Italy is not alone in this, as only a few monetary authorities have not acted likewise at one time or another. The point here is that, in the past, governments in such difficulties had no recourse to a Eurodollar market to borrow from. They had, if they were not willing to promptly take corrective measures, either to let the rate of exchange fall, or to try to borrow from the House of Morgan. Both actions were highly visible. The Eurodollar market provided ample (but temporary) resources smoothly and discreetly. Liability financing has often been used to 'doctor' official gold and foreign exchange reserves, a common and deplorable practice which hardly fools anyone any more.

Eurodollar interest rates, a few years later, went up well beyond Italian interest rates, so Italian banks found it then profitable to lend in the Eurodollar market rather than to borrow there. The authorities became alarmed at this outflow of capital and tried to stop it, but with limited success; the banks did not disobey the orders of the Bank of Italy (at least not openly), yet funds moved on a large scale away from Italy through non-banking channels. The Bank of Italy thought that it was stronger than the Eurodollar market, however, it turned out that the Eurodollar market was stronger than the Bank of Italy. The Bank of Italy found that the nation was sensitive to the impact of monetary tensions abroad, especially those in the United States. It could not successfully adopt monetary policies in conflict with that market's trend. Italy had lost part of its monetary sovereignty.

The German Bundesbank had similar problems in 1960, though in this case the situation was reversed, as it extended exchange cover to promote the export, rather than the import of short-term funds. It bought forward dollars at a premium above the rate charged on the spot market. This premium was set at 1 per cent per annum in August 1960 and raised to 1½ per cent in September. This created a paradise of a sort for speculators: 'Heads we win big, tails we still win something'.[44]

The purpose of the move was to induce German importers to borrow foreign exchange from the Bundesbank, through the intermediation of commercial banks, rather than from abroad, as they had been recently doing in large volume. It was also a special inducement for banks to hold dollars abroad, under these swaps, rather than convert them into D. marks.[45] As Emminger has stated, the attempt was a 'total failure'. The following description of the total failure, by Paul Einzig, shows the crucial role of the Eurodollar market:

> Eurodollar facilities have been used extensively not only for speculation against a currency, but also for speculation in favour of a currency. This was done, for instance, in 1961, when Eurodollars were borrowed and sold against D. Marks and Swiss francs in anticipation of a revaluation of these currencies, rather than a devaluation of the dollar.
>
> The German monetary authorities, by supplying the Eurodollar markets with dollar deposits through the intermediary of German banks, increased the difficulty of their own task in resisting the pressure for a second revaluation. In fact they initiated and maintained a vicious circle when lending their unwanted dollars to the German banks, and, through them, to the Eurodollar market, for much of the self same dollars were sold by the borrowers against D. Marks, so that they found their way back into the Bundesbank's reserves, only to be re-lent again to the Eurodollar market through the German banks.[46]

Indeed, one of the most bizarre stories concerning Eurodollars is that of the central banks when they deposited, either directly or through the intermediation of the BIS and of their commercial banks, unwanted dollars in the Euromarket. Through their own action, the central banks were reluctantly buying up dollars in amounts several billion dollars larger than the increase in US liabilities to them: a startling process where Eurodollars are multiplied in such a way that he who wants to get rid of one dollar ends by buying two or three, a throughly self-defeating process.[47] In spite of the agreement of May 1971, it is said that some of this redepositing still takes place.

The above-mentioned episodes (others could be noted) show clearly that when the volume of international liquidity is vast and growing without control, the central banks find it increasingly difficult to control the liquidity of their respective commercial banks and economies, as well as the rate of growth of the national stocks of money. Few central bank governors would now subscribe to the view that: '. . . the London banking community has earned the gratitude of all the countries which have directly or indirectly benefited by the new device (the Eurodollar market)'.[48]

Rather, they would agree with one of their own, Governor Otmar Emminger, that the Euromarket has made monetary management far more difficult and complex at both the national and the international level, and that from the point of view of the stability of the international monetary system, the negative aspects are certainly more significant than the positive aspects.[49]

THE EURODOLLAR MARKET AS A BRANCH OF THE NEW YORK MONEY MARKET

Every book or article with a historical review of the Eurocurrency market repeats that what gave a strong impulse to that market was the 1957 British decision to impose restraints on sterling credits to countries engaging in third-party transactions *within* the sterling area, and to raise the Bank rate to 7 per cent. This was, at the time, regarded as a very high rate, whereupon British banks went on financing this type of business with cheaper and easily available dollars.

Although every author says so, was it of importance? The Radcliffe report, which contains a detailed description of the 1957 sterling crisis, has no more to say on this point than this: '. . . and the restrictions on the provision of credit for overseas borrowers were tightened . . .'[50] In other sections the Radcliffe report has this to say:

> A few acceptances relate to trade that never touches the shores of the United Kingdom; this is often mentioned in illustration of the international services (and income) of the City of London . . . We were informed that the amount is at present small.[51]

And, about overseas and foreign banks, the Radcliffe Report stated:

> They grant credits to finance the movement of goods between the United Kingdom and the other countries in which they operate (and exceptionally, trade which does not touch the United Kingdom at all).[52]

One gets the impression from this that there was not much third party financing before 1957, partly because it was already restricted by the authorities. One also gets the impression that further restrictions in this field were but a minor aspect of the 'package', and that the sharp increase in the British bank rate alone would have justified the switch to dollars for such modest financing.

If the policy decisions of the British government have had but a modest influence on the growth of the market, the policy decisions of the Federal Reserve System, especially about Regulation Q, have been of considerable importance.[53] Marcello de Cecco writes:

> The voluntary restraint measures and the credit squeeze of 1966 marked the beginning of the American banks' takeover of the Eurodollar market. Up to 1964, this had been the preserve of the London banks ... The American banks began to integrate the Eurodollar market more completely into the pattern of their normal credit operations ...[54]

In the same way, Paul Einzig observed: 'For all practical purposes, the London Eurodollar market became the London branch of the New York money market over a long period'.[55]

The history of Regulation Q is one of malfeasance at home and abroad. From the earliest days of banking in America, the bank lobbies have tried, just as in other countries, to obtain from the authorities a prohibition of interest payments to demand deposits, putting forward as an argument, with no small degree of hypocrisy, the interest and safety of depositors.[56] The prohibition was finally adopted for demand deposits in member banks in the Banking Act of 1933, and for demand deposits in other insured banks in the Banking Act of 1935. Regulation Q of the Board of Governors which has regulated interest rates on time deposits was quite modest when it first appeared. It provided that where state banking authorities had fixed maximum interest rates payable on time deposits at figures lower than those set by the Board of Governors, the lower state figure became the maximum which could be paid by member banks located in these states. The relevant, modified text is that of Section 19 (Bank Reserves). It provides explicitly that Regulation Q does not apply to any deposit payable only outside of the United States.[57] It is the irony of history that commercial banks, which had lobbied so long in favour of such interest rate limitations, later found that they were a hindrance to them in the competition for these deposits with alternative institutions, particularly savings banks and savings and loans associations.

The heart of the matter is that up to 1966, maximum rates of interest on time deposits were almost meaningless because the Federal Reserve had willed it so: whenever the prime commercial paper rate was going close to the ceiling, the Federal Reserve systematically pushed the ceiling up, so that, in effect, it was no ceiling at all, and everyone in banking was aware of this. In the early 1960s, the Federal Reserve deliberately raised Regulation Q ceilings on large CDs to encourage the growth of time deposits within the banks. A rapid growth of CDs did, indeed, take place. When, in the middle of the 1960s, open market rates on short-term paper rose to the level set by Regulation Q, it could be expected that this maximum would be raised as usual. However, it was not raised as expected in the middle of 1966, and this created a credit crunch of a new kind. Large banks experienced a rapid run-off of large CDs as depositors could secure higher returns from non-bank sources. In the face of high loan demands from their customers, they found not only that they could not raise additional funds, but also that they were losing resources. The remarkable point about the episode was not that the Federal Reserve was tightening credit, a reasonable attitude in the circumstances, but that it was using a highly questionable method to do so. There was no need to use Regulation Q, as the Federal Reserve could have used its traditional instruments.

One reaction of the large American banks to the credit crunch of 1966 was to open up branches in London, sell CDs there and then make the funds available to the head office. This, of course, pushed up the Eurodollar rate and created additional difficulties for the pound, as noted above.

The 1966 episode was just a rehearsal for the events of 1969. Market rates receded at the end of 1966, then rose in the second half of 1967. As they were hitting the ceiling, the Federal Reserve raised the ceiling. But, in 1969, as interest rates further increased, the Federal Reserve refused to do it again. Charles A. Coombs had this comment:

> Virtually all Federal Reserve officials at the time conceived of Regulation Q as providing 'the sharp cutting edge' of credit restraint. As a lone dissenter concerned over the whipsaw effects internationally, I could find no one who took my worries seriously.[58]

What was the motivation of the Federal Reserve? From an internal point of view, the policy was self-defeating. It had no sharp cutting edge at all, since the purpose of reducing banking liquidity was successfully defeated by the borrowing in London and by other means.[59] Federal Reserve policy was, in fact, circumvented with the consent of the Federal Reserve itself: no US bank could have opened up branches in London or any foreign place without the consent of the authorities. Unless the American authorities did not know what they were doing, which is unlikely, the explanation must be sought in their concern with the balance of payments difficulties of the United States.[60]

After the rehearsal of 1966, the Federal Reserve could be sure that the large banks would again borrow in London. Therefore, such borrowing may be considered to have been a policy objective in a short-term approach to the chronic balance of payments difficulties, regardless of the consequences abroad. The outstanding liabilities of US banks to their overseas branches rose from about $3 billion early in 1968 to a maximum of over $12 billion at the end of 1969. Until the second half of 1969, the Federal Reserve took no action. Their action turned out to be quite mild: 10 per cent reserve requirements against *additional* borrowings from overseas branches. Discussing Eurodollars from the point of view of the American balance of payments, E. M. Bernstein observed that the US surplus of 1968 and 1969, based on the 'official-reserve-transactions' definition was entirely due to the borrowing abroad of American banks.[61]

The US recession of 1970 reversed the tight credit conditions which had brought about the huge capital inflows of 1968 and 1969. As interest rates fell sharply in the US, while boom conditions existed in several other major countries, US banks set about repaying their earlier heavy borrowing in the Eurodollar market. Over 1970 as a whole, the banks paid back some 6 to 6.5 billion dollars. The overall deficit reached $29.8 billion on the official reserve transactions basis. Because of interest rate differentials, and, even more importantly, due to expectations of exchange rate changes (primarily a devaluation of the dollar), the rules of the game became: sell dollar physical assets and claims, and buy non-dollar physical assets and claims. Even better: get into dollar debt in order to purchase non-dollar claims, and dollar devaluation will make you rich. Americans and foreigners alike were flying from the dollar. The new outflow of short-term private capital in the first half of 1971 became enormous. At this point, both the importance of the Eurodollar market and the desire of US authorities to use it as much as possible for balance of payments reasons is indicated by the issuance, from January to April 1971, of special securities at favourable yields to the foreign branches of American banks by the US authorities.[62]

Everyone knows of the suspension of dollar convertibility into gold by President Nixon on 15 August 1971, and its sequel. The Bretton Woods system collapsed because of American budgetary, fiscal, financial and monetary laxity in combination with fixed exchange rates and a fixed price of gold (set in 1934) and not because of the Eurodollar market. But the Eurodollar market, a factor of instability in the international monetary system, did help, much as in the case of sterling in 1967. It initially made it easier to postpone the unavoidable adjustment, and then accelerated the panic. The losses inflicted on dollar holders turned out to be larger than they would otherwise have been.

CONCLUSION

This paper has not tried to discuss every aspect of Eurodollars; for instance, the important connection between the balance of payments surpluses of oil producing countries and the Eurodollar market has not been reviewed, as this paper is primarily concerned with the lending activities of Eurobanks.

That something should be done to improve methods of operation in international banking has been made obvious by the vast amount of country default which took place in 1982 – a strong jolt to the complacency hitherto manifested, yet apparently not strong enough to induce some banks concerned to enter into their profit statements the provisions it calls for. Reform should be concentrated on three points, (a) accounting practices, (b) regulation of foreign lending, (c) bank supervision in all offshore centres.

Swift action is needed to eliminate fictitious banking profits and dividends through realistic loan-loss provisions. So far central banks have declined to give guidance, at least in public, beyond non-operational statements. This is understandable. The monetary authorities, in assuming this new responsibility, might be blamed sooner or later, rightly or wrongly. Perhaps a committee of wise men might be selected from central bankers, commercial bankers and economists to determine what range of specific loan-loss provisions would be called for, whether tax deductible or not.

Next, rules concerning foreign lending should be tightened, especially to countries with a history of default, for prudential reasons, not in order to reduce international capital flows and international trade. Thus the amount of foreign loans as a percentage of capital funds or total assets could be reduced, as well as the amount loaned to a single country or a single foreign firm.

Further efforts should be made to improve the co-ordination of national banking regulation, especially in the matter of provision for weak sovereign loans. It would be embarrassing if, for a given situation, there should be widely different regulations between regulating countries. As, in certain circumstances, the banker might be more knowledgeable than the supervisor, representatives of commercial banks should be appointed to advise the supervisors.

Perhaps most difficult would be, from a political rather than technical point of view, the control of the Euromarkets. Such control has been proposed on various occasions by national authorities, usually within the framework of the Bank for International Settlements at Basle. The American authorities proposed in 1980 the universal adoption of compulsory reserve requirements analogous to those usually in force within national banking systems. One of their motivations probably was the concern that the Euromarkets might once again be used to circumvent their policy decisions. These proposals were not adopted. The British were opposed to any change that would reduce the role of the City. The French were reported to be more sympathetic, but averse to what appeared to them as an extension of the American regulatory system. It is believed that the decision of the Federal Reserve System to create, in the United States, the so-called International Banking Facilities, was the direct outcome of their failure to obtain a consensus at Basle.[63]

It is reasonable to assume that the proposals presented in 1980 by the Federal Reserve authorities were very close to the plan published in the fall of 1979 by Henry C. Wallich, a governor of the Federal Reserve System. The main features of the Wallich reserve requirement plan are as follows:

(1) The requirements would have to be imposed by each participating country on its banks and their foreign branches and subsidiaries, wherever located,
(2) Reserve requirements would have to be the same in all currencies, although they could differ by maturity,
(3) The deposits subject to reserve requirements would be those owed to private non-banks, central banks, other official institutions, and banks of non-participating countries,
(4) Required reserves would be held in the currency of deposit, either in the central bank of the currency in question, in the central bank of the location of the deposit, or in the central bank of the head office of the Eurobank or branch carrying the deposit.[64]

The obvious purpose of the plan is that no participating country should have an advantage.

The Wallich plan has been criticised by Dr Masera, of the Bank of Italy, on two grounds:

(a) Some important countries, notably the United Kingdom, do not use methods of control hinged on the monetary base and on non-interest bearing compulsory reserves.

Governor Wallich was, of course, aware of this. He pointed out that where new legislation is needed, the process of establishing requirements would be a slow one. However, during a transitional period, what is achieved by one country with reserve requirements can be achieved approximately to the same extent by other methods, say capital ratios. The will to achieve the result is more important than the techniques used.

(b) If reserve ratios are identical for all Eurobanks, irrespective of currency denominations, Eurobanks would have an incentive to carry reserves in the currency with the lowest interest rates, in order to minimise cost. Transactions would be entered in their books in that currency, yet, through forward contracts, the banks could provide their clients with any currency effectively requested.

Governor Wallich was also aware of this. In his opinion, if the reserve requirements are modest, i.e. in the range of perhaps 2 to 5 per cent, and if the interest rate differentials among currencies are not extreme, these roundabout, cost minimising transactions are unlikely to develop to any great extent. If necessary, the practice of carrying business in one currency and carrying the reserves in another, for the purpose of circumventing the regulation and saving on the interest differential, might be prohibited and punished by a hefty fine of a multiple of that savings. Unless the banks were to engage in a wholesale falsification of their books, which is unlikely, it should be easy to find out, upon inspection, whether they engage in the practice, or not. Each bank might be required to indicate from time to time the breakdown of its deposits according to currency denomination, and maintain reserves in the same proportion.

In short, the technical difficulties indicated by Governor Wallich himself, and picked up by Dr Masera, are not without some foundation, yet they are not the main obstacle to the implementation of the Wallich plan. Had this plan, or a variant of it, been adopted, in principle, at the Basle meeting of 1980, it would have met the hostility of numerous commercial bankers, if only because they are hostile to inspections, declarations, or other interference in their business, and fear some obstacle to profit maximisation. These were the real reasons why the American Banking Association so bitterly fought for over a quarter of a century all schemes of deposit insurance.[65]

The banking panic from October 1907 to January 1908 brought losses to depositors. This led to the emergence of a strong movement in favour of deposit guaranty schemes, and eight states actually created deposit guaranty funds.[66] Today, the success of the Federal Deposit Insurance Corporation is universally recognized, and many concur with Milton Friedman and Anna J. Schwartz that:

> The major change was the enactment of Federal deposit insurance in 1934. This probably has succeeded, where the Federal Reserve Act failed, in rendering it impossible for a loss of public confidence in some banks to produce a widespread banking panic involving severe downward pressure on the stock of money; if so, it is of the greatest importance for the subsequent monetary history of the United States.[67]

Yet, few people are aware of the fierce hostility of most commercial bankers to what is today so generally praised. At the 1908 convention of the American Banking Association in Denver, Colorado, the President of the Association, Colonel J. D. Powers, said to his fellow bankers that deposit insurance was an attempt:

> to depreciate their [the bankers'] intelligence and dwarf their manhood, no less than to beguile them into an un-American unrighteous and undemocratic political trap, set solely for political game, and bated with false hopes, false doctrine and false pretence.

Almost everyone concurred with Colonel Powers. One Festus J. Wade denounced deposit insurance as an 'utterly absurd, silly, weak, unsound, socialistic doctrine'. The Federal Legislative Committee of the American Banking Association adopted in 1908 and 1909 the following resolution:

> Resolved,
> That the American Bankers Association is ulalterably opposed to any plan looking to the mutual guarantee of deposits, either by a State or the Nation, for the following reasons:
>
> 1. It is a function outside of State or National Government.
> 2. It is unsound in principle.
> 3. It is impractical and misleading.
> 4. It is revolutionary in character.

5. It is subversive to sound economics.
6. It will lower the standard of our present banking system.
7. It is productive of, and encourages, bad banking.
8. It is a delusion that a tax upon the strong will prevent failures of the weak.
9. It discredits honesty, ability and conservatism.
10. A loss suffered by one bank jeopardizes all banks.
11. The public must eventually pay the tax.
12. It will cause and not avert panics.

Only one banker dared defend the principle of deposit insurance, observing that, with such a guarantee, there would be no point in hoarding, that people would place their money in banks, which would be good for bankers. That was a good point to make, just after the sharp decline of the deposit–reserve ratio and the deposit–currency ratio. Surely all bankers would welcome additional deposits from people previously hoarding in fear of possible loss. This banker, named Schuette, said: 'Why should we allow our banking methods to continue on the same rules which, time and again, have brought disaster? Why not adopt a measure so easily obtainable?' Schuette was shouted down. Opposition to deposit insurance was so strong that it was with much difficulty that the advocates of a guarantee system succeeded in writing into the Banking Act of 1933 certain clauses providing for insurance of bank deposits.[68]

Considering that largely unsupervised foreign banking in the Euromarket resulted in 1982 in some degree of disaster, why not adopt measures so easily attainable? This question had been raised, in 1970, by Governor Otmar Emminger, in the following way:

> Such a massive concentration of short-term capital in an immense international market seems to call for some sort of surveillance and control on a world scale. Yet, nothing of the sort is envisaged. Each central bank must fight this 'monster' the best it can.[69]

An effort has been made in this paper to raise the same question again.

NOTES AND REFERENCES

1. I am much indebted to Dr Edward K. Smith for reading this paper, eliminating errors and making valuable suggestions. Responsibility for remaining defects is entirely my own.
2. Antonio Jorge, Jorge Salazar-Carillo and René P. Higonnet (eds), *Foreign*

Debt and Latin American Economic Development (New York: Pergamon Press, 1982).

3. E. Borchard and W. H. Wynne, *State Insolvency and Foreign Bondholders* (New Haven: Yale University Press 1951).
   Max Winckler, *Foreign Bonds, an Autopsy: a Study of Default and Repudiations of Government Obligations* (Philadelphia: Roland Swain Co, 1933).
   Ilse Mintz, *Deterioration in the Quality of Foreign Bonds, Issued in the United States 1920–1930* (New York: NBER, 1937).
4. Irving S. Friedman, in *Foreign Debt and Latin American Economic Development*, 'The Role of Debt Rescheduling', pp. 55–60.
5. Organization for Economic Cooperation and Development, 'Diagram 7', *Economic Surveys, United States*, November 1979, p. 45.
6. In the *Financial Times*, 18 Feb. 1983, John Plender writes that bankers and auditors are fiddling while the banking edifice threatens to burn, that some banks really do think they can fool all of the people all the time, and that various rescheduled loans look like being perpetually rescheduled. See his paper, 'International Bank Debt – of profits and imprudence'. But in the same newspaper of 10 Feb. 1983, Anthony Harris feels that the bankers are scapegoats 'in a play of illusion mounted by the governments and monetary authorities of the developed world . . . who should now be pelted with rotten eggs . . .' – The Micawber approach to debt.
7. William Hall, 'Citicorp ahead in Brazil despite difficulties', *Financial Times*, 16 March 1983.
8. 'British clearing banks, the manana bug, and the Ostrich position', *Economist*, 19–25 March 1983, p. 95.
9. Alan Friedman, 'Problem foreign loans focus scrutiny on bank profits', *Financial Times*, 23 March 1983.
10. Quoted by John Plender, *Financial Times*, 18 Feb. 1983.
11. See Henry C. Wallich, 'LDC Credit Risk and Bank Regulation', in *Foreign Debt and Latin American Economic Development*, p. 87.
12. Yoko Shibata, 'Discontent over Ministry of Finance guidance – Japanese banks take a new look at loans to sovereign borrowers', *Financial Times*, 8 March 1983. In the last few years, Japanese banks have engaged in vast 'balance of payments' loans (versus the more conservative 'project' loans). They will have real luck if they lose no more than 5 per cent.
13. See William Hall, 'Holes in the Supervisory Net', *Financial Times*, 17 Nov. 1982.
14. Lamberto Dini, *Financial Problems of the World Economy*, Lecture given at the Istituto Centrale di Banche e banchieri, Rome, 24 Nov. 1982.
15. R. Masera, 'Comments on Helmut W. Mayer's Paper', Proceedings of a Colloquium on 'The European Capital Market: Problems and Outlook' held in Milan on 27–28 Nov. 1980, published in *Giornale degli Economisti e Annali di Economia*, Università Commerciale Luigi Bocconi, Sept.–Dec., 1981.
16. As of late fees have tended to increase at the expense of the spread over Libor, the current practice of immediate inclusion of fees into profit is all the more to be deplored.
17. See H. Baschnagel, 'Neue Fragezeichen am Eurogeldmarkt, Euromarkte

heute', *Neue Zürcher Zeitung*, Supplement, 23 Nov. 1982. Of the total, 75 per cent was in dollars, 12 per cent in Deutsche marks, and 6 per cent in Swiss francs.

18. Henry C. Wallich, 'Why the Eurocurrency Market Needs Restraint', *Colombia Journal of World Business*, Fall 1979.
19. Data taken from Victor Argy, *The Postwar International Money Crisis, An Analysis* (London: George Allen & Unwin, 1981). A classic paper is Helmut W. Mayer's, 'The BIS concept of the Eurocurrency market', *Euromoney*, May 1976. It makes clear that the measurement of outstanding Eurodollars raises difficult conceptual and practical problems. To a large extent it is based on guesswork.
20. Paul Einzig, *The Eurodollar System, Practice and Theory of International Interest Rates* (London: Macmillan, 1965) p. 64.
21. Apparent or real surprise? The existence of dissimulated debt was '*le secret de Polichinelle*'. This is discussed in my paper on Latin American debt, *Foreign Debt and Latin American Economic Development*.
22. R. G. Hawtrey, *A Century of Bank Rate* (London: Frank Cass, 1962) pp. 83–5 and pp. 105–10.
23. Alan Friedman, of the *Financial Times*, notes that this subsidiary 'was widely believed to have been left largely unsupervised by the Luxemburg authorities'. It is in response to these difficulties that a new international banking supervisory code has been drafted and is expected to replace the Basle Concordat of 1975. See the *Financial Times*, 19 March 1983.
24. P. A. Wellons, *Borrowing By Developing Countries on the Eurocurrency Market* (Paris: Development Centre of the OECD, 1977).
25. A. Brandle, 'Chancen und Risiken in Syndizierten Eurokreditmärkte Heute', special supplement of the *Neue Zürcher Zeitung*, 23 Nov. 1982.
26. Lamberto Dini, *Financial Problems of the World Economy*, *ibid.*
27. Karl Otto Pohl, 'Durststreckte fur Schuldnerländer Verstärkte Spannungen an den Internationalen Kreditmärkten', *Neue Zürcher Zeitung*, 23 November 1982.
28. J. M. Keynes, 'The Great Slump of 1930', *The Nation and Atheneum*, 20 and 27 December 1930.
29. That was the experience of the Italian taxpayer some fifty years ago. See Ernesto Rossi, *I Padroni del Vapore*, ch. 6, La socializzazione delle perdite, pp. 120–45, Editori Laterza, 1957.
30. Alan Friedman, 'The Search for a Banking Lifeboat', *Financial Times*, 15 March 1983.
31. Alan R. Holmes and Fred H. Klopstock, 'The Market For Dollar Deposits in Europe'. *Monthly Review*, Federal Reserve Bank of New York, November 1960.
32. For a thorough discussion of risk and interbank deposits, see the excellent paper of Robert Z. Aliber, 'Monetary Aspects of Offshore Markets', *Columbia Journal of World Business*, Fall 1979.
33. In their book *The International Money Market* (Englewood Cliffs NJ: Prentice-Hall, 1978) Gunter Dufey and Ian H. Giddy state on p. 115, that the US balance of payments has little or no effect on the growth of the Eurodollar market. At the other extreme of the spectrum of opinions, Jean Denizet finds the explanation of the growth of the Eurodollar market in the

1960s in the American balance of payments deficit; see, *Inflation, Dollar, Eurodollar* (Paris: NRF Gallimard, 1971), p. 59. Henry C. Wallich writes: 'It is perfectly true that OPEC funds, or funds originating in the US payments deficits have at times flowed into the Eurodollar market. But the market is not dependent upon such special resources. A slightly rising interest rate resulting from strong demand for funds will draw virtually unlimited amounts from national markets into the Euromarket', in 'Why the Eurocurrency Market Needs Restraint', p. 20.

34. Jane Sneddon Little, *Euro-dollars, The Money Market Gypsies* (New York: Harper & Row, 1975) pp. 99–100.
35. Robert Triffin, 'The American Response to the European Monetary System', reprinted in R. E. Baldwin and J. D. Richardson (eds), *International Trade and Finance* (Boston: Little, Brown, 1981), pp. 479–80.
36. Paul Einzig, *The Eurodollar System*, p. 5.
37. Subsequently, the extremely low cost of opening a 'shell' in Nassau, the Cayman islands, or similar places, made it easier for smaller banks to operate in the Eurodollar market presumably borrowing from the larger banks. Jane S. Little, *Euro-dollars, The Money Market Gypsies*, p. 130, describes an American bank whose Nassau branch, consisting of a plaque, a walk-in closet, a file cabinet and a telephone, accounted for 8 per cent of the bank's pretax profit in 1971. All the business is negotiated in the US and merely recorded in Nassau. This is now common practice and is, of course unsound banking.
38. See Gabriel Ferras, 'Les Banques Centrales et le Marché de l'Eurodollar' *L'Eurodollar*, Herbert V. Prochnow (ed.) (Paris: Calman-Lévy, 1971) pp. 69–87; and, Paul Einzig, *The Eurodollar System* (London: Macmillan, 1965), ch. 13, Attitudes of Central Banks, pp. 112–23.
39. Charles O. Hardy, reviewing central banking in the 1920s concluded that there had not been much co-operation among central banks, and he considered this to be beneficial, for the pressure to co-operate represented a pressure to pursue unsound policy, to escape the consequences of one's own poor decisions. C. O. Hardy, *Credit Policies of the Federal Reserve System* (Washington, DC, 1932), reprinted by Garland Publishing Co., Renè Higonnet and Mira Wilkins (eds), 1983.
40. François Perroux, Jean Denizet, Henri Bourguinat, *Inflation, Dollar, Eurodollar* (Paris: NRF Gallimard, 1971) pp. 67–8.
41. Leland B. Yeager, *International Monetary Relations: Theory, History and Policy* (New York: Harper & Row, 1976, 2nd ed.) p. 458.
42. Otmar Emminger, 'Le marché des eurodevises: facteur de stabilite ou d'instabilité monetaire', *L'Eurodollar*, Herbert V. Prochnow (ed.) (Paris: Calmann-Lévy, 1971) pp. 273, 282, 287. See also *Eurocurrencies and the International Monetary System* (Washington, DC: American Enterprise Institute, 1976) p. 24: 'The combination of fixed exchange rates and the rapid flow of information regarding security prices through the Eurodollar market, implicit in the dollar's role as an effective supranational money, guaranteed in time to produce massive international capital flows'.
43. Alberto Ferrari, 'Le point de vue de l'Italie', *L'Eurodollar*, presentation de Hubert V. Prochnow Paris: Calmann-Lévy, 1971) p. 233.
44. Leland B. Yeager, 'The German struggle against imported inflation',

International Monetary Relations, ch. 24, pp. 497–8. Gerhard Fels, *Der Internationale Preiszusammenhang, eine Studie den Inflations-import in der Bundesrepublik* (Cologne: Heymanns, 1969). According to Fels, there is no historical example of a swap of spot for forward funds policy working as desired, p. 42.
45. Milton Gilbert, *Quest for World Monetary Order, The Gold-Dollar System and its Aftermath* (New York: John Wiley 1980) p. 102.
46. Paul Einzig, *The Eurodollar System, Practice and Theory of International Interest Rates* (London: Macmillan, 1965) 2nd ed. p. 117.
47. Fritz Machlup, 'The magicians and their rabbits', *Morgan Guaranty Survey*, May 1971, pp. 3–13. Leland B. Yeager, *International Monetary Relations*, pp. 435–6.
48. Paul Einzig, *The Eurodollar System*, p. 8.
49. Otmar Emminger, 'Le marché des eurodevises', p. 287.
50. Radcliffe Report, *Committee on the Working of the Monetary System-Report*, Cmnd 827, (London: HMSO, 1959) par. 424, p. 147.
51. Radcliffe Report, par. 184, p. 65.
52. Radcliffe Report, par. 424, p. 147.
53. For a good detailed account of Regulation Q and the CD market, see J. O. Light and William L. White, *The Financial System* (Homewood, Illinois: Richard D. Irwin, 1979), pp. 268 *et seq*.
54. Marcello de Cecco, 'International Financial Markets and U.S. Domestic Policy since 1945', *International Affairs*, p. 398. See also his essay, 'New Dimensions for International Lending', *The World Today*, September 1974.
55. Paul Einzig, *The Destiny of the Dollar* (London: Macmillan, 1972) p. 47.
56. See Milton Friedman and Anna Schwartz, *A Monetary History of the United States*, 1867–1960 (Princeton, NJ: Princeton University Press, 1963) pp. 443–4.
57. Federal Reserve Act, as amended through 1976, Washington, Dec. 1976, p. 41.
58. Charles A. Coombs, *The Arena of International Finance* (New York: John Wiley, 1976) p. 206.
59. The way in which the large American banks defeated the squeeze is described by Fred H. Klopstock, 'L'emploi des Eurodollars par les Banques des Etats-Unis', *L'Eurodollar*, pp. 93–4.
60. It became clearer and clearer that direct controls were not working. See George P. Shultz and Kenneth W. Dam, *Economic Policy Beyond the Headlines* (New York: W. W. Norton, 1977) p. 112. Gunter Dufey and Ian Giddy have argued, contrary to most writers, that the Eurodollar market did not grow in the 1960s because of US capital controls, but in spite of them. See *The International Money Market: Perspective and Prognosis*, pp. 259–68.
61. Edward M. Bernstein, 'Les eurodollars: les mouvements de capitaux et la balance americaine des paiements', *L'Eurodollar*, Herbert V. Prochnow (ed.) (Paris: Calmann-Lévy, 1971) p. 205. This is a period of American history when the authorities were 'doctoring' balance of payments data. See Milton Gilbert, *Quest for World Monetary Order*, (New York: John Wiley, 1980), p. 140, and when the President of the United States claimed

authority under the Trading with the Enemy Act of 1917 to implement disguised forms of exchange control.

62. Cf. Milton Gilbert, *Quest for World Monetary Order*, p. 152. According to Charles A. Coombs, *The Arena of International Finance*, these issues amounted to $3 billion and were made first by the Export-Import Bank, and then the US Treasury, in response to suggestions by the New York Federal Reserve Bank, p. 207. Official policy was a mixture of benign neglect and intervention, in short it was incoherent.
63. These issues are discussed in Ramses, '*Rapport Annuel Mondial Sur le Système Economique et les Stratégies*', Institut Français des Relations Internationales (Paris: Editions Economica, 1982) pp. 161–2.
64. Henry C. Wallich, 'Why the Euromarket needs restraint', *Columbia Journal of World Business*, Fall 1979, pp. 17–24.
65. Wilbert M. Schneider, *The American Banking Association, Its Past and Present* (Washington, DC: Public Affairs Press, 1956), pp. 228–30.
66. Milton Friedman and Anna J. Schwartz, *A Monetary History of the United States, 1867–1960* (Princeton, NJ: Princeton University Press, 1963) pp. 171–2. Victor Morawetz, *The Banking and Currency Problem in the United States* (New York: North American Review Publishing Co., 1909) pp. 72–9. A. Piatt Andrew, 'The essential and the unessential in currency legislation', Page lecture, Yale University, 1 May 1913, *Yale Review*, June 1913. Andrew Jay Frame, *Insuring Bank Deposits is Purely Theoretical, Impractical, Revolutionary, and Fatal to Conservatism, History Condemns It* (Waukesha, 1908). Fritz Redlich, *The molding of American Banking* (New York: Hafner, 1951) vol. 2, part II, pp. 215–17.
67. Milton Friedman and Anna J. Schwartz, *ibid.* p. 11.
68. Louis A. Rufener, *Money and Banking in the United States* (New York: Houghton Mifflin, 1938) p. 715.
69. Otmar Emminger, 'Le marché des eurodevises: facteur de stabilité ou d'instabilité monétaire', *L'Eurodollar* (Paris: Calmann-Lévy, 1971) p. 288.

COMMENT

JANE SNEDDON LITTLE

In his paper, René Higonnet provided an interesting review of many of the events which contributed to the development of the Eurodollar market. Now I think it might be useful to suggest a framework to help us to link these events together and to view them in a broader context. Basically, the Eurodollar market developed because bankers and their customers carefully cultivated it as a means of avoiding increasingly expensive national regulations. The creation of the Eurodollar market was a pioneering effort in the banking industry's continuing struggle to escape restrictions by means of financial innovation whenever regulatory costs outweigh their benefits. The post-war stream of financial innovations started by a few Eurobanks has culminated in the wave of deregulation currently sweeping the banking industry – particularly in the USA but also, to a much more limited extent, abroad.

The prerequisites for a flourishing Eurodollar market are: (1) that Eurobanks must be able to operate profitably with narrower margins between deposit and loan rates than banks in the United States; and (2) that all actors must have access to foreign currencies. As Mr Higonnet has pointed out, the existence of banking regulations, such as Regulation Q and reserve requirements, within the United States and their complete or partial absence in the Eurocurrency market fulfil the first condition. Although Mr Higonnet did not mention the second requirement, the need for access to foreign currencies, it certainly was equally important and was not met until the European countries restored convertibility in 1958–9. Accordingly, foreign exchange controls prevented episodic Eurocurrency transactions from acquiring the characteristics of an organised market until the late 1950s.

By then an embryonic Eurodollar market already existed, for according to M. S. Mendelsohn,[1] the new Chinese Communist government began holding its dollar balances with a Soviet bank in Paris in 1949 to prevent the United States from seizing these assets. This was the Banque Commerciale Pour L'Europe du Nord – the famous 'Eurobank'. When the United States actually did block Chinese assets during the Korean War, the Soviet Union also began placing and then borrowing dollar balances in Western Europe. Of course, the separation of currency from country risk which is inherent in a Eurodollar transaction is no longer a driving force behind the growth of the market. At times, however, this separability returns to centre stage as the Iranian hostage crisis and the Falklands War reminded us.

While the development of the Eurodollar market clearly received some further impetus from the sterling crisis of 1957, Mr Higonnet has a point in questioning the importance of the Bank of England's ban on the use of sterling to finance non-sterling trade. The impact of these restrictions may have been more symbolic than practical, a signal that sterling's days as the major international currency were indeed over and that London's future lay in applying her financial expertise and her foreign branch network to transactions denominated in another currency.

Clearly, many private and official British bankers had been working throughout the 1950s to restore sterling and the City of London to their former positions at the centre of world finance. Accordingly, when Sir

George Bolton left the Bank of England to become Chairman of the Bank of London and South America in 1957, one of his first decisions in the face of the new restrictions on the international use of sterling was to prepare 'a deliberate withdrawal from sterling activities in the belief that the international use of sterling would virtually cease'.[2] The fact that the 1959 Radcliffe Report – though it did not mention Eurodollars – did say that it mattered less whether international trade be financed in pounds than that it be financed through London suggests that Sir George Bolton's goals were shared more broadly in official as well as in private British circles – as Mr Higonnet has suggested.

Nevertheless, Mr Higonnet is undoubtedly correct to stress the relatively great importance of the rise in the British Bank rate to 7 per cent. From 1932 to the mid-1950s, the US authorities rarely allowed short-term rates to rise above a level of 1 or 2 per cent; thus, money management was not really worthwhile. In conjunction with the return to convertibility, however, the advent of higher interest rates in Europe and in the United States from the mid-1950s made banking regulations such as reserve requirements increasingly expensive and spurred financial innovation and active money management. For example, in addition to early Eurodollar transactions, 1961 witnessed the introduction of negotiable CDs by the First National City Bank of New York.

Having mentioned regulation, I would like to interrupt the historical flow to stress that the Eurobanks' relative freedom from regulation does not necessarily mean that they are unsupervised. Although many supervisory gaps persist, the situation does not appear to be quite as bleak as Mr Higonnet suggests, and progress towards a co-ordinated and co-operative approach to surveillance of the international banking system is being made – thanks largely to the efforts of the Committee on Bank Regulations and Supervisory Practices (the Cooke Committee). For instance, most countries now endorse the principle of parental responsibility for the solvency of their foreign branches and to a more limited extent of their foreign subsidiaries. Accordingly, most authorities are beginning to use consolidated data in addressing prudential and supervisory issues concerning banks headquartered in their countries. Moreover, some authorities – the German, Japanese and US – do conduct routine or periodic on-site examinations of foreign branches and, in the case of the United States, subsidiaries.[3] Further progress in this area would, of course, be most welcome.

Mr Higonnet has also questioned the soundness of the Eurobanks' tendency to borrow short to lend long. Surely, maturity transformation

– to a degree, at least – is one of the functions we expect financial intermediaries to fulfil. Moreover, according to a summary measure developed in 1976 by Niehans and Hewson,[4] the amount of maturity transformation performed by Eurobanks in the United Kingdom in mid-1982 had declined considerably from its 1977 level. And even then that volume was below the amount of maturity transformation which estimates suggest the domestic US commercial banking system undertakes.[5]

To return to the chronology of Eurodollars, as Mr Higonnet has indicated, few US banks were active in the Eurodollar market until the tight money periods of 1966 and 1969, when domestic money market rates rose above the levels permitted on bank deposits by Regulation Q. Accordingly, banks with foreign branches bid vigorously in the Eurodollar market in an effort to replace funds lost at home. Contrary to Mr Higonnet's assessment, however, I remain convinced that, for US banks as a group, this effort to circumvent the Federal Reserve's restraint was largely futile because banks borrowing Eurodollars were merely reshuffling among themselves reserves already available within the US banking system. The expansionary impact which resulted from the substitution of reserve-free Eurodollars for reserve-bearing deposits (usually time deposits) was relatively minor. While individual banks with foreign branches and their large corporate customers may have gained a competitive advantage from these Eurodollar borrowings, these large firms could also have obtained funds through the commercial paper market. As you may remember, the issuance of commercial paper by bank holding companies also came into vogue at this time.

Basically, as Helmut Mayer has stressed,[6] because the dollar serves as the international transactions currency, in an era of fixed or managed exchange rates capital flows in and out of this country do not change the quantity of reserves available within the US banking system. Unfortunately, such capital movements do affect the availability of reserves in other countries – a fact which has not always been adequately appreciated in the United States. Moreover, while the Eurodollar market provides an extremely efficient channel for capital movements, it does not change the direction of those flows. Capital would move from low-return to high-return investments whether or not the Eurodollar market existed. Accordingly, sterling and the dollar would have suffered foreign exchange crisis and the developing countries would have attracted funds with or without the Eurodollar market.

Another temporary spur to the development of the Eurocurrency market during the 1960s was the imposition of exchange controls, such as the Voluntary Foreign Credit Restraint Program and the Foreign Direct Investment Regulations, which the United States imposed to protect the dollar. Because these regulations required most US foreign investment to be financed from abroad and limited loans to foreigners from banks in the United States, US banks had additional incentives to establish overseas branches to tap the Eurocurrency market. The Eurodollar market has continued to thrive since the removal of these controls in 1974, however; thus, these regulations seemingly gave only 'infant industry' protection to the market and helped spread awareness of its many advantages.

Indeed, the fundamental reason for the growth of the Eurodollar market has been the advantages – primarily in terms of interest rates but also in terms of risk and convenience – which it offers over the domestic US money market. Of course, these advantages stem largely from the relative weakness of regulation in the Eurodollar market. Basically, thus, the Eurodollar market is an offshore competitor, an increasingly popular offshore competitor, of the domestic US money market. For instance, US non-banks had $14.9 billion in loans outstanding from Eurobanks in September 1982. That is an amount equal to about 9 per cent of C + I loans at large commercial banks. At times, such as late 1981, foreign branch loans to US non-banks have risen as much as 50 per cent in a single quarter because the Eurodollar rate was substantially below the US prime rate. Similarly, US non-bank holdings of Eurocurrency deposits have also been growing rapidly. In September 1982 US non-bank businesses held $90 billion in Eurodollar deposits. Such deposits grew 70 per cent from late 1980, or four times as fast as US M2. Clearly, therefore, a growing share of US financial transactions is occurring offshore as more and more money managers become sensitive to the price advantages of using these facilities.

Of course, the rapid growth of the Eurocurrency market is just one example of the widespread transfer of US financial transactions to comparatively unregulated channels. Other examples of this trend first established by the early Eurobanks are the increased importance of the markets for commercial paper and repurchase agreements, the growth of the money market mutual funds and the provision of financial services by non-bank firms like Sears and Shearson-American Express. This development is exerting pressure, in turn, for gradual deregulation of the US banking industry. The elimination of Regulation Q interest rate ceilings legislated by the Depository Institutions Deregulation and Monetary Control Act of 1980 and the arrival of Super Now and money market accounts are cases in point. The regulations permitting the establishment, in late 1981, of international banking facilities free from reserve requirements and interest rate ceilings on non-resident deposits is another example.

Similarly, the possibility of tapping the Eurodollar market has also undoubtedly made it easier for foreign banks to penetrate the US banking market without developing a domestic deposit base. Competition from foreign banks, which, prior to the passage of the International Banking Act in 1978, were able to locate in more than one state, has been one force leading to the re-examination of the McFadden prohibitions of interstate banking. Of course, the expansion of foreign banks in this country does not rival the geographic spread of domestic multibank holding companies through their non-bank subsidiaries. However, the unequal treatment of foreign and domestic banks prior to the passage of the International Banking Act seems to have brought the interstate banking issue into focus. Indeed, that legislation required a study of the McFadden restrictions.

Although the Eurocurrency markets have spurred financial innovation and deregulation primarily in the United States, they have also exerted similar pressures abroad. According to a recent paper by David Howard and Karen Johnson,[7] for instance, the Bank of England's 'corset' or limit on the growth of each bank's interest-bearing deposits was undermined by increased use of the offshore Eurosterling market, particularly after the abolition of exchange controls in 1979. Once the British authorities recognised that this scheme was fostering financial innovation and disintermediation, the corset was removed. A similar story can be told about the Canadian Winnipeg Agreement which set interest-rate ceilings on large Canadian dollar CDs of up to 364 days maturity from 1972 to 1975. By contrast, swapped US dollar accounts at Canadian banks had no interest rate ceilings or reserve requirements. Accordingly, such deposits grew from C$171 million in September 1972 to C$2 865 million in September 1974. The Bank Act of 1980 has subsequently set a reserve ratio of 3 per cent on non-Canadian dollar deposits and legislated the gradual reduction of reserve requirements on Canadian dollar deposits.

Despite some major steps towards deregulation of the domestic banking industry, the offshore markets retain some significant advantages, such as the absence of reserve requirements. The discrepancies amount to discriminatory taxation of domestic as opposed to offshore transactions and are hard to justify and complicate the conduct of monetary policy. Unfortunately, I do not share Renè Higonnet's optimism about the ease with which non-distorting controls could be placed on the Eurodollar market – given the significantly different approaches to banking regulation and the different attitudes towards international banking, in general, held in various countries. We know that the Eurodollar market grew in response to domestic banking regulation. Indeed, in an era of high interest rates, regulation seems to lead almost inevitably to financial innovation; thus, an emphasis on regulating the Eurocurrency market itself could well be counter-productive. Instead, further deregulation of domestic markets – perhaps in conjunction with the payment of interest on reserves – and increased harmonisation of banking regulations internationally is the more likely course. Limits to the process of deregulation do exist, however, since some regulations are, after all, deemed to be worth their cost. Most bankers would probably agree that deposit insurance and bank examination are current cases in point.

NOTES AND REFERENCES

1. M. S. Mendelsohn, *Money on the Move; The Modern International Capital Market* (New York: McGraw-Hill, 1980) p. 18.
2. Sir George Bolton in an interview with *The Banker* of February 1970, quoted in *A Banker's World: The Revival of the City 1957–1970: Speeches and Writings of Sir George Bolton*, edited by Richard Fry (London: Hutchinson, 1970) p. 28.
3. For further detailed information see Richard Dale, *Bank Supervision Around the World* (New York: Group of Thirty, 1982).
4. Jurg Niehans and John Hewson, 'The Eurodollar Market and Monetary Theory', *Journal of Money, Credit and Banking*, VIII (February 1976) pp. 1–27.
5. Jane Sneddon Little, 'Liquidity Creation by Eurobanks: A Range of Possibilities', *The Columbia Journal of World Business*, XIV (Fall 1979) pp. 41–2.
6. See, for instance, Helmut Mayer, 'The Eurocurrency Market and the Autonomy of US Monetary Policy', *The Columbia Journal of World Business*, XIV (Fall 1979) pp. 32–7.
7. David H. Howard and Karen H. Johnson, 'Financial Innovation, Deregulation and Monetary Policy: The Foreign Experience', a paper presented at a Conference on Interest Rate Deregulation and Monetary Policy, Monterey, California, 28–30 November 1982.

COMMENT

RAINER S. MASERA

In these comments I shall address three points raised by Mr Higonnet, indicate basic differences in approach to Eurodollar issues between Mr Higonnet and myself, briefly discuss prudential control and finally end with a concluding observation.

Firstly, according to Mr Higonnet 'bankers and economists discussing Eurodollars are much like their predecessors of the heroic age of British monetary theory one hundred and fifty years ago . . . The story of Eurodollars is a mystery story of puzzled magicians pulling unexpected rabbits out of hats where they had previously hidden chickens'.

Mr Higonnet's paper purports to solve the mystery by throwing light on the culprits and by suggesting what course of action should be taken to prevent new crimes being perpetrated. In a nutshell, it is Mr Higonnet's 'uncharitable view' that the Eurodollar is an 'unnecessary' system, which thrives on the combination of 'unsound banking' by commercial banks and the connivance – indeed, the complicity – of central banks, willing to pursue 'unsound policies' through the intermediary of the Eurosystem. It is accordingly, Mr Higonnet's belief that the market's growth should be 'immediately', although belatedly, checked, before a disaster occurs, by imposing reserve requirements at an identical level for all Eurobanks, irrespective of currency denomination.

This commentator's views on the role and functions of the Euromarkets are far more positive than Mr Higonnet's. Of course, this is not to deny the gravity of today's problems nor that a more appropriate mix might have been selected in the well known trade-off between the cost and allocative efficiency of financial intermediaries and the implementation of an appropriate degree of control by the monetary authorities on their credit-creation potential and in the prudential field.

Rather than providing a detailed critical analysis of the many points on which I find myself in disagreement with Mr Higonnet, I shall concentrate on two specific issues – the first one of prudential character and the second one of monetary policy nature. These will allow me to highlight, in the final part of my comments, some key questions on the problems of the efficacy and control of the Euromarkets.

Secondly, Mr Higonnet states that 'the Ambrosiano disaster has revived alarm about the behaviour of central banks'. He quotes press articles saying that 'Two hundred and fifty international banks involved in the collapse of the Banco Ambrosiano bitterly blame the Bank of Italy for not having extended its guaranty to the debts of an Italian bank'.

In addressing the question of the Banco Ambrosiano – which by the way obviously does not pertain to the early history of the Eurodollar market – two clear-cut distinctions should be made: the first is between obligations of the Banco Ambrosiano itself, directly or via branches abroad, and obligations of banks abroad owned by holding companies, also based abroad, of which the Banco Ambrosiano was a majority shareholder. The second is between parental responsibility in the case of commercial and central banks.

As to the latter point, it must be emphasised that the 1975 Concordat, to which Mr Higonnet makes reference in this context, did *not* address the issue of the moral or legal commitment of central banks to pay the debts of a collapsing bank. Its aim was rather to ensure that banks' foreign establishments were adequately supervised.

Having agreed on the need for consultation and co-operation between host and parent supervisory authorities, central banks also recognised in the Concordat that it was not possible to define clear-cut rules for determining exactly where the responsibility for supervision should be placed in any specific situation. A number of general guidelines could, however, be agreed upon concerning the prudential aspects of liquidity, solvency and foreign exchange positions.

On the specific question of the sharing of responsibility for supervision in the case of solvency controls, the relevant points made in the Concordat are the following:

> For foreign subsidiaries and joint ventures, primary responsibility rests with host authorities; but, in addition parent authorities must take account of the exposure of their domestic banks' foreign subsidiaries and joint ventures because of those parent banks' moral commitments to those foreign establishments. For foreign branches, solvency is indistinguishable from that of the parent bank as a whole. It is therefore essentially a matter for parent supervisory authorities.

It is clear from this excerpt that the question of the moral or legal commitment of central banks was not addressed in the Concordat. The problem of responsibility was discussed only with reference to commercial banks.

As regards this point, a clear-cut distinction was drawn between branches and subsidiaries. As to the latter, a moral commitment to those foreign establishments was mentioned for parent commercial banks. It is evident, however, that the question of the moral commitment of the parent bank is clearly not applicable in the case of the Banco Ambrosiano, since the Banco Ambrosiano itself went into liquidation.

Mr Higonnet refers perhaps to the G-10 Governor's press communiqué issued in September 1974, which addressed the problem of the lender of last resort in the Euromarkets, rather than to the 1975 Concordat. Here again, however, no reference was made to the questions of any central bank 'payment' of the debts of a collapsing bank, as was explained in Dr Dini's paper[1] to which Mr Higonnet makes references. The focus was exclusively on the problems of illiquidity.

Recalling the precise words of the communiqué, 'The Governors . . . recognised that it would not be practical to lay down in advance detailed rules and procedures for the provision of temporary liquidity. But they were satisfied that means are available for that purpose and will be used if and when necessary'.

Any commitment of the domestic monetary authorities to repay debts incurred through fraudulent activities by foreign establishments owned by holding companies incorporated abroad, over which no direct supervision could be exercised, would only result in a stimulus to irresponsible risk-taking activities by commercial banks, thereby contributing to a global deterioration of standards.

As to the Banco Ambrosiano's direct foreign liabilities, the Italian monetary authorities made it possible for the new bank which was created after the liquidation of the Banco Ambrosiano to repay all the latter's outstanding debts.

Thirdly, I come to a specific critical assessment of Mr Higonnet's concluding remarks on the need to check the growth of the Euromarkets by setting reserve requirements at an identical level for all Eurobanks irrespective of currency denomination, but varying according to maturity. In his opinion, this would ensure that no banking system would have an advantage over any other

It is not entirely clear on what analytical grounds Mr Higonnet advocates his compulsory reserve plan. In particular, he does not seem to subscribe to the 'bank multiplier approach' to the analysis of the Euromarkets.

Be that as it may – I will come back to this general point later – it is easy to show that the scheme he proposes is technically questionable.

To start with, it should be noted that the abolition of competitive advantages between domestic financial systems and the corresponding Euromarkets would require (a necessary but not a sufficient condition) also integration of internal methods and tools of control in all the main countries. However, some important countries, notably the UK, do not use methods of control hinged on the monetary base and on non-interest bearing compulsory reserves.

But quite apart from this difficulty, the basic technical reason why Mr Higonnet's plan does not appear to be feasible in practice is that the introduction of non-interest bearing reserve ratios identical for all Eurobanks, irrespective of currency denominations, would place different burdens on each of the currencies, depending on the existing spreads of market interest rates.

Non-interest bearing compulsory reserves can be taken to represent an indirect tax, the actual rate of which is given by the product of the reserve coefficient and the interest rate that could be obtained in the market. The additional cost per unit of deposit which a Eurobank would have to bear in the event of a common uniform reserve requirement, by operating in one currency rather than another, would therefore be given by the product of the reserve coefficient and the interest rate differential. The Eurobanks would tend, therefore, to enter all transactions in their books in the currency with the lowest nominal interest rate. Forward contracts would, of course, make it possible to provide their clients with any currency effectively requested at the time of the expiry of the credit contract.

Let me now try to state in a more positive way the fundamental differences between my approach and that of Mr Higonnet to the questions of analysis and control of the Euromarkets.[2]

To start with, I would submit that the theoretical understanding of the working of Euromarkets has made substantial progress. I would, indeed, go as far as to say that broad consensus has emerged in the literature on an interpretation based on portfolio lines.

Explanation of the growth of the Eurosystem should in principle be found in the context of a general equilibrium worldwide portfolio model of financial intermediation. In this context, the business of Eurobanks is likened to that of non-bank financial intermediaries, who offer liquid liabilities for which the Eurobanking system can actually provide alternatives.

These 'portfolio' or 'credit' models to Eurobanking show the inappropriateness of the so-called fixed coefficient multiplier approaches.[3]

The initial deposit multiplier approach is not helpful from a heuristic point of view because it focuses on the repercussions of an initial flow of deposits, for given interest rates and behaviour and leakage coefficients, as if the market could be considered in isolation from the overall process of deposit and credit creation within banks and non-bank financial intermediaries in the national economic systems.

The portfolio approach also helps to recognise that more meaningful analysis of deposit and credit multipliers conducted in the framework of a multi-stage banking system requires modification in order to allow for portfolio adjustments to shifts in asset preferences between imperfect substitutes. Additionally, any such shifts to Eurodeposits tend to lower their relative yield.

These models indicate, in fact, that the first round deposit multiplier tends to be less than unity, i.e. *a divisor*. The full response – which relates the overall 'final' change in Eurodeposits to an original shift of deposits from domestic to Eurobanks – must, however, take into account the positive impacts resulting from redeposits in the Euromarket and the possible savings of monetary base reserves.

If this analytical framework is adopted, the question that has still to be answered is why Eurodeposits have shown such a rapid growth, compared to other financial assets.

The explanations I would give are twofold. To start with, I would stress the relevance of the interaction of inherent competitive advantages of Eurobanks, due to the lower degree of regulation than is commonly applied in domestic markets, and the efficiency of Eurobanks themselves in spurring financial innovation. A second argument is that far from being unnecessary as Mr Higonnet claims – demand for net Eurocurrency deposits (as proxied by the so-called 'net' market size) has been primarily related to world trade and worldwide payments imbalances.[4] Since these variables have shown very rapid growth in the past twenty years, they help to explain why the Eurocurrency market has shown such substantial expansion throughout the 1960s and the 1970s.

If an analytical approach along 'portfolio' lines is adopted, it then follows that a uniform system of reserve requirements on all Eurodeposits, such as the one proposed by Mr Higonnet, is not called for, quite apart from the question of its technical feasibility.

This, however, is not to say that one should be totally against any form of reserve requirement. In the technical discussions that took place in Basle in 1979–80 on control of the Euromarket I suggested, for instance, that a case could be made for either interest bearing or for differentiated reserve requirements (according to the currency of the deposit) in respect to Eurodeposits which are close to transactions balances – i.e. sight and very short-term (up to 1 week or 1 month) non-bank deposits.[5]

I find the views expressed at that time reinforced by the enactment of the Depository Institutions Deregulation and Monetary Control Act and by greater reliance on monetary control in the US, which by leading to high nominal interest rates, increases the cost advantage to Eurobanking intermediaries in respect of demand deposits.

Finally, I address the question of prudential control. It is in this area that, as is now evident, efforts to achieve better control of the market and reduce competitive advantages *vis-à-vis* domestic financial intermediaries should have been more incisive.

Quite a few economists and central banks alike saw in the 1979–80 that a potentially dangerous situation was developing in the international financial system, although many were too complacent at the time. Indeed, it was precisely in reaction to such complacency that I wrote in 1980,

> The prudential aspect of the Euromarkets is the one that deserved more attention and more immediate consideration: the combination of maturity transformation and sovereign risk in a world payments system characterized by sizeable and lasting imbalances, and by the large inherited debt positions of many countries, suggests that risks incurred by the Eurobanks may be high and their position vulnerable. A weak dollar, accompanied by negative real rates of interest no doubt reduced the burden of outstanding debts after the first oil shock. The second shock . . . is accompanied by determined efforts of the US authorities to combat domestic inflation. The adjustment path of the world economy . . . may not be immune to the opening up of crisis point.

Evidence of the recognition of perspective dangers can, in fact, be found in the Basle Communiqué of April 1980, where the Governors stated their will to give high priority to ensuring that banks' international business be supervised on a consolidated basis, country risk exposure be better monitored and more comprehensive and consistent data for monitoring banks' maturity transformation be developed.

But evidently this was not enough. With the benefit of hindsight it is, however, fair to admit that the size of the real interest rate on dollars and the length of the world recession were not easy to foresee.

What appear now to have been imprudent policies by commercial banks are partly the result of major shifts in economic policies – and notably monetary policies – which were not easy to anticipate.[6]

I conclude by observing that, in my opinion, we are now moving along a narrow and dangerous path. However, if (i) domestic policies in major industrial countries will not choke the feeble recovery now beginning to manifest itself, if (ii) sufficient financial resources are promptly made available to the Bretton Woods institutions, notably to the IMF, and if (iii) commercial banks act coolly by not attempting hasty and counter-productive withdrawals of funds from developing countries, it should be possible to sail out of dangerous waters with relatively few scars.

Three big ifs, but the attainment of these goals is well within our reach.

NOTES AND REFERENCES

1. See L. Dini, 'Financial Problems of the World Economy', lecture given at the Istituto Centrale di Banche e Banchieri, Rome, 24 November 1982. On this question, see also C. Ciampi, 'Il sistema creditizio e il riequilibrio dell'economia', paper presented at the Forex Club Italiano, Turin, 2 October 1982.
2. The points made here are necessarily sketchy. For a more comprehensive presentation, see R. Masera 'Deposit Creation, Multiplication and the Eurodollar Market', in *A Debate on the Eurodollar Market*, Ente per gli Studi Monetari Bancari e Finanziari 'L. Einaudi', December 1972 and 'The Eurocurrency Markets: their Development, the Problem of their Control and their Role in the International Monetary System', paper prepared at the invitation of the External Financing and Development Branch of Unctad and published in *Mercati Monetari Internazionali e Inflazione*, Università degli Studi di Roma, Facolta di Scienze Politiche, Istituto di Studi Economici Finanziari e Statistici, Rome, 1981.
3. On these points see, for instance, A. Swoboda, 'Credit Creation in the Euromarket: Alternative Theories and Implications for Control', Group of Thirty Occasional Paper, no. 2, New York, 1980.
4. For empirical evidence on these lines, see R. Williams, 'International Capital Markets: Recent Developments and Short-Term Prospects', IMF Occasional Paper, no. 7, Washington DC, August 1981; R. Masera, 'Determinants of the Growth of the Eurocurrency Markets', in *Recent Developments in the Economic Analysis of the Euromarkets*, Bank for International Settlements, Basle, September 1982 and H. Terrell, 'International Banking Facilities and the Eurodollar Market', paper

presented at the International Conference on Eurodollars held at Florida International University, Miami, 3–4 February 1983.

5. On this point, see R. Masera, 'Comments on Helmut W. Mayer's Paper', Proceedings of a Colloquium on 'The European Capital Market: Problems and Outlook' held in Milan on 27–28 November 1980, published in *Giornale degli Economisti e Annali di Economia*, Università Commerciale Luigi Bocconi, no. 9–12, September–December 1981.
6. Admittedly, frequent instances of complacent lending by commerical banks can be found. But, in broader terms, it must also be recalled, as Carli does in his comprehensive policy assessment of the Euromarkets (G. Carli, 'Eurodollars: Policy Analysis', paper delivered at the International Conference on Eurodollars held at Florida International University, Miami, 3–4 February 1983, p. 21), that in the Venice summit the heads of State and government of the seven most industrialised countries did assign to commercial banks a primary role in the recycling process. A more balanced division of responsibilities between international official organisations and international banks would no doubt have been desirable.

COMMENT

HELMUT W. MAYER

Mr Higonnet's stimulating paper on the early history of the Euromarket presents a rich fabric of facts, with interpretations and qualitative judgements. Although I do not always find it easy to agree with him, he makes a large number of lucid and shrewd observations. What I do rather miss in this essay, however, is a balanced overall view of international banking and its past development. Such an overall view would be essential for a realistic interpretation, since to base one's conclusions only on isolated aspects chosen according to one's very personal predilections is bound to result in a rather biased picture of the Euromarket and its economic consequences.

Looking back over the history of Eurobanking, three general features emerge. One is the broad and, in part, rather heterogeneous set of influences which have been responsible for the rapid growth of the Euromarket. At the outset, there was, of course, Regulation Q, the 'voluntary' US balance of payments restraint programme, and today there are still numerous regulatory advantages such as the exemption from minimum reserve requirements, interest ceilings and various other macro, micro and fiscal constraints which constitute an artificial incentive for the growth of the market. This, however, is only part of the story and there also have been other important influences at work.

Very generally, it may be said that the growing importance of the Euromarket has been just one aspect of a much broader development, namely the increasing economic and political integration of the world as a whole. In the early years of the market the academic literature laid heavy emphasis on the fact that credit intermediation in this market was effected, from the point of view of the location of the agent banks, in foreign currency, the so-called xenocurrency market. This emphasis diverted attention from a much more significant institutional development with which the emergence of the Euromarket was inseparably bound up, namely the internationalisation of banking. The big banks, which had formerly focused their activities primarily on their domestic markets, set up a network of affiliates around the world, adopting an outlook and engaging in activities that were truly universal. In microeconomic terms, therefore, the Euromarket is not a self-contained entity but just one facet, albeit a very important one, of the banks' very much broadened international outlook. This internationalisation of banking, in turn, has been closely related to the growing importance of multinational corporations and the increasing weight of international trade. I feel rather uncomfortable when Mr Higonnet says that basically the Eurocurrency market is unnecessary; I think it would be more correct to say that, given the direction in which the world was moving, the emergence of a truly international banking market was unavoidable. Perhaps within a different regulatory framework this international market might have assumed a slightly different institutional shape. However, basically the Euromarket is just the financial counterpart to the increasing global interdependence we have been witnessing in other areas, owing to free trade, technological developments entailing increased international division of labour, and vast technical progress in the field of transport and communications.

Looking at the same phenomenon from a somewhat different angle, one cannot deny that the growth of the Euromarket has largely occurred in response to genuine international financing and intermediation needs, both for large investment projects and balance of payments as well as development finance. Of course, supply factors may have been of considerable importance, too – for instance, the regulatory constraints, the competition from alternative channels of domestic financial intermediation and the weakness of domestic investment demand which, in several instances, limited the banks' scope for expansion in their domestic market and thus induced them to try to develop their international business. And the market's competitive efficiency, its wholesale character and its innovative capacity also certainly had something to do with its rapid growth. Nevertheless, in the absence of a huge international demand potential, these supply factors and regulatory biases could not, by themselves, have accounted for all of the very rapid growth of the international banking market.

I noticed that Higonnet in his essay takes a rather dim view of the usefulness and genuine macroeconomic importance of this role of the Euromarket as an international financial intermediary. However, there can be no doubt that a large volume of international capital flows will always be an essential part of an efficiently functioning highly integrated world economy. While there may be abuses, maladjustments and policy problems – on which Mr Higonnet, indeed, focuses in his paper – one cannot simply ignore the positive macroeconomic functions performed by these capital flows. I shall come back to this point later on.

This brings me to the second main feature which emerges from the past development of international banking, namely the highly polyvalent character of this market. For one thing, the Euromarket acts as an international money market for the banks themselves in which they can place their liquidity surpluses and meet their own needs for loanable funds. Secondly, the Euromarket serves as a financial intermediary for the private non-bank sector, acting either as a *parallel* market to the domestic market or as a source of finance for international trade and investment. And, thirdly, the Euromarket is used by the official sector as a source of balance of payments and development finance and as a deposit outlet for official reserves. Moreover, as a further complication, these various functions of the market cannot be clearly distinguished from each other, since to a large extent they overlap. Analysts who, as has quite often happened in the past, focus on just one or two of the functions of the market, while claiming general validity for their findings, therefore, are bound to come up with biased conclusions.

I suspect a little of such one-dimensional thinking surfaces in Mr Higonnet's comments on the international banking statistics, which he apparently thinks are grossly inadequate. He says, for example, that no one really knows the volume of outstanding Eurodollars and that the most interesting estimate was produced by Henry Wallich, who found that at the end of 1978 the ultimate monetary liabilities to non-banks in the Eurocurrency market were about $160–170 billion. It should, however, be clear that Governor Wallich had only one limited aspect of the Euromarket in mind, namely its role in offering a substitute for domestically held money or liquidity balances. While, particularly from the point of view of monetary analysis, this is undoubtedly a legitimate interest, it would certainly not justify gearing all the Eurocurrency statistics to this one aspect alone and dropping, for example, all interbank figures. If that were done, the Eurocurrency statistics would no longer show the role of the Euromarket in balance of payments and development finance which, I would venture to say, are equally or even more important aspects of the market's international activities. The truth is that there is no single figure which could do full justice to the broad spectrum of the Euromarket's macroeconomic functions and adequately measure the size of the market. The particular statistical aggregate on which one focuses will depend on the aspect of the market one is interested in. This need for eclecticism in the use of the international banking statistics is, however, by no means a reflection on their adequacy and quality. In comparison with other international statistics, such as balance of payments and international trade statistics, the quality of the Eurocurrency statistics is in fact quite good. While there are gaps and there is much room for further improvement, the main weakness of the present international banking statistics is certainly not their insufficiency and incompleteness, but their lack of timeliness. Although, even in this respect they compare favourably with most other statistics on international financial relationships.

The third conclusion to be drawn from the history of the market is closely related to the preceding two. Since the relative importance of the various growth impulses and different macroeconomic roles of the Euromarket changes over time, the overall economic impact of the Euromarket is not constant either, but will depend very much on the general world economic constellation. This means, that it is not possible to evaluate the overall macroeconomic performance of the Euromarket on *a priori* grounds, but that the market always has to be seen in the light of a specific world economic context. The past performance of the Euromarket and of international banking in general, provides ample illustration of this point.

In 1968–69, at the time of the US credit crunch, the Euromarket, as aptly described in Mr Higonnet's paper, acted mainly as a channel for capital flows from the rest of the world to the United States. These capital flows helped to finance the US balance of payments deficit and, by keeping down foreign official dollar accruals or actually leading to some reserve losses, exerted a restrictive or even deflationary influence on the rest of the world. In the United States, by contrast, because of the reserve currency role of the dollar, this capital inflow did not give rise to a major increase in the monetary aggregates or in credit availability, though there may have been undesirable distributional side effects. Globally speaking, therefore, the impact of the Euromarket during this period was mildly deflationary and supportive of the US dollar.

Subsequently, this situation was emphatically reversed with the unwinding of the US credit squeeze. In 1970 and 1971 reflows of funds from the United States to the Euromarket and the diversification of official reserve holdings away from the United States to the Euromarket added to the other sources of US payments outflows and to the downward pressure on the dollar, thereby materially contributing to the explosive reserve and liquidity build-up in the rest of the world, without a corresponding restrictive effect in the United States. It cannot be denied that during this period the impact of the Euromarket was, on balance, destabilising and a contributing factor in the surge of inflation around the world.

The scenario changed once more with the oil price explosion in late 1973, when the international banking sector began to play a leading role in the intermediation of the OPEC surpluses. Given that there were no other major international channels commensurate in size to the OPEC surplus, there is a fairly broad consensus that without the Euromarket's contribution the disruptive influence on world economic activity and on the growth performance of broad groups of developing countries would have been much more serious.

This helpful and stabilising role was subsequently reenacted in the wake of the second, 1978–9, wave of oil price increases. Moreover, even after the rapid erosion of the renewed OPEC surpluses, the international banking sector continued to exert a stabilising influence on the world economy, in so far as very large banking outflows from the United States and the placement of US corporate funds in the Euromarket provided an offset to the other types of capital that were flowing to the United States for interest rate and security reasons. Without these massive capital exports from the United States via the international banking sector – for the 30-month period from March 1980 to September 1982 the volume of these funds amounted to about $140 billion on a net basis – the upward pressure on the dollar and on interest rates outside the United States would have been even more pronounced, and so would the deflationary pressures emanating from the restrictive US monetary policy stance on the rest of the world.

It is, of course, true that more recently the tensions and cracks in the international credit structure have cast doubts on the international banking sector's past role in development and balance of payment finance, and there is a serious danger that an all too sudden withdrawal of the banks from this business might throw the world economy into even deeper recession. Mr Higonnet states in this context that history shows that we, and he apparently means especially the bankers, learn nothing from history. However, another 'half-truth' says that history never repeats itself. And in fact, the scenario at present is in many respects quite different from what it was in the 1920s.

While there were undoubtedly some misjudgements and abuses, the fact is that the main reason for the present difficulties in international credit relations is not any basic contradiction in the logic of international bank lending, but policy failures within the principal industrial countries themselves. Hardly anybody a few years ago would have dared to predict the sad shape that the world economy is in at present: protracted near zero, or even negative, growth rates, stagnation of international trade, an extremely high level of capacity under-utilisation and unemployment with correspondingly dire consequences for export volumes and prices in the developing countries and – despite all this – until very recently unusually high interest rates. If that were the scenario with which banks usually had to reckon, there would hardly be any bank credit growth at all. Conversely, it is quite clear that most of the debtor countries' external payment problems would fade away if the principal industrial countries were to return to reasonable rates of economic growth and activity. This makes it quite clear where the principal responsibility for the present tensions and cracks in the international credit structure lies.

All this is not to deny that in the past there have been exaggerations in international bank lending and that the funds borrowed have not always been put to the best use. Moreover, in view of the increased stretching of banks' gearing ratios and the rapidly growing weight of country risks in banks' balance sheets, some slowdown in the pace of international bank lending was indicated in any case. However, this is not the time for a U-turn. At present the banks, in their own interests will have to go on in their lending assuming that the present slump in the world economy is only temporary and will once again give way to sustained economic growth and reasonably high levels of economic activity. It is when this recovery has come – and let us hope that it is not too far away – that there will be time for the banks to show that they have learned from the past and will exercise the necessary self-restraint. If this should not be the case and the gloom should be directly replaced by a renewed wave of euphoria in international bank lending, then perhaps there would be a time for what Mr Higonnet seems to have in mind when he says that the Euromarket's growth should be checked and Eurobanks brought under ordinary bank controls. What I do, however, doubt, although I must admire Mr Higonnet's optimism, is whether the implementation of such a control mechanism would really be 'technically not very difficult', as he claims.

Of course, in the microeconomic field, that is in the field of banking supervision, such controls are already in place or in the process of being put into place. The agreement on the international division of supervisory responsibilities, the so-called Concordat, the principle of supervising banks on an internationally consolidated basis, and the agreement on the confidential exchange of information between national supervisors – all worked out by the Basle Committee of banking supervisors – are intended to ensure that no bank with a head office in the G-10 countries and no banking office within the G-10 countries escapes adequate supervision.

In the field of macroeconomic controls, however, the extension of the domestic instruments to the banks' international business would be much more problematic. The reason for this lies in the large international differences between national control systems, which means that an extension of the domestic controls to the banks' international business would tend to impose a serious competitive handicap on those banks with head offices in the more restrictive countries. On the other hand, imposing an internationally uniform set of regulations on banks' international business, even if that were possible from a legal point of view, would discriminate between the same banks' domestic and international business and thereby give rise to new distortions and circumvention efforts.

Reserve requirements, which are apparently the candidate for Mr Higonnet's international control system, are a good case in point. The rate at which they would be applied would probably have to be a kind of average of national rates. This would mean that in countries with high required reserve ratios the incentive for shifting business to the international market would remain intact, whereas in countries with low or no reserve ratios there would be an incentive to book the business through the domestic market. Moreover, in the case of non-interest bearing reserve requirements, the cost of which for the banks would depend on the level of nominal interest rates, there would always be the incentive to denominate the funds with the help of swapped deposits in the currency with the lowest interest charge. On the other hand, in the case of interest bearing requirements, it would be very doubtful whether they could significantly slow down the growth of the Euromarket. Unlike in the national market, there is no well-defined and controllable monetary base for the Euromarket. The banks could always avail themselves of the required reserves in the US market without exerting much of a tightening effect there. But controlling the US monetary aggregates with a view to checking Euromarket growth would really amount to the tail wagging the dog and this might not only have undesirable effects on the US domestic monetary scene but also destabilising effects on the world economy as a whole.

Perhaps the only macroeconomic instrument that would be able to effectively curb the growth of Eurocurrency credit would be some sort of direct quantitative controls on the growth of such credit. But I need not point out to you here that such a measure would open up a Pandora's box of problems, conflicts, abuses and inefficiencies.

Whatever control devices may be used in the future, however, it should be clear that the aim should not be to stop the growth of international bank credit altogether. However one might strain one's phantasy looking for alternative channels, it seems clear to me – and here I may differ sharply from Mr Higonnet – that international bank lending will continue to have an important role to play in balance of payments and development finance, although hopefully on a somewhat more modest scale and in a more co-ordinated way than in the past.

Part II

2 Eurodollars: an Economic Analysis

ROBERT Z. ALIBER

The rapid growth of the Eurodollar market in the last several decades has raised intriguing questions about the impacts on exchange rates, monetary control, and the world price level. The articles and books written on the growth of the offshore market in deposits and other financial instruments denominated in the US dollar, the German mark, and other currencies reflect a process of discovery, much like the reports from the explorers of the New World in the fifteenth and sixteenth centuries to their sponsors on the manners and morals of the Indian tribes, the flowers and the fauna, and the geological features. Early maps suggest the difficulties inherent in extrapolating the configuration of the coastline of the Americas from a cursory sample. Similarly the early explanations and analysis of the Eurodollar market bear only a vague relationship to the current understanding of why this market developed, and some of its implications, especially for the traditional issues of monetary control and regulation.

This article reviews the state of analysis of the Eurodollar and traces the development of this understanding. Throughout, the term Eurodollar refers to the offshore bank deposits which may be denominated in any of the several currencies; these deposits may be produced in Panama, or Singapore or other centres outside Europe, as well as in London and in Luxemburg. The institutional basis for the development of the offshore market is discussed in the first section. The impact of the growth of the offshore market on competition within the banking industry is considered in the second section. The impacts of the growth of the offshore market for deposits and other financial instruments on the relationships among currency areas are analysed in the third section. The implications of the growth of the offshore deposits on monetary control, the supplies of money and credit, and the world price level are discussed in the fourth section.

I THE INSTITUTIONAL BASIS OF THE OFFSHORE BANKING MARKET

The current story

The key institutional feature that explains the growth of the Euromarkets or offshore markets in bank deposits is differential national regulation of financial transactions. The regulations that apply to a particular transaction in one national jurisdiction differ from those that apply to the same transaction in other national jurisdictions. As a consequence of differential regulation, a set of financial transactions denominated in one currency are shifted to a jurisdiction where regulation is less restrictive. The transactions may involve the production of financial liabilities by banks or by non-banks; if banks are involved, the transaction is an offshore banking transaction and the locations in which these transactions occur are offshore banking centres.

Offshore banking centres are the monetary equivalent of flags of convenience in the shipping business or of tax havens; within these centres, transactions denominated in foreign currency are less extensively regulated than comparable transactions denominated in the same currency in its home country. Competition among centres to attract transactions denominated in foreign currencies, like competition among tax havens, leads to a lowest-common denominator approach to the regulation of offshore transactions; as a result, offshore deposits tend to be produced in centres where the restrictions are minimal – or non-existent.

Individual countries cannot readily regulate transactions in offshore centres in their own currencies, for a currency is a unit-of-account, like the mile and metre, and not a property right subject to licensing. What countries can do is to regulate the shift of funds between other jurisdictions and their own. The possibility or likelihood of such regulations either might deter or, alternatively, stimulate such shifts.

By definition, the financial assets produced in offshore banking centres are close substitutes for those produced in various domestic centres; indeed, they are identical in one attribute, currency of denomination, and they may be identical in others, such as maturity or default risk. The financial assets produced in the offshore centres differ from those produced in the domestic centres and denominated in the same currency in terms of their susceptibility to various types of regulations – interest rate ceilings, reserve requirements, exchange controls, expropriations, withholding of interest income for tax and disclosure requirements. Moreover, the arrangements or conventions that limit interest rate competition in various domestic markets may not extend to offshore markets. The types of regulations that may handicap the expansion of banks in their domestic markets or the entry of foreign banks into various domestic markets frequently do not apply to their entry into offshore markets.

In addition, the distinctions among currency areas may also parallel or reflect distinctions in the preferences of depositors or of banks, and of borrowers. Thus, the Europeans may have a somewhat different attitude towards certain risks than the Americans. And offshore branches of banks may have different asset preferences than domestic branches or the head office – especially if there are regulatory or tax asymmetries.

Some of these regulatory factors affect the return attached to assets, others the risk attached to these assets. Two different types of risk distinguish domestic and offshore deposits. One is the risk of owning a particular asset in different jurisdictions, which involves the exchange controls or expropriation or some other act of one or another set of national regulators. Investors may differ on their estimates of the risks attached to these deposits. A few investors may believe the risks of offshore deposits to be lower than the risks of domestic deposits; hence they might prefer offshore deposits in terms of both risk and return. Most investors believe that the risks of offshore deposits are higher than those of domestic deposits; otherwise, no one would own domestic deposits if offshore deposits offer higher returns. The secular increase in offshore deposits may reflect that the returns associated with offshore deposits have increased, or that the risks associated with these deposits have declined. A second is the risk attached to the deposit associated with the institution that produced the deposit, a type of default risk. Since most of the institutions which produce offshore deposits also produce domestic deposits, the differences in the firm-specific risks are not important in explaining the secular increase in the demand for offshore deposits. Although there may be differences in the costs of producing similar financial assets in a domestic centre and in various offshore centres, such differences appear modest relative to the differences that result from differential regulation.

The necessary condition for distinction between risk and return on offshore and on domestic deposits reflects the demarcation of the world into different political jurisdictions. The sufficient condition for the growth of offshore deposits is that the cost-savings that are possible because of the regulatory differentials are larger than the cost increases from using the offshore habitat. Thus the use of tax havens incurs additional legal and accounting costs, but the increase in costs is usually smaller than savings in tax payments. Because the producers of offshore deposits are not subject to reserve requirements or interest rate ceilings, the returns on offshore deposits are higher than those on domestic deposits. The differences in reserve requirements mean that the costs of 'producing' deposits are lower in the offshore banking centres than in the domestic banking centres, since offshore deposits were not subject to this 'tax on deposits'. The higher the reserve requirements, the greater the financial incentive to acquire offshore deposits.

The growth of offshore deposits relative to domestic deposits resulted both from the increase in the return available on offshore deposits, relative to domestic deposits, during a period of inflation and from reductions in the estimates of the risks of offshore deposits. More effective risk assessment probably would have meant that offshore deposits would have grown, even if the interest rate differential were constant. During a period of increasing interest rates, the magnitude of the reserve requirement 'tax' increased – and so the financial incentive to acquire offshore deposits increased.

The growth of money market funds in the United States provides an analogy to the growth of offshore deposits. The assets of these funds increased from \$4 billion in 1977 to \$200 billion in 1982 – a rate of growth much higher than that of Eurodollar deposits. The common feature is that the money market funds were not obliged to hold reserves, so the interest rates paid by the funds exceeded those that domestic banks could pay. Moreover, interest rate ceilings were much more important for owners of small deposits than for those with large deposits. In effect, the money market funds provided an investment option for the owners of small deposits comparable to that provided by offshore banks for owners of large deposits. Thus the money market funds were competitive with the banking system as financial intermediaries; in effect, they were the domestic equivalent of offshore banks.

Earlier stories

In the early 1960s, the growth of Eurodollar deposits was attributed to the desire of the Russians to hold dollar-denominated deposits at a time when they feared that the US authorities might apply exchange controls to any deposits held in banks in the United States. The Russians would have held offshore dollar deposits, even if the return had been lower than on domestic dollar deposits. Subsequently, however, the development of an offshore market in deposits denominated in various currencies was traced to the 1920s (Einzig).

In the mid-1960s, the US balance of payments deficit was frequently cited as the 'cause' of the growth of Eurodollar deposits. The story was that the deficit led to an increase in the dollar holdings of foreign central banks, which had a stronger preference to hold offshore dollar deposits than did US residents. However, the US balance of payments deficit might have increased if US residents had shifted funds from domestic dollar deposits to offshore dollar deposits; the story is that under the then prevalent liquidity approach to the measurement of the payments balance, the increase in US residents holdings of claims on foreigners was not included in the measurement of the payments balance, while the increase in foreign residents claims on the United States was so included. The shortcoming of this explanation was that deposits denominated in the Swiss franc and the German mark were increasing about as rapidly as deposits denominated in the US dollar – and Germany and Switzerland usually had balance of payments surpluses.

Another explanation for the growth of the market was attributed to the desire of banks headquartered in Europe to invade or participate in the sale of dollar deposits in competition with US banks, which hitherto had a monopoly on the sale of dollar-denominated deposits (Swoboda). The foreign banks could establish branches and subsidiaries and agencies in the United States; indeed, many foreign banks had such affiliates. Presumably the entry costs associated with the sale of dollar deposits in Europe was below that associated with the costs of selling dollar deposits in the United States. Then US banks established offshore offices as a defensive measure to prevent a decline in their share of the dollar deposit business. Yet a few US banks headquartered in New York or San Francisco might as easily taken the initiative to establish offshore offices as a way to circumvent two different types of limitations on their expansion in the US deposit market. One was the formal restraint in expansion which both within states like Illinois and New York and across state boundaries. The second was that more aggressive initiatives to increase domestic market share might have raised the interest costs of the domestic deposits extant.

The shortcoming of these arguments is that they confuse the motives for the purchase or sale of offshore deposits by the different investors or agents with the institutional features that facilitate the growth of an offshore market for deposits. None of these earlier stories is wrong or exclusive. There can be numerous motives for the increase in the demand for offshore deposits and for the increase in the supply, although each can be expressed in these risk and return calculations. The motives for the growth of offshore deposits either reflect the demand for returns higher than those available on domestic deposits or the demand for lower risk. Most investors acquire offshore deposits because of increased return; a few because of reduced risk. If investors, in general, believed that offshore deposits were associated with reduced risk as well as higher returns, the demand for domestic deposits would be modest; domestic deposits would be an 'inferior good'.

II THE EXPANSION OF THE EURODOLLAR SYSTEM AND COMPETITION WITHIN THE BANKING INDUSTRY

The traditional industrial organisation question is whether changes in government regulations affect the price and the output of a particular industry. Thus when the US domestic airline industry was deregulated, attention was given to the frequency of the service between various city-pairs, the level of fares between these city-pairs, and the entry of new firms into particular markets. Some major carriers previously identified with service between the East and West coasts, such as United and TWA, began to enter the Florida and Texas markets. Eastern, in contrast, developed routes on an East–West axis. Braniff expanded so rapidly it landed in the bankruptcy court. New firms emerged as discount operations on established runs; Midway Airlines, Jet America, Peoples Express, and Air Florida are in this group. One result of airline deregulation was that the cross-subsidisation from heavily travelled city-pairs to lightly travelled city-pairs declined; fares tended to fall between the first group of city-pairs and rise between the second group. Jet America's presence in the Chicago–Los Angeles market meant that United Airlines could no longer use profits on this route to keep fares low on the Chicago–Saginaw route. At the normative level, deregulation raises questions about consumer welfare and economic efficiency.

The US banking industry has not been deregulated, at least in a formal sense not until 1980; however, the expansion of the offshore offices of US banks represents a back door, informal, and partial approach to deregulation.

Thus banks which are regulated in one jurisdiction expand and compete in other non-regulated jurisdictions. The question for the banking industry is how the growth of offshore banking has affected the volume of output of the banking industry, and the price at which various bank products are available.

The growth of offshore banks has affected both the numbers of banking offices and the location of particular transactions in ways that are self-evident. The opportunity to branch abroad has enabled US banks to circumvent domestic restrictions on expansion. Thus banks in Illinois which had not been able to establish branches within the state (but which could set up Edge Act Subsidiaries in New York and other seaport centres) were able to establish branches abroad. Similarly, banks headquartered in New York or California could establish branches in various foreign jurisdictions. US banks found it much easier to branch across national borders than to branch across the borders among states.

Because of the growth of offshore banks, there is increased competition among banks for deposits denominated in the major currencies. More banks compete in the major financial centres for offshore deposits than compete in the domestic market for deposits denominated in the same currency. Thus the London market for offshore dollar deposits may have more major suppliers or producers than are in the New York market for dollar deposits.

Moreover, the expansion of offshore banking has enabled banks to circumvent the restraint on entry into markets for deposits denominated in certain currencies. For example, entry into the deposit market in Canada traditionally was constrained, yet offshore banks could offer to sell deposits denominated in the Canadian dollar in New York, London, and various other offshore centres. So the options available to Canadian investors expanded, provided that they were willing to incur the costs and risks associated with these deposits.

Finally, once a bank had been established to sell offshore deposits, the additional cost of the entry into the domestic market in the centre in which it is located is modest – and substantially below the cost that the firm would face if it were to enter the domestic market first. Thus the branches of US banks established in London to compete for dollar deposits subsequently began to compete for sterling deposits. As a result, the sterling deposit market became more competitive, especially for larger depositors.

At any moment, various factors limit the size of individual banks – their capital, reserve requirements, and the market area in which they might sell deposits. Some banks might have excess capacity in one of these factors. For example, reserve requirements might be the dominant limit to the size of Bank X; if required reserves were lower, Bank X would be able to sell more deposits within its established markets given its capital. In contrast, Bank Y might be limited in its ability to expand by the size of their capital; depositors might believe that its capital cushion is too slender, so Bank Y would find the interest rate it would have to pay to sell more liabilities would be too high to be profitable. (But a few might nevertheless pay these rates, although like Braniff they would expand themselves out of business.)

The informal backdoor approach to deregulation facilitated by the offshore market permits banks with 'excess capital' (at least with capital which is excess relative to their domestic market opportunities) to expand more rapidly, much as if the banking had been deregulated in the domestic jurisdiction. However, to the extent that individual banks do not have capital which is excessive relative to their deposits, then the shift to offshore banking or the reduction in domestic reserve requirements would not enable them to expand; the establishment of offshore offices only would affect the centre in which they produce deposits. In contrast, if some banks have excess capital, then the relaxation or elimination of the reserve requirement may permit them to grow more rapidly than would otherwise have been possible, provided they are not too dominant a factor in the domestic market. So the growth of offshore banks has almost certainly led to increased competition as those banks with 'excess capital' have sought to expand deposits as a way to reduce their capital–deposit ratio. And the banks with the greatest incentive to expand abroad have been those with relatively more excess capital.

Hence the development of offshore branches enables banks to circumvent the domestic limits on growth. Inevitably some banks will 'follow the herd'; they will establish offshore banks because other banks that they seek to compete against have established such offices. Yet unless the second group of banks have 'excess capital', growth in offshore deposits will be at the expense of growth of domestic deposits.

Thus the development of offshore banks has meant that the banking industry is larger than it would otherwise be; the banks are larger relative to other types of financial intermediaries, and to direct financial transactions between borrowers and lenders. In addition, the market shares of those banks which have the most adequate capital in the domestic context, increase.

Borrowers benefit from the expansion of the banking industry, for the interest rates at which they can sell their debts will decline. Some depositors also benefit, since they receive higher interest rates than they would on domestic deposits. As a group depositors are better off, since banks are able to pay higher interest rates to the extent they are not required to hold reserves against offshore deposits. But, as the deposits of banks have increased relative to their deposits, the adequacy of the capital cushion has declined, and the depositors must pay relatively more attention to assessing the risks associated with deposit liabilities of individual banks.

III THE GROWTH OF THE EURODOLLAR MARKET AND THE RELATION AMONG CURRENCY AREAS

This question is whether the growth of offshore deposits denominated in the dollar and various other currencies has affected the level of exchange rates, and especially the foreign exchange value of the dollar. If the growth of offshore deposits has no significant impact on the exchange rate or the official reserve flow between central banks, then the policy issues raised by the growth of offshore banks are better considered under the headings of industrial organisation and financial regulation and monetary policy than under the heading of international finance.

A popular argument is that the unanticipated increase in the volume of dollar deposits had led to a decline in the foreign exchange value as a result of excess production of dollars. At one level, the argument is almost tautological – since the exchange rate is the relative price of two monies, any innovation which affects the supply or the demand for assets denominated in a particular currency should affect the exchange rate. Yet a similar argument might be made about the implications of the unanticipated increase in the volume of offshore mark deposits and offshore Swiss franc deposits. That the foreign exchange value of the mark might increase because of excess production of dollars and that the foreign exchange value of the mark might decline because of excess production of the mark is not possible, at least not at the same time. Conceivably the US dollar, the German mark, the Swiss franc, and other currencies with significant volumes of offshore deposits might depreciate relative to those currencies in which the volume of offshore deposits is trivial. Yet this argument seems *ad hoc*, no attention is given to the demand for loans denominated in the US dollar, the German mark, and various other currencies.

Before inferences can be made about the impacts on exchange rates of the growth of offshore deposits, two questions must be resolved. One involves the specification of the contra-factual situation. Was the growth of the reserve base in each country independent of the growth of offshore deposits denominated in its currency, or did the authorities reduce the rate of growth of the reserve base because of the growth of offshore deposits? Is it possible that the authorities in various countries reacted differently to the growth of offshore deposits denominated in their currencies?

The second question to be resolved before the impacts of the growth of offshore deposits denominated in various currencies on the foreign exchange value of the dollar can be answered involves the type of transactions that led to the increase in offshore deposits denominated in the US dollar, in the German mark, and in the Swiss franc. Thus the growth of offshore deposits denominated in the US dollar might result from a shift from domestic dollar deposits to offshore dollar deposits. Or alternatively, the growth of offshore deposits denominated in the German mark, or the Swiss franc, or some other foreign currency. In the second case, the growth of offshore dollar deposits leads to an increase in the foreign exchange value of the dollar; in the former, however, there is no immediate impact on the foreign exchange value of the dollar. There may be an indirect impact to the extent growth of offshore deposits affect the interest rates on dollar loans and dollar deposits.

The growth of offshore deposits denominated in the dollar might be associated with an increase in the foreign exchange value of the dollar; in this case the story would be that some investors had shifted from assets denominated in the German mark or the Swiss franc or any other foreign currency into offshore dollar deposits when they might not otherwise shift into New York dollar deposits. The excess of the interest rate on offshore dollar deposits would provide the incentive for this shift. However, a counterpart argument might be made about the shift from dollar assets into offshore mark assets, and so the net of these two arguments would have to be determined. This argument might be resolved if the data show that the excess of interest rates on offshore deposits relative to domestic deposits is larger in the dollar segment of the offshore market than in the segments denominated in other currencies. Alternatively, the growth of the offshore dollar deposits might be associated with a decline in the foreign exchange value of the dollar if the growth of the dollar-denominated monetary aggregates is larger than anticipated because the US authorities focus only on the domestic dollar-denominated aggregates, while the foreign authorities consider the aggregates denominated in their currencies on a worldwide basis.

A taxonomy might be developed which would project changes in the foreign exchange value of the dollar in terms of combinations of answers to various assumptions about the management of the reserve base in various currencies and the assets that investors sold when they acquired offshore deposits. Sorting through the taxonomy would lead to a large number of possible answers, but it would not resolve the central question. The foreign exchange value is the price that clears the market in assets denominated in the several currencies – in the outstanding stocks of these assets. While the *rate of growth* of offshore dollar deposits during any period may be quite large relative to the rate of growth of domestic dollar deposits, the *increase* in the volume of offshore dollar deposits in any period is small relative to the outstanding *stock* of dollar. Since the issue about the exchange rate impacts resolves to the *differences* in *stocks* of assets denominated in the dollar and in other currencies attributable to the growth of the offshore deposits, the inference is that the exchange rate impacts will be modest.

IV THE MONETARY IMPLICATIONS OF THE GROWTH OF OFFSHORE DEPOSITS

The current story

The growth of offshore banks has led to extensive debate about the monetary implications, and especially about the impacts of the growth of offshore dollar deposits on the effectiveness of monetary control, aggregate spending and the world price level. Two extreme views about the credit implications can be identified – one is that one of the major causes of the increase in the world inflation rate is the unanticipated growth of offshore deposits denominated in the US dollar; those who subscribe to this view generally believe that there is substantial volume of credit creation in the offshore market. The competing view is that the impacts of the growth of offshore deposits on the world price level are modest, either because virtually all offshore deposits involve interbank transactions, or because the leakages from the offshore system to the domestic system are so large; the second group believes that credit creation by offshore banks is trivial relative to credit creation by domestic banks. Between these extremes there are a number of intermediate positions which differ primarily because of the differences in the model of the offshore banking system and the relation of offshore banks to domestic banks.

The current story is that the monetary implications of the growth of offshore deposits are comparable to those associated with the shift of funds from deposits in large banks in New York or Chicago to deposits in much smaller banks, for the former are subject to a reserve requirement of 12 per cent while the latter are subject to a reserve requirement of 3 per cent. For a given reserve base or a given volume of high-powered reserves, the potential credit creation is larger, the lower the effective reserve requirements. From the viewpoint of monetary analysis, that the offshore banks are in Europe or indeed offshore is irrelevant; the only relevant phenomena is that they are subject to a lower level of required reserves (indeed, a zero level). For the analysis of monetary phenomena in the United States, the deposits of offshore banks denominated in the US dollar are relevant, both those in offshore offices of US banks, as well as the offshore offices of non-US banks. Similarly, for the analysis of monetary phenomena in Germany, the deposits of offshore banks denominated in the German mark are relevant, including those in the offshore offices of US banks, Swiss banks, and French banks, as well as of German banks.

The offshore market for deposits in each national currency is a geographic extension of the domestic market for deposits denominated in that currency, with the major difference that offshore deposits are not subject to reserve requirements. So the effective reserve requirement in the dollar area is the weighted average of the mandated reserve requirements on dollar deposits produced by banks located in the United States and the zero reserve requirement on dollar deposits produced by banks located outside the United States, including the offshore branches of US banks. Over the decade, as offshore dollar deposits have increased relative to domestic dollar deposits, the effective reserve requirement in the dollar area has trended downwards. From the point of view of the impacts on the volume of credit, it is as if the authorities had reduced the reserve requirement applicable to dollar-denominated deposits in the United States if there had been no offshore dollar deposits.

The increase in the volume of credit associated with the expansion of the dollar deposits of offshore banks exaggerates the aggregate increase in volume of credit in the dollar credit area. The story is straightforward – if investors had been denied the opportunity to buy offshore dollar deposits, their demand for money market funds would have increased more rapidly. So would their demand for other substitutes for domestic deposits.

One feature of the operation of Eurobanks is that they hold no reserves or no significant amount of reserves. Holding reserves would reduce the income of offshore banks, and hence their ability to compete for deposits. The need to hold reserves is reduced significantly by matching the maturity structure of assets with those of liabilities. And while offshore banks might be subject to unanticipated withdrawals of call deposits, these banks can always 'buy-in' more deposits by raising the interest rates paid. Or they can obtain funds from their domestic parents.

The growth of the liabilities of money market funds provides an analogy to the growth of the liabilities of offshore banks: the money market funds are not obliged to hold reserves. The money market funds use the monies realised from the sale of their liabilities or shares to buy loans from business firms; in this way the money market funds create credit. Similarly, to the extent the offshore banks buy loans from commercial borrowers, the volume of credit increases.

The impacts of the growth of offshore deposits denominated in the dollar on monetary control and on the US price level depends on two factors – one is whether changes in the volume of offshore dollar deposits relative to changes in the volume of domestic dollar deposits are stable and predictable or variable and non-predictable. The second is whether the magnitude of the increases in offshore dollar deposits is large relative to the increase in domestic dollar deposits. If the increase is predictable and large or non-predictable and small, the growth of offshore dollar deposits would not pose problems for monetary control. However, the evidence suggests the growth of offshore deposits *is not* predictable and is large; and if so, the growth of offshore deposits does present a problem for monetary control.

From the point of view of monetary control, spending and the price level, offshore deposits are just like domestic deposits with the difference that they are subject to the zero reserve requirement. The effective reserve requirement in each currency area is weighted by the volume of each type of deposit; the fractional reserve credit multiplier is the reciprocal of the reserve requirement. The authorities set the monetary base; but just as in a domestic monetary system the supply of credit depends on the demand for deposits subject to different reserve requirements, so it does in a system which integrates offshore deposits denominated in a particular currency with domestic deposits.

That the offshore system is a geographic extension of the domestic system is evident in the arrangement for clearing payments. Thus dollar payments from offshore banks are cleared through the mechanism of the New York Clearing House, much like the payments from a bank in Albany, New York to a bank in Trenton, New Jersey. There is no separate payments clearing arrangement for offshore banks. (Indeed, payments from the offshore branch of one US bank to another offshore branch of the same bank may be cleared through New York Clearing House, while payments from one domestic branch of the bank to another are likely to be cleared within the bank.) Payments initiated by offshore banks denominated in a currency other than the dollars are not cleared through New York.

The question of whether the growth of the Eurodollar system has been associated with an expansion of money and credit is quite independent of whether the Eurocurrency multiplier is a meaningful concept. Thus at the conceptual level, it might be argued that there is a multiplier, but the credit expansion is trivial – or it might be argued that there is a significant impact on the level of credit, even though the multiplier has no 'stand-by-itself' significance. And the current story is that the growth of the Eurodollar system has been associated with a significant increase in money and credit – in effect the multiplier in the dollar credit system is higher than might be inferred from the required reserve ratio for domestic deposits.

The earlier stories

One traditional story is that the growth of offshore deposits had no impact on commodity price levels because virtually all offshore loans are interbank credits. The issue is primarily factual. Most offshore credits do represent interbank loans. But to the extent that offshore banks make loans to commercial borrowers and governments, and the increase in these loans is significant relative to the increase in such loans from domestic borrowers, the growth of offshore deposits affects the level of spending.

Usually the question about the credit implications of the growth of offshore banks and offshore deposits centres on the concept of the fractional credit reserve multiplier. In the domestic context, the multiplier relates the increase in the aggregate money supply with the increase in the monetary base, the deposits of the commercial banks in the central bank. One approach towards the measurement of credit creation in the offshore banking system involves the increase in the credit from the offshore banks with the increase in their reserves. A second approach towards the measurement of the multiplier involves the total or aggregate increase in the volume of offshore deposits or credit for each autonomous increase of one dollar in the volume of offshore deposits. This is the Euromarket equivalent of an increase in the capital inflow to the British financial system or the Canadian financial system of one dollar.

In his classic article 'The Euro-Dollar Market: Some First Principles', Friedman writes

> the existence of the Euro-dollar market increases the total amount of dollar balances to be held by non-banks throughout the world for any given amount of money (currency plus deposits at the Federal Reserve Banks . . . by permitting a greater pyramiding on this base by the use of deposits at US banks as prudential reserves for Euro-dollar deposits.

If pyramiding means that the multiplier in the dollar currency area is lower, the statement is consistent with the story of this section. If pyramiding means that Eurobanks hold deposits at New York banks in the same way as New York banks hold deposits at the Federal Reserve, there is an inconsistency. Elsewhere in the article the description suggests that Friedman leans towards a segmented offshore system.

In a *Wall Street Journal* article, Laffer applied a 'double-decked' pyramid model. Thus US banks hold reserves at the Federal Reserve and offshore banks hold reserves at the New York banks. So an increase in the monetary base is supposed to lead to an increase in the liabilities of US deposit banks by the multiple inferred from the domestic reserve requirements, while the liabilities of the offshore banks would increase by the multiple inferred from the implicit reserve requirement of the offshore banks. The shortcoming of these approaches is that there is an implicit assumption that the volume of liabilities of the offshore banks is determined by the willingness of these banks to buy loans, rather than by investor demand for the liabilities of these institutions. Moreover, there is the assumption that the offshore banks hold reserves seems inconsistent with the pricing of their deposits.

Various attempts have been made to estimate the multiplier in the offshore market. Two sets of data would be needed to estimate the multiplier in the offshore market – one set, the volume of offshore deposits, is readily available. The second set, the reserves of the offshore banks have eluded several attempts at measurement. One inference from the difficulty in finding the reserves of the Eurobanks is that these reserves do not exist; if these reserves were there, then the reserves of the Eurobanks should not be so difficult to identify or measure.

For more than a decade, a series of articles on the need to include the Eurodollar multiplier have been produced by economists and officials associated with the Bank of Italy. The authors are Fratianni and Savona, Magnifico and Savona, and Carli and Savona. These two propositions are not necessarily logically related. Eurodollars should be included in the measurement of the US money supply and Euromarkets in the measurement of the German money supply, with the appropriate adjustment for interbank deposits. But accepting the proposition that dollar deposits produced by offshore banks should be included in the measurement of the US money supply does not mean that there is a separate monetary base for the Eurodollar system, any more than there is a separate monetary base for the money market funds or the credit unions.

Textbooks attempt to synthesise current knowledge. Ethier asks, 'What is the Eurodollar Multiplier?' After repeating the traditional formula, that the 'Eurodollar analog to reserves in a national banking system is the deposits of Eurobanks in US banks'. Ethier continues, 'Estimates of the actual multiplier have varied enormously [*sic*], but in recent years a consensus seems to be forming that it is not greatly above unity, and that a high multiplier is thus not a source of instability'. If this conclusion is correct and the multiplier is one, then the reserves of the Eurobanks in the US banks should approximate the level of Eurodollar deposits, or perhaps $200 or $300 billion. Finding $200 to $300 billion of reserves should not be difficult. The second shortcoming of this approach is the association between a multiplier 'not greatly above unity' and 'a high multiplier'. The third shortcoming of this approach is the assumption that inferences can be made about the stability of instability from the constancy of the multiplier; such a conclusion would be warranted only if the proceeds from Eurodollar loans were spend outside the United States.

A series of articles and books are associated with Hewson, occasionally in collaboration with Sakakibara or Niehans. One central theme is that the fixed coefficient fractional reserve multiplier is irrelevant. Following Niehans' distinction between the roles of banks as creators of liquidity (banks borrow short and lend long) or as middlemen or distributors of liquidity (banks match maturities of loans and deposits), and evidence that Eurobanks match the maturities of their loans with those of their deposits, Hewson concludes 'that the Eurobanking system functions primarily as a distribution system for existing liquidity rather than as a system that creates new liquidity' (p. 33). One minor shortcoming of the observation is that a non-trivial proportion of the liabilities of the Eurobanks are call deposits; at issue is whether these deposits as a minimum might be associated with liquidity creation. The focus on the liquidity creation – liquidity distribution distinction slights the relation between the liquidity distribution in the domestic market and liquidity distribution in the offshore market; Hewson suggests that the liquidity distributed in the offshore market is a substitute for liquidity which is distributed in the domestic market. This conclusion does not follow from the previous steps in the argument; if it did, then the growth of Eurobank deposits would appear to be associated with a decline in the loans of domestic banks.

McKinnon concludes that there are several reasons 'for not worrying about excess liquidity creation in the Euromarkets'. The first, following Hewson and Niehans, is that a sharp increase in the 'flow of deposits to Europe will bid down Eurodeposits rates of interest that are unregulated and are ultra-sensitive to demand and supply'. This conclusion would be correct if *both* of the following conditions hold: first that banks consider the domestic and offshore deposit markets partially segmented, and secondly that borrowers consider the domestic and offshore markets partially segmented. If the deposit markets are partially segmented, but the loan markets are fully integrated, McKinnon's conclusion is unwarranted; similarly the conclusion is unwarranted if the deposit markets are fully integrated. A second and more basic reason that McKinnon offers for not worrying about excess liquidity creation is that most Eurobanks deposits involve interbank transactions – or that most Eurobank loans are to other Eurobanks. At the end of the chain of deposits and loans, there must be non-bank borrowers; McKinnon's sanguine conclusion would be warranted only if the *increase* in loans to non-banks from Eurobanks were trivial or modest in relation to the *increase* in loans to non-banks from domestic banks, currency area by currency area. The data suggest that the ratio of these two first differences is neither trivial, nor modest.

Swoboda's most recent essay usually distinguishes a multistage banking system approach to multiplier from an initial-deposit multiplier and from a world-money-stock approach. Swoboda appears to favour a combination of the multi-stage banking approach and the world-money-stock approach. Moreover, he appears to believe the impact of the growth of offshore deposits on the level of spending depends on whether the incremental depositor is a central bank or some other investor. His own conclusion is that the 'Eurodollar market has not created tremendous amounts of credit and that it has not made, in itself, a high difference in the world or national money stocks'. This conclusion is much too gross; Swoboda must decide whether the growth in loans to non-bank borrowers from offshore banks is large or small relative to the growth in the loans to comparable borrowers from domestic banks. Unless offshore banks somehow link particular types of loans with central bank deposits, the issue is a red herring; given the length of the interbank deposit chain, it seems unlikely that such linkages exist.

V CONCLUSION AND POLICY IMPLICATIONS

The development and growth of the Eurodollar market and of offshore banking transactions results from the demarcation of the world into multiple political jurisdictions. As a consequence, current and prospective regulations applied to transactions in some jurisdictions are less extensive than those applied in other jurisdictions. The volume of offshore deposits increases whenever the returns associated with acquiring an asset in a jurisdiction where current or anticipated regulations are less severe dominates the additional cost, with appropriate adjustment for any differential risks. The expansion of offshore deposits has been especially rapid when the opportunity cost of holding domestic deposits has been high; when interest rates have increased, the cost of reserve requirements has increased. The rapid growth of money market funds in the United States in the last five years provides an analogy to the growth of offshore banks; the money market funds avoid the interest cost of reserve requirements. Some investors shift their wealth to these funds to benefit from the higher returns, while others believe the higher returns inadequate relative to the increased risk.

The expansion of banks has resulted in a much more competitive international banking industry. In many countries the expansion of banks was constrained by government regulations; in others, by the cartel-like organisation of markets. Thus in countries dominated by a small number of banks – most countries other than the United States, Italy, and Japan – efforts by banks to increase their size and market share may have seemed too costly. Federal and state regulations limited the domestic expansion of US banks. Banks which had the capital to expand, but were constrained from doing so in their domestic markets could expand more readily in the offshore market. Such an expansion of banks in the offshore market might have occurred even in the absence of differential reserve requirements; however, the impact of lower reserve requirements on offshore deposits led to a surge in the growth of offshore banks – which are primarily the branches and to a lesser extent the subsidiaries of the major domestic banks in each country. Inevitably the customers of banks – both depositors and borrowers – have benefited. Similarly, the owners of the money market fund deposits have benefited from the higher returns on these funds. And the alternative of a very competitive money market fund industry induced banks to respond by introducing new products – and by seeking to reduce their regulatory handicaps.

Determining whether the expansion of offshore deposits denominated in various currencies has affected the foreign exchange value of the US dollar, or of the German mark, or of the Swiss franc is complex; the question can be answered only by assumptions about the contra-factual developments in the absence of an offshore market and, especially, both the growth of the reserve bases in the several currency areas and the growth of other substitutes for domestic deposits. Moreover, to answer this question, information would be needed on the currency denomination of the assets that investors would have held, if they had not acquired offshore deposits. To the extent the excess of the interest rate on offshore deposits over the interest rates on domestic deposits is generally larger on the dollar than on most other currencies (because reserve requirements in the United States are higher than in most other countries), there would be more of an incentive to shift into offshore deposits denominated in the dollar from domestic deposits denominated in other currencies. However, the probable impact of the growth of offshore deposits on the foreign exchange value of the dollar is modest because the exchange rate is the price which equalises the demand for and supply of stocks of assets denominated in the several currencies, and the *increase* in offshore deposits in any period is small relative to the total *stock* of dollar assets extant.

The question of whether the growth of US money market funds has affected the foreign exchange value of the dollar might seem playful or even absurd. Yet this question is the counterpart of the question of whether the growth of offshore deposits has affected the foreign exchange value of the dollar. Higher interest rates on money market funds induces two forms of substitution; one from other dollar assets and one from non-dollar assets. The second type of shift should tend to cause the foreign exchange value of the dollar to increase. Of course, to the extent the Germans develop money market funds, then some investors might switch from dollar assets into mark assets.

Much the greatest concern about the expansion of the offshore deposits centres on the domestic monetary implications, especially regarding impacts on the price level and on monetary control. The view of this paper is that the offshore banks are no more than geographic extensions of domestic banks – situated in the centres where deposits are not subject to reserve requirements. There is no offshore banking system *as a system*; rather there are offshore extensions of the several national banking systems. From the viewpoint of monetary control, the key question is whether the authorities can predict or forecast the growth of offshore deposits relative to domestic deposits denominated in their currencies; if they cannot and the increase in the volume of offshore deposits is not trivial, relative to the growth in domestic deposits, then the development of offshore deposits has led to a decline in the effectiveness of monetary control – the authorities must be less confident of the impact of changes in the reserve base on the monetary aggregates. Determining the impact of the growth of offshore deposits on the commodity price level requires attention to two aspects of the contrafactual scenario; one is whether the growth of the monetary base was less rapid than would otherwise have occurred in the absence of the development of the offshore market, and the second is whether (or how rapid) some other substitute for domestic bank deposits might have increased if the offshore deposits were not available.

The domestic counterpart of this question is whether the growth of money market funds has affected domestic monetary controls. For most investors, claims or deposits in these funds are extremely close substitutes for deposits in banks; the implication is that the money market funds should be included in the monetary aggregates for the purpose of monetary control. Ultimately that question is empirical.

This interpretation of the monetary implications of the growth and development differs from most previous interpretations in that no significance is attached to the fractional reserve multiplier in the offshore banking system. There is no meaningful multiplier in the offshore system. Instead, the growth of offshore dollar deposits subject to a zero reserve requirement means that the effective fractional reserve credit multiplier in the dollar currency area is lower than would be inferred from US reserve requirements. A similar statement could be made about the German mark currency area, and each other national currency area. Holding reserves is costly to interest income; offshore banks avoid holding reserves by matching the maturity dates of assets with those of liabilities. Those who have argued that there is a mutiplier in the offshore banking system should be able to measure the reserves of the offshore banks, especially if this would-be multiplier is low; then the reserves of the offshore banks should be quite large – if they exist. Even if the multiplier is high, the reserves of the offshore banks would be in the tens of billions of dollars, sufficiently large to be readily measured – if these reserves exist.

If the growth of the offshore market in bank deposits is primarily a result of differential regulation, the policy implications are straightforward – the regulatory incentives for shifting from domestic deposits to offshore deposits should be reduced or eliminated. There are three basic ways this objective might be attained – reserve requirements and interest rate ceilings might be applied to offshore deposits, or the reserve requirements on domestic deposits might be reduced, or interest might be paid on domestic deposits. The first, applying reserve requirements to offshore deposits, is not feasible, both because of issues involving extra-territoriality and of competition among monetary havens. The second, reducing reserve requirements, has already been adopted for international banking facilities in the United States and for bank-sponsored money market funds. The likelihood that the third, the payment of interest on required reserves, might be adopted in the United States seems low, and due to political reasons; Congressional objections to mandating that the Federal Reserve pay interest to commercial banks at the cost of paying profits to the US Treasury are likely to be both strong and widespread. The likelihood then is that the favoured approach to reducing regulatory differentials is to define more and more domestic deposits so that they are not subject to reserve requirements.

BIBLIOGRAPHY

Aliber, Robert Z., 'Radio Luxembourg and the Euro-Dollar Market Are Both Offshore Stations', The *International Money Game* (New York: Basic Books, 1973).

Aliber, Robert Z., 'The Integration of Offshore and Domestic Banking Systems', *Journal of Monetary Economics*, Oct. 1980.

Altman, O., 'Foreign Markets for Dollars, Sterling and Other Currencies', *Staff Papers*, Dec. 1961.

Bank for International Settlements, *Annual Report 1982* and earlier years, Basle.
Carli, G., 'Eurodollars: a Paper Pyramid?', *Quarterly Review*, Banca Nazionale del Lavoro, June 1971.
Clendenning, E. Wayne, *The Euro-Dollar Market* (Oxford: Clarendon Press, 1970).
Einzig, Paul, *The Euro-Dollar System* (London: Macmillan, 1961).
Ethier, Wilfred, *Modern International Economics* (New York: Norton, 1982).
Fratianni, M. and Paolo Savona, 'Euro-Dollar Creation: Comments on Professor Machlup's Propositions and Developments', *Quarterly Review*, Banca Nazionale del Lavoro, June 1971.
Friedman, Milton, 'The Euro-Dollar Market: Some First Principles', Morgan Guaranty Survey, Oct. 1969.
Hewson, John and Eisuke Sakakibara, 'The Euro-Dollar Deposit Multiplier: a Portfolio Approach'', *Staff Papers*, July 1975.
Holmes, Alan R. and Fred H. Klopstock, 'The Market for Dollar Deposits in Europe', *Monthly Review*, Federal Reserve Bank of New York, Spring 1960.
Klopstock, Fred H., 'The Euro-Dollar Market: Some Unresolved Issues', *Essays in International Finance*, no. 65, Princeton, 1968.
Machlup, Fritz, 'Eurodollar Creation: a Mystery Story', *Quarterly Review*, Banca Nazionale del Lavoro, Sept. 1970.
Mayer, Helmut, 'Some Theoretical Problems Relating to the Eurodollar Market', *Essays in International Finance*, no. 79, Princeton, 1970.
McKinnon, Ronald I., *Money in International Exchange* (New York: Oxford University Press, 1979).
McMahon, C. W., 'Controlling the Euro-markets', *Quarterly Review*, Bank of England, Mar. 1976.
Niehans, Jurg and John Hewson, 'The Eurodollar Market and Monetary Theory', *Journal of Money, Credit and Banking*, 1976.
Savona, Paolo, *Eurodollars* (Miami: Florida International University, 1982).
Swoboda, Alexander, 'The Euro-Dollar Market: an Interpretation', *Essays in International Finance*, no. 64, Princeton, 1968.
Swoboda, Alexander, 'Credit Creation in the Euromarket: Alternative Theories and Implications for Control' (New York: Group of Thirty, 1982).

COMMENT

PETER M. OPPENHEIMER

It seems to me that an overriding merit of Professor Aliber's paper is that he stresses that the economics of Eurocurrencies is a matter primarily of financial structure and efficiency and only secondarily of international payments and exchange rate determination. And while I would like to supplement what he says and suggest a few shifts of emphasis, I do not have any fundamental disagreements with his analysis. There is one point I would like to make at the outset, though, and that is that he does attempt at each stage in his paper to contrast what he calls the current story about Eurocurrencies with what he calls earlier stories. This, however, I do not find convincing. I do not think the basic story has actually changed.

If I may be permitted a little egocentric indulgence, I first began to take an active interest in the nature and significance of the Eurodollar market over twenty years ago, when I was at the BIS. The systematic collection and reporting of Eurocurrency statistics to the BIS was begun in 1963 and the regular chapter on the Euromarkets in the Bank's annual report appeared for the first time in 1964. It fell upon me at that time to do most of the leg work on that first occasion and *inter alia* to devise a workable definition of the so-called net size of the market.

We found, in fact, that the only practical possibility of getting to such a definition was to exclude those interbank deposits which did not represent a net transfer of foreign currency funds from one country to another. For example, if French banks reported liabilities of $100 million to German banks, and German banks report $60 million of liabilities to French banks, then the net figure would be a French liability of $40 million, 100 minus 60. And that is really all there was to it.

The term net size gave rise later to some misunderstanding by those who jumped to the conclusion that the term must signify some net addition to national money supplies and therefore, to inflationary forces in the world economy. Now, even if that were correct, in a statistical sense, it would not, as Professor Aliber pointed out in his paper, be correct as a proposition in economics. It would be misleading, in fact, unless it were accompanied by an analysis of the counter-factual alternative, that is to say, if the Euromarket had not developed, then how would other financial aggregates have behaved? But actually the point was not even statistically correct, in fact, as Helmut Mayer explained in a very good piece in *Euromoney* some years ago in 1976. Essentially, a substantial part of that net figure for the size of the Eurodollar market, as calculated by the BIS, still represents an interbank transfer mechanism, in my example from, say, German banks to French banks, and not a measure of additional liquid assets in the hands of non-banks.

This begins to focus our attention of course, as Richard Herring did, on the interbank market, and I shall have something to say about that too in a moment. In any case, the point I want to emphasise, at this stage, is that the potential implications of the Euromarkets for financial efficiency and stability were specifically recognised at the outset, even though the relative size of the Euro network was, at that time, tiny by today's standards, and other features of the world financial scene were also radically different from those of today. Thus, just to give some examples of what I mean by what was recognised, reference to the analogy between the Euromarket and non-bank financial intermediaries and the consequent limited relevance of credit multiplier models will suffice. The significance of the interbank mechanism is, on the one hand, for spreading risk among lending institutions, and on the other, possibly allowing individual debtors to overborrow, and thus increasing risk. The new competitive pressures were brought to bear on domestic banking systems by the growth of the Euromarkets, as well as the uncertain implications of the Euromarkets for exchange rates and balance of payments positions. All these were noted, not only in the BIS, but by Altman and Klopstock and other people, and were discussed at that time, albeit in rather cursory fashion. The fuller analysis was provided in the later 1960s and early 1970s by people in the BIS and elsewhere, Helmut Mayer, Warren McClam, Rainer Masera, Alexander Swoboda and others and also the rather impressive theoretical underpinning of Niehans and Hewson. All this should be seen, in my view, as a development of aspects that were all present in embryo in the early years.

So much for the indulgence, let me now turn to the central contentions of Professor Aliber's paper. First, he attaches prime importance to the stimulus which freedom from reserve requirements, interest rate ceilings, and other regulatory restraints have given to offshore banking. And he compares this freedom with that afforded by tax havens and flags of convenience. He also might have added, I think, by export processing zones which is another example of the same sort of thing. Relative risk considerations, positive or negative, must also be brought in. Secondly, he emphasises the importance of rapid inflation in enhancing the return available on interest bearing offshore deposits relative to domestic deposits which Ian Giddy has spelled out more fully for us already. Thirdly, Professor Aliber brackets the growth of offshore deposits with other structural innovations in the financial system, such as the development of money market funds, NOW accounts, and the shift of deposits in the US from large to small banks with consequent reductions in the required reserve ratio for the banking system as a whole. Pulling these points together, his overall conclusion is that, and I quote, 'The offshore banks are no more that geographic extensions of domestic banks.'

I have no specific quarrel with any of that, but I feel that his treatment underemphasises two other factors which are equally important. One is the significance of the interbank mechanism in transmitting information, and thereby lowering transaction costs, independently of reserve requirements or any other regulatory burdens, and here I shall take up a theme which Richard Herring discusses in Chapter 3. The other point which is closely connected with the first one is the specifically international nature of much of the market's activity. Now the point about information and transactions costs is bound up with a key structural feature of the Euromarkets, mainly, the distinction between, on the one hand, the flow of funds from initial depositors to ultimate borrowers and, on the other, the interbank mechanism in the middle. Bankers in one country do not typically find it cost effective to acquire information about the creditworthiness of commercial enterprises in another country. And historically, this factor has been an important barrier to international credit flows. By historically, I mean that, going back a hundred years or more, the main international credit flows, until the Euromarket, consisted of acquisition of foreign government and public utility bonds by non-bank investors and also of course, trade credit and commercial bank acquisition. However, the main sort of predominant flow, say, from Britain was the acquisition of bonds by non-bank investors mostly in the public sector. Today, in the world's banking community, one institution is prepared to trust its colleagues with enormous sums on the strength of a name, and then leave the colleague to parcel out these sums to retail borrowers at the end of the line. Thus, in the interbank network, the world's bankers have stumbled on a highly effective defrictioning device for international credit flows.

I think the word stumbled on really is right, if I could interject a historic note here. The point about the late 1950s was that the British banks were more or less the only set of national banks which had anything resembling a worldwide network of credit institutions. And they were anxious to put them to use again. I think people have forgotten that the United States international banks were almost non-existent at that time, it is a slight exaggeration, but the overwhelming majority of US bank offices, branches, subsidiaries, overseas date from the period since the mid 1960s. And initially, it was this inherited institutional structure which pushed the British into seeking new ways of doing this business. Now, once all of this consideration's aspects are appreciated, then the specifically international significance of the Euromarket comes immediately into greater prominence. I think

Professor Aliber's paper did somewhat encourage us to view the Eurodollar market as the offshore window of the US banking system and the Eurosterling market as the offshore window of the UK banking system, and so forth. In addition to this, we need to recognise the system's special capacity to intermediate between countries and the fact that the relative role of different currencies in the balance sheets of the banks in the Eurosystem, at any moment, is to a certain extent a matter of chance, dependent on the currency denomination chosen by non-bank depositors and borrowers wherever they may happen to be.

The role of the market, if I could just develop this point slightly further, the two roles of the market are, as an offshore window of a particular country system and as an international intermediator. The role of the market as an offshore window of a particular country system is particularly apparent when that country's policy-makers are enforcing a credit squeeze, impelling its residents to turn to the Euromarkets for funds. The US example in 1968–9 and to a lesser extent, the last two or three years, come readily to mind. But it should also be said that the role of the Euromarkets in enhancing the competition within the banking sector stems also from its wider international liaison and does not depend on it being called in by borrowers in a specific country to circumvent a credit squeeze. A point that is worth mentioning here that has been previously noted is that the wave of bank mergers, for example, in Europe in the late 1960s and early 1970s certainly owed something to the increased competitive pressures emerging from the Eurosystem. In Britain we had a major bank merger, two of our big five and National Provincial and the Westminster merged, the big four in the Netherlands became the big two, the Ambro Bank and the Algemene Bank Nederland, as well as a similar merger in France. There was a definite wave of restructuring the banking system at that time which was partly triggered by the Eurocurrency market's competition.

Now, coming to the other side, the international, specifically, the international role, I need only gesture at the balance of payments financing problems of the past decade, to remind everybody of the great importance of the international banking network centred on the Euromarkets in the past decade. The official channels of balance of payments finance, the International Monetary Fund and so forth, simply could not be adapted swiftly enough to the new political and economic circumstances. The much bigger role for OPEC and for the newly industrialising countries in the Third World involved rather delicate political, as well as, financing problems, not just for the international institutions themselves, but for the Western governments which had the predominant political voice in running them and were reluctant to surrender it. In these circumstances it was the private markets which provided the flexibility necessary to shift the perspective of the international financing pattern and adapt it to the new circumstances.

I want finally to say something about multipliers and stability. Professor Aliber, towards the end of his paper, contrasts two extreme views about the role of the market in generating a lot of credit and in not generating a lot of credit because it is all interbank. I do not find that contrast is entirely consistent with other parts of his paper.

It seems to me that, everyone can agree that the Euromarket creates and/or transmits credit on a large scale. The question is whether the amounts involved are larger in size and/or different in direction from the credits that would alternatively be in place if the Euromarkets as we know them did not exist. Again, it is the old counterfactual. And if they are larger and different, is this good or bad based on some criterion. Now, my objection to the multiplier approach to these questions is not that the multiplier approach is wrong so much as it is unhelpful, it does not really enable us in a convincing way to answer any of these questions. I am very happy to concede that you can, if you wish to, describe the activities of the statistical facts about the Euromarket in terms of a credit multiplier. We have a general point lurking here about the nature of theoretical explanation. Towards the end of *The General Theory*, Keynes has a chapter in which he points out that for those who would like to state the whole of the preceding theory in terms of the quantity theory of money, that is open for them to do so. He simply does not think it is a very helpful way of understanding the system, but those who prefer that kind of language are at liberty to use it. Similarly, I understand from my theoretical physicist friends that Einstein could have used Euclidian rather than non-Euclidian geometry in special relativity, it just would have made it much more complicated and even less comprehensible. So it does seem to me that it is rather silly to argue about whether there is or is not a multiplier, what the proponents of that approach have to demonstrate, if they want to convince the rest of us, is that the multiplier focuses in a valuable way on the problems which the market throws out. However, I do not find that approach convincing.

Nevertheless, I think it is agreed by most people that the character and the activity of the Euromarkets do pose problems for prudential regulation and stability. And further, that there are some types of links, although as Professor Aliber stressed, not terribly direct ones. There are several kinds of links between the Euromarkets and the debt crisis that we face today. Let me suggest two links, one of which is particularly relevant, and then make a few final remarks about the nature of competition and the problem which this poses in the Euromarket in general.

It is useful to ask the question, what would have happened if we suppose that the IMF or other official institutions had done all the balance of payments financing, in the wake of the big rise in oil prices, that went through the private network? Would that official credit have gone so lopsidedly to so few countries, and with so little pressure on them to adjust, or would in fact, some of the other countries who have not been such big borrowers, have had access to some of it. Now, although I raise that question, I do not want to answer it because I am not sure what the answer is. But, it is at least possible that official financing with conditionality would have resulted in a more even and less problematic distribution of the given volume of debts around the world, than the one we actually face. If that is so, then it is possible to argue that the market process and the activity of the international banking markets in financing balance of payments disequilibria was a cause, a cause not the cause, of a maldistribution of credit.

The second possible link between the debt crisis and the Euromarkets, I think is clearly the other way around, that is to say, it is the debt crisis which has raised dangers and threats to the Western banking system. Even contrary to my first suggestion, if we take the geographical distribution of the present debts as given, if those debts of the Mexican and Argentinian and Brazilian governments and so forth were all owed to the IMF and to national governments, well then certainly, national tax payers might be feeling rather uncomfortable at the present moment, but at least the private banking systems would not be under threat. So, one can say that even if the debt crisis had nothing to do with the banking system, the fact that the banking system is right in there means that willy-nilly it is under threat because of the debt difficulties of these banks.

Now, let me pass on to the extent that the problem of stability, if there is one, is the problem of a competitive process in the Eurodollar market independent of the current banking crisis and further what does it precisely consist of? The main thing I want to stress and this reverts back to the remarks I made about the multiplier process, is that I do not think really it has anything at all to do with the uncontrolled growth of the money supply or uncontrollable inflationary pressures, or the determination of the general price level.

In remarking on this I would like to express my indebtedness, not only to historical writings of various kinds, but to a paper by Fred Hirsch in the Manchester School in 1977 on what he called the Bagehot problem. It was really applying the sort of nineteenth-century banking crisis analysis and Bagehot's comments on it to modern circumstances. Now, one has really said everything when one draws attention to the fact that the banking crisis of the mid-nineteenth century occurred against a background of secular price stability thanks to Britain's adherence to the gold standard. There were, of course, ups and downs of prices, but there certainly was not a problem of price level determination and long-term over-expansion of the quantity of money the way many people think there is today. The problem had something to do with the character of the competitive process within the banking system notwithstanding the fact that no sort of long-term price instability existed, and real interest rates were not a problem and so forth. It was the competitive process within the banking industry that posed problems and the need to keep prudential considerations properly in account.

In most markets other than the banking market, the ultimate sanction against those who are not prudent is that they go bankrupt. And that is the sort of ultimate sanction on the whole, that in the banking sector, we are very hesitant about, that is, letting a major bank go bust because of the external diseconomies, the public good aspect, the threat to the entire banking system, a point to which Richard Herring refers to in Chapter 3. This means that there have to be some limits on the competitive process in banking, all the more so, because the competitive process in banking seems to involve bandwagon effects, defective credit risk assessment procedures and so on. For example, Bank A lends because Banks B, C, and D are in it and if Bank C is in it, it cannot be bad. In any case, if we do not go in with them they will not come in next month on the New Zealand loan, so we had better go in. There is a kind of herd instinct about these things and this underlies the need to have some kind of restraint on the competitive process in banking.

I shall now revert to Professor Aliber's theme of integrating the offshore and domestic aspects of the banking system. In his 1977 paper, Fred Hirsch referred not merely to the international incidents such as Herstatt, Franklin National and all the rest of them, but also to the domestic, so-called secondary banking crisis in the UK in 1954 which was the result of over-enthusiastic competitive and speculative expansion of business, particularly in the property market. And all this was regulated to the tradition, which one can in a sense trace back to Walter Bagehot, that bank behaviour has to be regulated not merely by the formal instruments of reserve requirements and so on but, by a sort of code of behaviour that bankers must be gentlemen, not do too many of these naughty things that may end them up in the bankruptcy court if they go wrong.

Unfettered competition, in other words, is not desirable because, with the externality aspect that I referred to, it poses a danger to the whole system. And this, it seems to me is the dilemma of deregulation, that regulation in some form is necessary, and the currents of the last few years, and I do not mean the current debt crisis, but rather the Cooke Committee and discussions elsewhere around the Euromarkets which emphasises this point that regulation in some form is necessary for stability, yet in a flourishing market system, regulation tends to spawn deregulated centres because people want to get out from under, and escape to areas of greater freedom. The moral, I suppose, is that life will remain just as interesting for central bankers trying to cope with this problem, as it will for their commercial counterparts.

COMMENT

PAOLO SAVONA

Is it possible to reach a consensus on the necessary policy decisions to be made in the field of Eurobusiness starting with Professor Aliber's excellent contribution to this conference? This is what I propose to do while analysing his paper. In my opinion, the new development of balance of payments problems that banks operating in the international markets have to face, can hardly be solved by continuing the ongoing dispute about the possible existence of a multiplier in the Eurocurrency market.

A common base for policy decisions has to be established. The agreement reached in Paris by the Group of Ten (now 11, after Switzerland joined the Group) is not sufficient to fulfil the needs of international banks' activities.

The consensus analysis I have made consists of five major points which I want to propose.

1. Understanding the offshore monetary business is only possible

within the framework of a general equilibrium or disequilibrium portfolio model.

2. Many active forces determine the volume of the offshore business in the framework of a general equilibrium portfolio model, and the relevance of each force changes according to both time and different market conditions. By active forces I refer to a variety of phenomena such as the multiplier, switches from one currency to another, matching or mismatching of maturities and so on. All phenomena have been studied in the ongoing debate about Eurobusiness during the past 15 years. We have to accept the idea that each analysis of the individual force operating in the offshore monetary market has given a contribution to the dispute. It is not an eclectic view; it is instead a 'selective' view of the various forces. Eurocurrency analysis implies an understanding of the relevant forces in each moment of time and each area of the world market.
3. The world money multiplier – I agree with Professor Aliber's statement – that it is higher in the presence of an offshore market than in its absence, in consideration of the existing regulatory policies and the autonomous need for international money. I will delve into this aspect later.
4. The influence of the offshore market on exchange rates is modest in the long run – this point had not been made clear earlier – but it is relevant in the short run. We have not been able yet to state whether, in theory or practice, there is, indeed, a link between the short and the long run equilibria on exchange markets and the existence of Eurocurrencies and offshore markets.
5. The influence on inflation deriving from offshore markets is still to be understood; it is clear, however, that offshore credit activities influence the world supply schedule of real goods.

My proposal for a minimum consensus analysis requires an integration of just two different points in Professor Aliber's analysis.

He and others have explained offshore business only through institutional features: I would like to stress the relevance that different sets of information on domestic dollars have on both Eurodollars and offshore dollars. There seems to be room, therefore, for an international 'body' recognised as expert or 'well informed' in both real and financial markets; we can envisage such a feature in the Eurocurrency or offshore currency business. For example, if one were interested in the state of health of the Italian lira, one should not only consider the interest rates expressed in liras, but should also examine the Eurolira negotiated in, say, England. As a matter of fact the London market, where the lira is freely negotiated, is a source of reliable information, in that it reflects all of Italian regulation. The dollar in New York has maintained a domestic dimension of the information; London sends different messages on the dollar quotations reflecting the impact of international business.

One has to accept, therefore, the autonomous need for international money which derives from the existence of world trade, the integration of the markets and the needs of a higher level of information. The Euromarket is the reply of the market to these needs, not merely the result of institutional features.

Generally, I use the following historical definition of money: money is the Anglo-Saxon equivalent of the Latin word *moneta* which means 'she who informs'. The Romans used to refer to the goddess Juno as Moneta; she, in fact, always preannounced Jupiter's decisions. Juno's temple was located by the capitol, above the shop where the 'sestertii', the Roman currency, were minted. It is therefore natural (and surprising) that the Romans had already recognised the essence of the monetary function in information. I see the same characteristic in the Eurodollar.

The second point relates to the acceptance in Aliber's paper of the idea that the creation of the domestic reserve base is somehow influenced by the existence of offshore markets. I believe that even the opposite view can be maintained and that both of them influence the markets for goods, in both real and nominal terms. My analytical proposition on this issue is that the discrepancy between savings and investment schedules is influenced by the offshore markets which, in turn, influence the supply schedule of real goods.

I shall try to formalise some relationships:

Financial Accounts (flows)
Central Bank's balance sheet:

$$MB_s = MB_d$$

Households' and firms' consolidated balance sheets:

$$M2 + I = D + S$$

Real Accounts (excluding Government)

$$\text{GNP} + M = C + I + X$$

where MB is monetary base (s = supply; d = demand), $M2$ is money *lato sensu*, I is investment, D is debts or credits, S is savings, GNP is gross national product, M is imports, C is consumption, and X is exports.

Given that $\text{GNP} - C = S$, then

$$S - I = X - M.$$

i.e., a discrepancy between exports and imports is equal to an *ex-post* discrepancy between savings and investment. But $S - I$ is also equal to $D - M2$.

If an entity called IMB (international monetary base) does exist – or as Aliber accepted – if the creation of MB is influenced by offshore markets, then offshore markets do influence $S - I$ and, through this channel, the conditions of production.

If we abstract from the possibility to create monetary base through government budgets or relations with banks we can concentrate our attention on the potential creation of monetary base from the disequilibria between exports and imports. By further assuming a system devoid of intermediaries we can visualise such an entity whereby monetary flows ($D - M2$) are in equilibrium (disequilibrium) with real flows (S – I) only when no creation of monetary base exist. If there is such a creation, $S - I$ diverges; the conditions of production are influenced and so are the nominal and/or the real terms of global demand.

Let me conclude with a few comments on the attempts that Michele Fratianni and I have made to introduce the concept of international monetary base in the debate on the analytical foundation of Eurocurrency business.

Are there some international financial instruments – we have asked ourselves – whose increase in supply can bring about a reduction in international interest rates? Fratianni and myself are both aware that the well known liquidity effect works in the short run only; none the less, it is the indicator of the nature that characterises the instruments composing the monetary base.

Some operational and institutional definitions of MB are also valid; from the analytical point of view, however, the concept I expressed appears to be more appropriate. Monetary base consists of such instruments whose increase in supply induces a direct variation in the interest rate: money ($M2$) instruments operate in the opposite way, in that a variation in the interest rate induces an increase in their supply. (See Figure 2.1, overleaf, which indicates these relationships.)

We have then introduced a general equilibrium model with such an

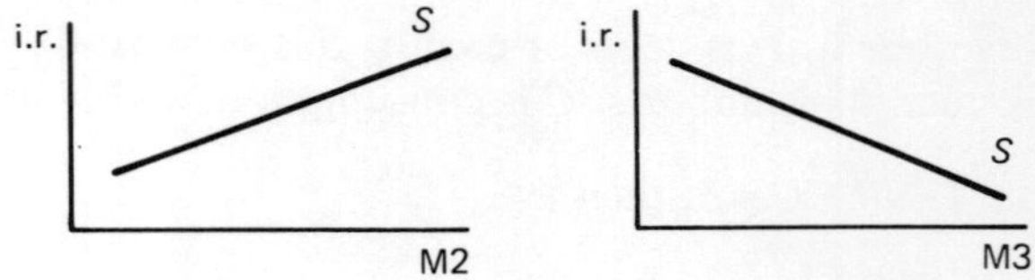

FIGURE 2.1

instrument which we envisaged – and, incidentally, tested econometrically – in US bank deposits held by non-residents. Our analysis is not indispensable to explain the Eurodollar business; in fact, other explanations appear just as valid. On the other hand, I would like to stress that the concept of international monetary base is very useful to: (i) forecast the likely future development of the Eurodollar market and, (ii) give a theoretical explanation out of 'adhockeries'.

A friend of mine who works in the commodity division of the World Bank has discovered that the most efficient definition of international money, in that it explains econometrically price movements of raw materials, is the Fratianni–Savona concept of IMB. So, while I am ready to admit that IMB is not the only tool of analysis, I would certainly recommend it as a highly useful concept.

3 The Interbank Market

RICHARD J. HERRING

The Eurocurrency market is fundamentally an interbank market. Interbank liabilities constitute from two-thirds to three-quarters of the aggregate liabilities of Eurobanks.[1] About one thousand banks from more than fifty countries are active in the market (Group of Thirty 1982a, p. 16).

Despite the prevalence of interbank transactions in the Eurocurrency market, most economists begin their analysis of the market by netting out interbank activity. Interbank activity is often treated as nothing more than an inconvenient amount of double-counting in the data. When the issue under analysis is the role of the Eurocurrency market in creating liquidity for the non-banking sector, it is appropriate to net out interbank activity; indeed, it is an indispensable aid to clear thinking. But too often analysis stops with the question of liquidity creation and interbank activity is ignored altogether.[2] The consequence is that much of the literature on the Eurocurrency market is irrelevant to most of the transactions that take place in the market. Yet in order to understand the full economic importance of the Eurocurrency system and the risks posed by Eurocurrency transactions to the safety and soundness of the world banking system, it is important to analyse the interbank market. Moreover, any market that surpasses $1 trillion in size deserves to be taken seriously in its own right. In the brief remarks that follow, I will begin to redress this traditional imbalance by focusing on interbank transactions and ignoring, for the most part, transactions between Eurobanks and non-banks.

Figure 3.1 depicts a stylised chain of interbank transactions. The first intermediary, I_1, accepts a deposit from a non-bank and lends it to the second intermediary, I_2. The deposit may be lent and relent from bank to bank a number of times, each at a margin as small as 1/32 per cent, until some intermediary – in Figure 3.1 the nth intermediary – I_n, lends the funds to a non-bank borrower. A survey conducted by the Group

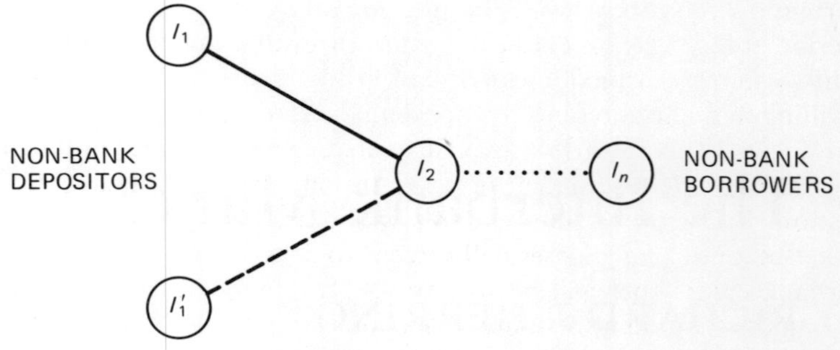

FIGURE 3.1 *An interbank chain of deposits*

of Thirty (1982a, p. 17) indicates that most banks redeposit more than 40 per cent (nearly 60 per cent in the case of the largest banks) of interbank deposits. The chain of deposits is the series of transactions among the intermediaries $I_1, \ldots, I_n$ and the interbank market is the volume of all such transactions. This market serves several economic functions indeed, an individual transaction may serve several functions but for simplicity we shall consider each function in turn.

LIQUIDITY ADJUSTMENT

The fundamental function of the interbank market is to redistribute liquidity worldwide between economic units with surplus funds and economic units with deficits. In general some banks will have an advantage in soliciting deposits from non-banks. This advantage may arise from a reputation for prudence and financial soundness or from propinquity to, or an ethnic identification with holders of large deposits (or large numbers of deposit holders). Alternatively the advantage may arise from a bank's location in a regulatory environment that depositors deem favourable, either because they have great confidence in the local supervisory authorities or the lender of last resort, or because the depositors are protected by secrecy laws from hostile acts by foreign governments, and perhaps, from taxation by any government.

Other banks, such as I_n, may have a special advantage in making loans to non-banks. This advantage may arise from historical ties to corporate or official borrowers or from a location in a region that is in current account deficit. These factors are likely to give a bank superior information about borrowers, but the advantage may also arise from a superior ability to process information in evaluating the borrower's creditworthiness. A final, more disconcerting possibility, is that I_n may be willing to make a loan to the non-bank at a lower cost than banks I_i ($i = 1, \ldots, n-1$) because it is less risk averse, or has a greater preference for risk, or under-estimates the risks in lending to the non-bank in question. Presumably such a bank will ultimately drop out of the market because heavy losses will force it to contract its activities or its interbank credit lines will be withdrawn. In the meanwhile, however, the bank's imprudent lending behaviour may make the interbank market vulnerable to credit shocks.

A bank that has special advantages in soliciting deposits may not have a comparable advantage in lending to non-banks and so it may place deposits in the interbank market where they can be channelled to a bank that has more attractive lending opportunities.[3] A number of transformations may take place before the funds deposited by the non-bank at I_1 finally reach the non-bank borrower. First, there will undoubtedly be a geographic transformation. For example, funds that were originally deposited in Bahrain may ultimately reach a non-bank borrower in Bolivia, Burma, or Bulgaria. The interbank market is a remarkably efficient mechanism for economising on transactions costs in linking non-bank depositors and borrowers separated by enormous distances. These transactions costs, imposed on both borrower and lender, include costs of collecting market information, costs of communication, taxes, costs of obtaining information about the creditworthiness of the borrower and the costs of monitoring and administering the credit agreement.[4] These costs are likely to be prohibitive for a direct credit transaction between a non-bank depositor and a non-bank borrower that are separated by great distance. And where there is an interbank chain of deposits, transactions costs are presumably greater for a credit transaction between I_1 and the non-bank borrower than the sum of transactions costs between each of the links in the chain and between I_n and the non-bank borrower.

Why are transactions between banks that reside in different nations less costly than between non-banks in different nations? One answer is that information about banks is cheaper and more reliable than information about non-banks and that it flows more readily between banks than between banks and non-banks. Another answer may be that the soundness of banks is more intensively monitored by officials than the creditworthiness of non-banks and, in the event of financial distress, banks are more likely to receive emergency assistance.[5] Moreover, there may be an expectation that in the event of a balance of payments crisis, interbank claims will have a higher priority for repayment than claims on non-banks. Thus, implicit guarantees may lessen the need for information about banks and, in part, account for the lower transactions costs among banks and the apparent willingness to deal on a 'name' basis. In addition, some geographic transformations take place within the branch system of individual banks where transactions costs are likely to be minimal.

Credit transformation is also likely to take place along the interbank chain, especially since the banks perceived to be soundest and most reputable tend to have an advantage in soliciting deposits from non-banks. The 1000 banks active in the interbank market can be classified in several risk categories and to some extent interest rates in the interbank market are tiered to reflect the standing of individual banks.[6] The usual range of interbank rates, however, is narrow. Ellis (p. 357) reports that the range is typically about $\frac{1}{4}$ per cent, although in times of stress such as the Herstatt crisis or the recent Mexican debt crisis, the range may extend to 1 or 2 per cent.[7] Most banks react to increases in the perceived riskiness of other banks by rationing or cutting back on interbank credit lines, rather than charging a higher differential.[8]

Currency transformation may also take place along the chain of interbank deposits if, for example, the non-bank depositor wants to hold dollars and the non-bank borrower wants to borrow Deutsche marks. Bank I_n may accept an interbank deposit of dollars from I_{n-1}, convert the dollars into Deutsche marks and lend them to the non-bank borrower. This transformation may enable I_n to develop a short position in dollars and a long position in Deutsche marks, or it may simply offset a position that the bank accepts from some other non-bank customer.

In addition, maturity transformations may occur along the interbank chain if the non-bank depositor prefers a maturity of, say, three months and the non-bank borrower prefers a maturity of five years. For example, bank I_{n-1} may accept an interbank deposit at three months' maturity and make an interbank placement with I_n at six months' maturity where it is lent to a non-bank for seven years on a six-month rollover basis.[9] As in the previous case of currency transformation, the transactions may enable the bank to take a position with regard to the three-month rate three months hence, or it may simply offset a position developed in other bank dealings.

Finally, some rescaling of deposits may take place along the interbank chain. Bank I_2, for example, may combine deposits from banks I_1 and I'_1 *and place the combined total deposit with* I_3. Or the reverse phenomena may occur. Bank I_n may, for example, fund loans to a number of different non-bank borrowers from a single large interbank deposit.

Thus several different transformations may be performed in redistributing world liquidity from surplus units to deficit units along the interbank chain-geographic transformation, credit transformation, maturity transformation, currency transformation or a rescaling of the flow of funds. The interbank chaining of deposits permits different banks to specialise in different transformations and may, thereby, permit the intermediation between non-banks to take place more efficiently. This increase in the efficiency of intermediation is the primary contribution of the interbank market to the world economy.

MANAGING FOREIGN EXCHANGE AND MATURITY POSITIONS

The second major function of the interbank market is to facilitate the management of foreign exchange and maturity positions. We have already noted that currency transformations and maturity transformations may take place in the intermediation between non-bank depositors and borrowers, but in addition quite apart from the intermediation function the interbank market provides a convenient mechanism for banks to manage their foreign currency and maturity positions. Herring and Marston (1976) have argued that the foreign exchange markets and the Eurocurrency market should be analysed as one integrated market and showed how Eurocurrency transactions can be substituted for foreign exchange transactions in hedging operations. For example, suppose that a bank has an unwanted long position in Deutsche marks for delivery in three months because of transactions with one of its customers. The bank may close this position either by selling Deutsche marks in the forward market or by borrowing Deutsche marks for three months in the interbank market, converting the Deutsche marks into dollars in the spot foreign exchange market and placing the proceeds in a dollar deposit in the interbank market.

Mayer (1976) and McKinnon (p. 17), especially, have emphasised the 'key foreign-exchange aspect' of interbank transactions. Using Bank of International Settlements figures for sources of funds for the Eurocurrency market in mid-1975, McKinnon (p. 18) estimated that foreign exchange transactions constituted as much as 60 per cent of the sources of funds, although he emphasised that existing reporting systems do not permit an accurate analysis.

Similarly the interbank market provides an efficient means for managing interest rate risk. Maturity mismatches resulting from the needs and preferences of non-bank customers can be hedged by transactions in the interbank market. In addition the interbank market presents the banks with the opportunity to develop a position at a particular maturity in order to take advantage of anticipated changes in interest rates. There is, however, considerable controversy over the extent to which banks actually do mismatch their interbank assets and liabilities. Some economists (for example, Niehans and Hewson, p. 11 and McKinnon, p. 19) have inferred from the Bank of England statistics on the maturity structure of claims and liabilities in non-sterling currencies that there is little position-taking in interbank transactions. Other economists (myself included) are sceptical of the appropriateness of the data for drawing inferences about the practices of individual banks.[10] The comments of bankers and reports in the press, moreover, indicate that substantial mismatching does occur.[11]

ARBITRAGING REGULATORY AND TAX DOMAINS

The third major function of the interbank market is that it facilitates the avoidance of taxes, constraints and other frictions in domestic money markets. This is, of course, the aspect of the market that Aliber has long emphasised. As early as the credit crunches in the United States in 1965 and 1969, it became obvious that a substantial volume of interbank activity in the Eurocurrency market was essentially domestic, rather than international in nature. In that period there were extraordinarily strong incentives to channel funds through the Eurocurrency market, since US bank deposit rates were constrained by the Regulation Q ceilings and borrowings from foreign branches were not subject to reserve requirements.

The essential feature of the arbitrage transactions is that domestic transactions are channelled through foreign offices in order to avoid domestic regulations or in order to profit from the difference in domestic and external returns that arise from the existence of domestic regulations.[12] The Securities and Exchange Commission (SEC) investigation of Citibank in response to the allegations made by a former employee, David Edwards, provides a virtual compendium of interbank transactions undertaken in order to avoid local regulations or, in the more discrete phrase of Citibank's counsel, Sherman and Sterling, 'in order to conduct business in compliance with local regulations'. For example, the SEC staff report details numerous 'round-trip' transactions that a Citibank auditor described candidly as '. . . the rinky dink deals which were resorted to by our branches to get round the local regulations and any locally imposed limits. It [sic] covers a wide area ranging from deals done to park positions . . . to making deposits and placement deals which improve the bank's liquidity ratios . . .'.[13] One example is the 'London round trip'. From about February 1975 to about April 1977, Citibank's London branch funded six-month interbank deposits with call borrowings. Because the resulting extent of the mismatching of maturities was contrary to the guidelines established by the Bank of England, the mismatched position was swapped to the Nassau branch by lending to the Nassau branch at the call rate and borrowing from the Nassau branch at six months' maturity. Thus the mismatched position was parked at the Nassau branch and the mismatch disappeared from the balance sheet of the London branch as did the tax liabilities.[14] Although Citibank was uniquely unlucky in having been compelled to reveal its practices to public scrutiny, there is no reason to believe that Citibank's uses of the interbank market were unusual. Undoubtedly a substantial, but unmeasurable, amount of interbank activity is simply arbitrage flows across the complicated international patchwork of regulatory domains.

SECONDARY FUNCTIONS

Because banks find it useful to participate in the interbank market to perform the three primary functions that we have discussed – to make liquidity adjustments, to manage exposure to foreign exchange and mismatching risks, and to profit from differences in regulatory and fiscal jurisdictions – a sizeable additional volume of activity takes place as a consequence of the trading activity that carries out these functions. In order to trade effectively in the world market, a bank must deal continuously on both sides of the market. An active trading presence is an indispensable means of keeping track of developments in the market – the 'intelligence' motive. Not only will a continuous flow of trading data enable the bank to track movements in market rates more effectively, but transactions relationships with other banks will convey information about other banks (such as indications of overtrading) that is not available in balance sheet and income statements on a timely basis. The bank is thus able to make better judgements about interbank credit lines. By bidding for funds on a continuous basis, furthermore, banks test their credit lines from other banks – the 'precautionary' motive. Since reliance on the issuance of liabilities for liquidity is subject to uncertainties over the availability of credit lines, drawing on those lines even when there is no pressing need for liquidity, but simply to turn over the deposits in the interbank market, provides a useful means of gauging the bank's liquidity. Moreover placements of deposits with other banks may cultivate reciprocal relationships that can be drawn upon in the event of a liquidity squeeze. Activity on both sides of the market also serves a useful strategic purpose – the 'strategy' motive. A bank that is both an active taker and placer of interbank deposits is more likely to get a competitive price from other banks if they recognise that the bank may 'hit' either the bid or asked quotation.

POLICY CONCERNS ARISING FROM INTERBANK ACTIVITY

From the preceding summary of the functions performed by the interbank market, it is clear that policy-makers face a dilemma in dealing with it. Although policy-makers appreciate the important role of the interbank market in increasing the efficiency of international financial intermediation (particularly when the policy-maker's country is borrowing in the market), they are undoubtedly distressed over the erosion of the effectiveness of national regulatory and fiscal policies that the market facilitates. While thoughtful policy-makers perceive the benefit of the interbank market in helping banks manage exchange rate and interest rate risks and thereby offer more efficient services to non-banks, they are also apprehensive that banks may use the interbank market to take excessive risks.

But most of all, the extent of interbank activity raises fears of contagion. The same channels that so efficiently transmit funds from surplus units to deficit units can also transmit shocks. In times of stress, the interbank market may become a primary source of contagion. Shocks may be transmitted in two separate, but related ways. First, if bank I_3 gets into trouble because of heavy exposure to a non-bank that defaults, bank I_2, which is a creditor of I_3, also can be in trouble. This is interbank credit risk. It is an especially difficult problem because any bank in the interbank chain is not likely to know the ultimate source or the final use of the funds deposited and redeposited. For example, undoubtedly several banks with claims on Brazilian banks were surprised and dismayed to learn that Brazilian banks were major creditors to Poland. Second, if bank I_3 gets into trouble, bank I'_2 may find it difficult to roll over its interbank deposits because other banks will fear either that I'_2 may have outstanding claims on the same non-bank borrowers as I_3 or because they fear that I'_2 is a creditor of I_3. These fears may be without basis in fact, but exposure figures are so difficult to verify that in the short run only the fears may matter. This is interbank funding risk.

The possibility of contagion demands that each country take an interest in the quality of supervision and the availability of lender of last resort facilities in other countries. Furthermore, the possibility of contagion means there is a public interest in the way in which banks manage their interbank credit lines. The policy consequences of these concerns over contagion are beginning to take shape in the work of the Cooke Committee. But if policy measures are to avoid being counter-productive, it is essential that we first achieve a fuller understanding of the functioning of the interbank market.

NOTES

1. It is extremely difficult to gauge the volume of activity in the interbank market. See Ellis, pp. 354–5, or Mayer, pp. 61–2, for a discussion of some of the problems in measuring the size and structure of interbank activity. In March 1982, liabilities to other banks constituted $1355 billion of the $1930 billion gross size of the Eurocurrency market (Morgan Guaranty Trust Co., p. 9).
2. As one can infer from the citations in this essay, neglect of the interbank market has not been without exception.
3. It seems likely that, other things being equal, banks with smaller, more geographically concentrated branch systems are likely to have a greater involvement in the interbank market (either as net takers or placers of funds) than banks with larger branch systems. A bank with a larger, widespread branch network would appear to be better able to intermediate between ultimate savers and primary borrowers within its own banking network with less recourse to the interbank market. In support of this proposition, Ellis (p. 356) reports evidence that involvement in the interbank market (measured as a proportion of total liabilities in foreign currencies) varies directly with the size of the bank. But the interbank market is so efficient that several very large international banks with worldwide branch networks use the interbank market rather than an internal, intrabank allocation mechanism to redistribute liquidity within the branch system, presumably because it is less costly. The Group of

Thirty Survey (1982b, p. 53) indicates that about half of the banks polled centralise global control of funding and about half permit decentralised local (profit centre) control.

4. See J. Niehans and Hewson for a network model based on minimising transaction costs.
5. The crisis involving Banco Ambrosiano Holding SA, a holding company subsidiary of Banco Ambrosiano, brought this assumption to light even though the reluctance of the Bank of Italy to provide assistance cast its validity in doubt
6. See Giddy (1981) for an interesting discussion of tiering and the financial statistics often used to evaluate an international bank.
7. The Group of Thirty (1982a, p. 17) reports that during the Herstatt crisis in 1974 some banks paid as much as 2 per cent above LIBOR.
8. See Guttentag and Herring for an analysis of rationing and tiering in response to increased concerns regarding a financial crisis.
9. Most discussion of the extent of maturity transformation *vis-à-vis* non-banks has been incomplete and misleading. Most analysts, perhaps following the lead of Niehans and Hewson, have concluded that the practice of lending at a floating rate on a roll-over basis implies that little maturity transformation takes place, except at the very short end of the yield curve. This, however, is much too narrow a view of the nature of maturity transformation. When a financial intermediary accepts a short-term deposit from a non-bank and makes a longer term loan to a non-bank borrower at a fixed rate of interest, the non-bank borrower derives two benefits: (1) the borrower has locked in the cost of funds over the period and (2) the borrower has assured the availability of funds over the period. When the loan is made at a floating rate – as is the usual practice in the Eurocurrency market – the interest rate risk is passed on to the borrower, but the funding risk is not. Thus the borrower retains one, but not both of the benefits of traditional maturity transformation. It is misleading to emphasise the interest rate risk component to the exclusion of the funding risk component.
10. See below for anecdotal evidence that a certain amount of window dressing may underlie the Bank of England statistics.
11. The increase in interest rate volatility that accompanied the Federal Reserve Board's shift to monetary targets made mismatching more hazardous. Indeed, during 1980 and 1981 substantial losses on mismatched positions were reported by a number of international banks (Group of Thirty, 1982a, p. 22). Undoubtedly other banks registered substantial profits from mismatching. But despite the increase in the volatility of interest rates, the Group of Thirty Survey (1982b, p. 53) indicated that most banks did not alter their maturity gapping practices in the Eurocurrency market.
12. For an up-to-date discussion of arbitrage see Kreicher (1982) or Ian Giddy's contribution to this volume.
13. Introduction to the SEC staff report, *Citicorp Report*.
14. These transactions are discussed at length in the SEC staff report, *Citicorp Report*, pp. 48–53A.

REFERENCES

Ellis, John G., 'Eurobanks and the interbank market', Bank of England *Quarterly Bulletin*, September 1981, pp. 351–64.

Giddy, Ian H., 'Eurocurrency Arbitrage', mimeographed, January 1983.

Giddy, Ian H., 'Risk and Return in the Eurocurrency Interbank Market', *Greek Economic Review*, August 1981, pp. 158–86.

Group of Thirty, *Risks in International Bank Lending*, New York, 1982a.

Group of Thirty, *How Bankers See the World Financial Market*, New York, 1982b.

Guttentag, Jack and Richard J. Herring, 'A Framework for the Analysis of Financial Disorder', in *Economic Activity and Finance*, Ballinger, 1981.

Herring, Richard J. and Richard C. Marston, 'The Forward Market and Interest Rate Determination', in *Eurocurrencies and National Financial Policies*, American Enterprise Institute, 1976.

Kreicher, Lawrence, 'Eurodollar Arbitrage', Federal Reserve Bank of New York *Quarterly Review*, Summer 1982, pp. 10–22.

Mayer, Helmut, 'The B.I.S. concept of the Eurocurrency market', *Euromoney*, May 1976, pp. 60–6.

McKinnon, Ronald I., 'The Eurocurrency Market', *Essays in International Finance*, No. 125, Princeton, December 1977.

Morgan Guaranty Trust Co., *World Financial Markets*, December 1982.

Niehans, Jurg and John Hewson, 'The Eurodollar Market and Monetary Theory', *Journal of Money, Credit and Banking*, February 1976, pp. 1–27.

SEC Staff, *Citicorp Report*, mimeographed, released September 1982.

4 Eurocurrency Arbitrage

IAN H. GIDDY[1]

INTRODUCTION

It is well known that alternative views of the nature of the Eurocurrency market have important public policy implications. What is less widely acknowledged is that these alternative views depend importantly on assumptions about the efficiency of arbitrage between the domestic and Eurocurrency markets. For example, whether central banks' deposits of their reserves in the Euromarket affect the size of the market depends on whether such placements are arbitraged back into domestic markets; and whether separate monetary intervention is needed to affect Eurodollar credit conditions depends on how readily domestic conditions are transmitted to the offshore markets. It follows that an understanding of the elasticity of arbitrage between the domestic and offshore markets, and among the different segments of the Eurocurrency market, might go a long way towards eliminating incorrect models of the Eurocurrency market, and therefore eliminating inappropriate policy prescriptions.

The evidence on relative interest rates presented here verifies the fact that the Eurodollar market is closely integrated with the domestic market and with other Eurocurrency markets. In the absence of capital controls, credit conditions in the offshore market are identical to those in the domestic market. The interest rate evidence suggests that interbank arbitrage dominates the linkages between domestic and Eurocurrency markets, and that perceived risk has little effect on relative rates. Relative quantities, on the other hand, may be the result of a stock adjustment of portfolios held by non-banks, whose behaviour may indeed be influenced by considerations of relative risk.

TWO SETS OF ARBITRAGE RELATIONSHIPS

Interest rates in the Eurocurrency market have gained in importance as the expanding market has captured an ever-growing share of international capital flows. Credit flows from one currency area to another tend to flow more and more through the Euromarkets: deposits from a national market are placed into the segment of the Euromarket that is denominated in the same currency, and the funds are then lent – with or without conversion into another country currency – to a borrower in another country; occasionally to the same country from where the funds originated. With the Eurocurrency market playing such a central role in the international transmission of interest rates, analysis must focus on two sets of relationships: (1) the link between a national credit market and its external segment, i.e., the Euromarket denominated in the same currency; and (2) the connection between two or more segments of the Eurocurrency markets denominated in different currencies.

The key to the analysis of the relationship *between domestic interest rates and external rates* is a clear understanding of what the Eurocurrency market is. Using the United States and its currency for illustration, the external (Eurodollar) and internal (domestic) market are merely competing segements of the total market for dollar-denominated credit, intermediated by financial institutions operating either internally (domestic banks) or externally (Eurobanks). The Eurodollar market competes with the domestic US bank market in the same way as, say, time deposits compete with bankers acceptances. Interest rates in any two segments of the credit market differ largely because of different risk characteristics as long as vigorous arbitrage is present.

As a consequence, the popular opinion that Eurodollar rates are peculiarly international, or that they are somehow determined by US rates, is misleading. The Eurodollar market is simply an integral segment of the total market for dollar credit, and interest rates in all segments are determined simultaneously. Arbitrage between the domestic and external segments of the dollar money market assures close correspondence both in terms of rate levels and in terms of rate changes in the absence of specific barriers and obstacles.

We now turn to the interest rate linkages resulting from competition *between the external market for funds denominated in different currencies*. How are Eurodollar interest rates linked to Euromark interest rates? As in the case of domestic-Euro interest rate linkages, we begin with the premise that competition will tend to equalise effective interest rates on similar securities, unless capital controls or other barriers prevent arbitrage between markets.

Arbitrage between Eurodeposits in the same banking centre, but denominated in different currencies, is not subject to capital controls. Nor are there necessarily differences in political or bank risk. Hence the persistent interest rate differentials that one does observe must be attributable solely to differences in currency of denomination. Funds in the Euromarket can readily be borrowed in one currency, and the principal plus interest sold forward for reconversion to the original currency. Such covered interest arbitrage should ensure that covered interest rate parity holds at all times between, say, Eurodollar and EuroGerman mark interest rates. Thus different *currency* segments of the Euromarket are perfectly integrated, thanks to the forward exchange market.

Putting these two influences together, one may see that the Euro interest rate in a particular currency is subject to two sets of influences – from the domestic market and from other Eurocurrency markets – that may sometimes pull in different directions. These tensions may be reconciled in one or two ways: (1) through *integration* of the international money market, i.e. by allowing Eurorates to equate *both* with effective interest rates in the domestic market *and* with covered rates on Eurodeposits denominated in other currencies, or (2) through *segmentation* of the international money market, i.e. by imposing capital controls that insulate the domestic money market, allowing the offshore rate to deviate from the effective domestic rate and to be determined entirely by covered interest parity with other currencies.

How exactly these influences reflect themselves in relative rates, and how these relationships have changed over time, is the subject of this paper.

DOMESTIC-OFFSHORE ARBITRAGE: EURODOLLARS

Among those who believe that arbitrage determines the relation between domestic and offshore interest rates, two strands of reasoning can be distinguished.[2]

The first is the market-price-of-risk view, which holds that the Eurodollar deposit rate should lie above the domestic rate a level given by the risk premium demanded by depositors, and that since depositors can readily arbitrage between domestic and offshore assets of equivalent risk, the Eurodollar premium should *only* be determined by relative risks. This approach implies that depositors' supply of funds to the Eurodollar market is infinitely elastic at the US deposit rate plus a premium attributable to the market price of risk. The premium is thus set in a portfolio context by depositors.

The alternative view is the cost of regulation theory – that the Eurodollar premium is purely and solely determined by the regulatory costs, such as taxes and reserve requirements, of offering domestic rather than offshore deposits. Banks, in this view, are indifferent between obtaining funds in the United States or the Eurodollar market, except for the regulatory cost differential, which is primarily the cost of holding non-interest-bearing reserve requirements.

An important paper on these arbitrage questions by Johnston[3] suggested that the interest differential is dominated by the relative cost of regulation. Johnston's technique was to adjust the US interest rate for the cost of reserve requirements and deposit insurance fees, and to plot the differential. He found that, at least during the late 1970s, the adjusted differential was insignificantly different from zero. Kreicher[4] refined Johnston's technique by constructing an 'arbitrage tunnel' within which, he argued, the Eurodollar deposit rate must lie if no arbitrage incentives exist. The limits of the tunnel were calculated by carefully incorporating the cost of reserve requirements on domestic deposits as well as those on Eurodollar borrowings by banks in the US, FDIC fees, and the bid-offer spreads faced by banks conducting onshore–offshore arbitrage. Kreicher's computations were based on two separate arbitrage assumptions.

First, outward arbitrage will take place unless the Eurodollar deposit rate available is less than or equal to the effective domestic cost of funds. The latter is measured by the dealer's bid rate for CDs in the secondary market, adjusted for reserve requirement fees.

Secondly, inward arbitrage will take place unless the effective cost of Eurodollar funds (including a reserve requirement on Eurodollar borrowing by US banks) equals or exceeds the effective cost of domestic funds, defined as before. Plotting the lower bound, the Eurodollar bid rate and the upper bound in relation to the midpoint between the upper and lower bounds, Kreicher found that for most of the post-1974 period the Eurodollar rate was a good dog, and lay within or close to the arbitrage tunnel. The exception was the last two years of the study, 1981–2. Kreicher hints that the deviations of this period may have resulted from fears about Eurobanks' country debt exposure. Yet is it not true that the disposition of banks' loans is independent of the funding source? As Aliber puts it, 'A US bank can buy an incremental dollar loan with funds realized from the sale either of an offshore deposit or of a domestic deposit' (p. 513).[5]

This raises an interesting point about their subject. Aliber's statement implies that the appropriate paradigm is the *quasi-arbitrage condition*: that banks already have a loan portfolio which they can fund in either the domestic or the offshore market. In fact, Kreicher's second (inward) arbitrage condition of this kind: he assumes US banks have a *domestic* loan portfolio which they may fund either domestically or offshore. The problem with this approach is that how one derives the arbitrage limit depends upon whether one assumes the existence of a domestic loan portfolio to be funded, or an international one, or both. For example, when banks fund domestic loans with Eurodollars they face a reserve requirement, but not when funding foreign loans with Eurodollars.

The alternative approach is to impose the *true arbitrage condition*, which makes no assumption about the existence of loan portfolios whose funding could be rearranged. Instead, true arbitrage starts from ground zero; banks have to borrow in one market (at the higher end of the bid-offer range) to invest in the other. This condition, which was the one imposed by Kreicher for outward arbitrage, is a stricter one.

In order to ensure consistency, I have adopted Kreicher's 'arbitrage tunnel' for an examination of arbitrage incentives, but based on the 'true arbitrage' condition, for three sets of markets: the domestic and offshore dollar markets, and the Eurocurrency markets denominated in dollars and German marks, the last pair being linked through the spot and forward foreign exchange markets.

Let us begin with the Eurodollar–US certificate of deposit (CD) market linkage. The true arbitrage limits are found as follows.

First, outward arbitrage will take place unless the Eurodollar deposit rate available is less than or equal to the effective domestic cost of funds. The latter is measured by the dealer's bid rate for CDs in the secondary market, adjusted for reserved requirements and deposit insurance fees. The condition is:

$$E\$_L \leqslant \frac{(CD_H + FDIC)}{(1 - RR_{CD})} \tag{1}$$

where the subscripts L and H stand for the lower and higher of the two rates, respectively, whenever a bid-offer spread is present, and $E\$$ is the Eurodollar rate, CD is the domestic certificate of deposit rate, $FDIC$ is the deposit insurance premium assessed on all domestic deposits and RR_{CD} is th domestic reserve requirement on CDs.

Secondly, inward arbitrage will take place unless the effective cost of Eurodollar funds (including a reserve requirement on Eurodollar borrowing by US banks) equals or exceeds the return obtainable by placing the funds in the domestic CD market. The second condition is:

$$\frac{E\$_H}{(1-RR_{E\$})} \geqslant CD_L \tag{2}$$

where $RR_{E\$}$ is the reserve requirement imposed on Eurodollar borrowings by US located banks.

Also we may define the Eurodollar spread as

$$E\$_{SPRD} = E\$_H - E\$_L \tag{3}$$

Combining (1), (2) and (3) and rearranging to put $E\$_L$ in the middle gives the boundaries for the Eurodollar bid rate – the 'arbitrage tunnel':

$$\frac{CD_L}{(1-RR_{CD})} \cdot (1-RR_{E\$}) - E\$_{SPRD} \leqslant E\$_L \leqslant \frac{(CD_H + FDIC)}{(1-RR_{CD})} \tag{4}$$

Monthly data for all the above variables were obtained from the *Financial Times* except for domestic CD rates and US reserve requirements and the effective FDIC premium which were obtained from the Federal Reserve Bank of New York. All rates are on three-month instruments traded in the interbank market. The upper bound, the lower bound and the actual Eurodollar bid rate ($E\$_L$) were then expressed as deviations from the midpoint between the two bounds, by subtracting (upper + lower)/2 from each. The resulting series are plotted in Figure 4.1.

Figure 4.1 should be interpreted as follows. The two lines varying symmetrically about the zero line are the theoretical limits. When the actual bid rate exceeds the upper bound, there is an apparent outward arbitrage incentive; points below the lower bound suggest an inward arbitrage incentive. The reader may be surprised at the number of deviations that appear. Outward arbitrage incentives in 1972 and 1973 reflect the remnants of the US capital control programme, and in 1974–5 the aftermath of Bankhaus Herstatt's collapse. The deviations in 1980–2, although less consistent than those in the Kreicher study, are not easy to explain; perhaps they do represent the additional incentive

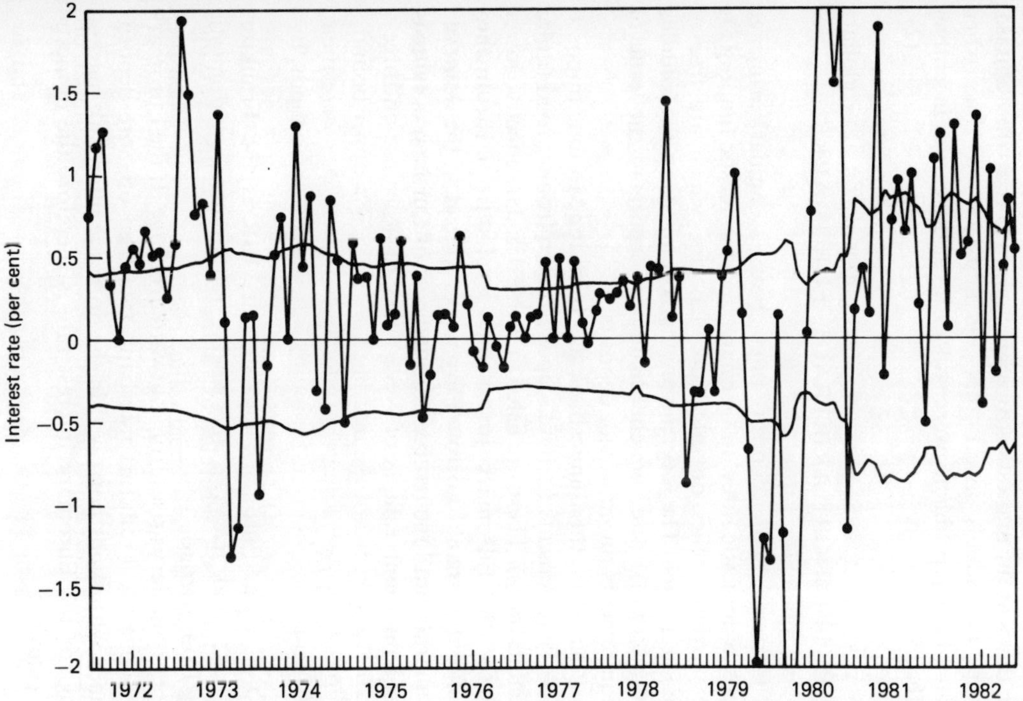

FIGURE 4.1 *Eurodollar arbitrage tunnel. Deviations from midpoints of bid limits (January 1972 to December 1982)*

required to place funds in offshore deposits during a period of international banking uncertainties. Another explanation lies in balance sheet constraints imposed by bank regulators of the developed countries – there existed at the time a reluctance to see banks' assets and liabilities increase without a corresponding increase in their capital. Whatever the reason, market participants confirm that they existed. These same individuals assert that by mid-1983, a time when international banks' problems were still with us, the earlier incentives had vanished.

DOMESTIC-OFFSHORE ARBITRAGE: EUROMARKS

Offshore German mark deposit rates bear a similar arbitrage relationship to domestic rates. In Germany, most domestic funding for wholesale purposes relies on interbank deposits, which are free of reserve requirements. The key money market rate is therefore the Frankfurt interbank rate, which already incorporates the cost of reserve requirements on non-bank deposits.

On the other hand, the Bundesbank has from time to time imposed steep reserve requirements on bank deposits taken from abroad (up to 100 per cent at times). These are listed in Table 4.1. The effective lower boundary for the Euromark invest rate results from the inward arbitrage incentive: banks borrow Euromarks to lend in the domestic interbank market until the reserve-adjusted cost of Euromarks exceeds the domestic interbank rate, i.e.

$$\frac{EDM_{\mathrm{H}}}{(1-RR_{\mathrm{EDM}})} \geqslant FIR_{\mathrm{L}}$$

where EDM is the Euromark deposit rate, FIR is the Frankfurt interbank rate, and RR_{EDM} is the reserve requirement on domestic borrowing from abroad.

The upper boundary arises from outward arbitrage. If the Euromark rate rises above the Frankfurt interbank rate then offshore deposits may be made with funds borrowed in the domestic interbank market. The ceiling for the Euromark interest rate is therefore the domestic interbank rate:

$$EDM_{\mathrm{L}} \leqslant FIR_{\mathrm{H}}$$

Thus the true arbitrage limits for the Euromark bid rate, EDM_{L}, are

TABLE 4.1 *Reserve requirements on non-resident deposits in German banks*

	Applicable from	Minimum reserve (%)
1972	July 1	35.0
1974	Jan. 1	30.0
	Oct. 1	27.6
1975	July 1	24.85
	Aug. 1	9.35
1976	May 1	9.85
	June 1	10.35
1977	March 1	10.45
	June 1	9.95
	Sept. 1	8.95
1978	Jan. 1	15.0
	June 1	9.0
	Nov. 1	9.0
1979	Feb. 1	10.3
1980	May 1	9.45
	Sept. 1	8.5
1981	Feb. 1	7.95
1982	Oct. 1	7.15

SOURCE Deutsches Bundesbank, *Monthly Bulletin*, various issues.

$$FIB_L(1-RR_{EDM})-EDM_{SPRD}\leqslant EDM_L\leqslant FIB_H$$

A quasi-arbitrage study by Dietmar Klein of the Deutsches Bundesbank confirms that the Eurorate lies within its proper bounds at almost all times.[6] I have reproduced that study using original data from the *Financial Times* and employing the true arbitrage condition. The deviations-from-midpoints plot of the arbitrage limits and the actual Euromark bid rate are displayed in Figure 4.2.

The chart provides evidence consistent with the cost-of-regulation view. If relative rates were determined by depositors' views about relative risks, then the Luxemburg subsidiaries of German banks would certainly be regarded as riskier than their domestic parents after the failure of Italy's Banco Ambrosiano to prevent its Luxemburg unit from defaulting on its deposit liabilities. One would therefore expect that Euromark rates would exceed domestic rates during the second half of 1982; but even this event did not succeed in pushing Euromark rates above their upper limits.

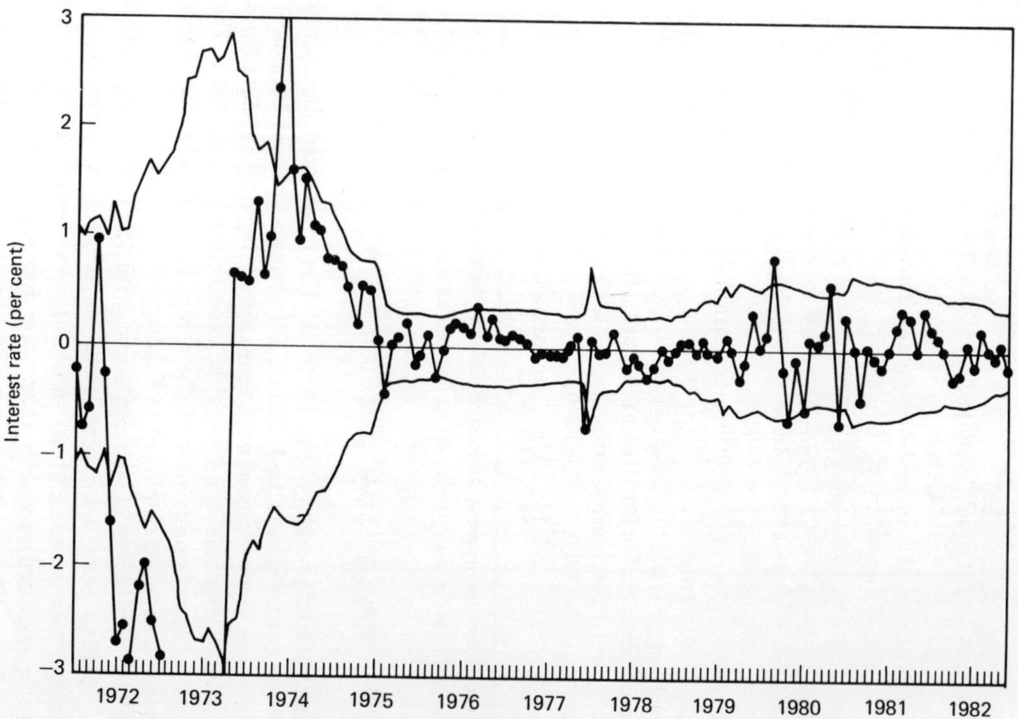

FIGURE 4.2 *Euro-German mark arbitrage tunnel. Deviations from midpoints of bid limits (January 1972 to December 1982)*

Thus both Eurodollar and EuroGerman mark interest rates behave in a manner consistent with the theory that relation between domestic and offshore interest rates is cost-determined.

CROSS-EUROCURRENCY ARBITRAGE

As was noted earlier, the interest rate on any Eurodeposit is influenced not only by the domestic market but also, through covered interest arbitrage, by the other Eurocurrency interest rates. As long as arbitrage is as free to cross currency boundaries as it is to cross jurisdictional boundaries, we should expect close parity between covered interest rates on two different Eurocurrencies.

Indeed, a test of the true arbitrage condition for, say, EuroGerman marks can be constructed in a manner matching that of the onshore-offshore arbitrage tests. Given the bid and offer rates for Eurodollar, the bid and offer rates for EuroGerman marks, the bid and ask rates for spot and forward foreign exchange, and the spread in the Euromark interbank deposit market, we are able to construct a *second* arbitrage tunnel for the Euromark bid rater. The method is as follows.

Capital will flow from dollars into German marks if a bank can profitably borrow dollars at the Eurodollar offer rate, buy marks spot at the ask rate, sell marks forward at the bid rate, and deposit in marks at the Euromark bid rate. This produces this interest rate parity (IRPT) upper bound for the Euromark bid rate (EDM_L):

$$EDM_L \leqslant E\$_H - (1 - E\$_H)\frac{(F_L - S_H)}{S_H} \cdot \frac{365}{T} \cdot 100$$

where S is the spot exchange rate, dollars per German mark, F is the forward exchange rate, dollars per German mark and T is the days to maturity.

Similarly, arbitrage capital will flow from German marks into dollars unless

$$EDM_H \geqslant E\$_L - (1 - E\$_L)\frac{(F_H - S_L)}{S_L} \cdot \frac{365}{T} \cdot 100$$

Using the relationships between bid and offer rates and spreads, this gives the Euromark bid rate's lower boundary:

$$EDM_{\mathrm{L}} \geqslant E\$_{\mathrm{L}} - (1 - E\$_{\mathrm{L}})\frac{(F_{\mathrm{H}} - S_{\mathrm{L}})}{S_{\mathrm{L}}} \cdot \frac{365}{T} \cdot 100 - EDM_{\mathrm{SPRD}}$$

Once more, we gathered data from the *Financial Times* for the period 1972–82, and computed the month-end IRPT upper and lower bounds for the Euromark bid rate. These were then transformed by subtracting the midpoint of the upper and lower bounds, to produce the graph shown in Figure 4.3. One may readily see that the all-powerful covered interest arbitrage condition suffers from occasional irregularity, at least as measured by data taken from daily newspaper quotations. Perhaps this is not surprising, considering the sensitivity of such arbitrage relationships to the precise timing of the quotations – which, in any case, are not actual transactions data. More interestingly is the fact that from 1979 onwards, the Euromark bid rate bumps up against the top boundary, frequently exceeding it. This suggests that the foreign exchange market pressure on the mark's interest rate was *downward*, opposing the *upward* influence on the German domestic rate.

Since covered interest arbitrage is widely felt to hold perfectly almost by definition, it is probable in any case that one may safely attribute small deviations from inter-Eurocurrency covered interest parity to data inadequacies. If this is the case, then *all* the arbitrage tests reported here are subject to errors as large as half of 1 per cent. If that is the case, we can dismiss almost all the inexplicable deviations from onshore–offshore parity as attributable to the same data errors as the covered interest parity test. And if almost all the deviations we have found here are illusory, then there is a strong case for saying that all four sets of markets – the two domestic markets and the two Eurocurrency markets – are very tightly integrated indeed.

CONCLUSION

This paper has adduced evidence favouring the view that domestic and Euromarket interest rates in the same currency are linked in a fairly mechanical fashion through the relative cost of regulation faced by banks issuing deposits in the two sets of markets. The logical implication of this evidence is that changes in risk perception, familiarity with the market, and other factors will not change the Eurodollar premium. No matter how much, or how little, depositors are prepared to offer at various interest rates, they always get the same rate relative to the US rate. How in this context, does the Eurodollar

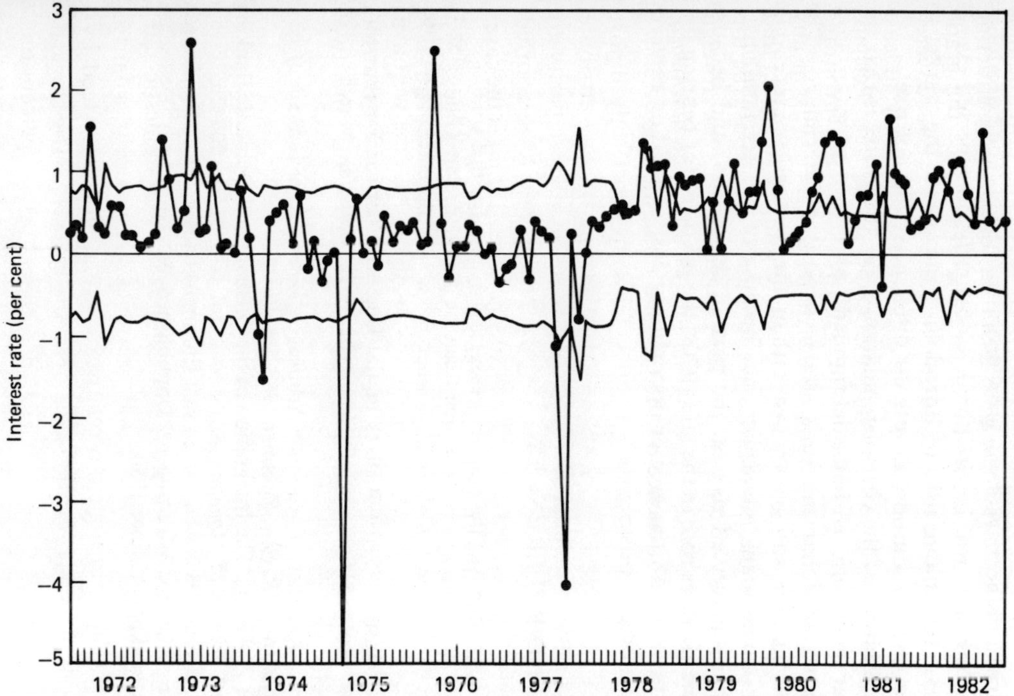

FIGURE 4.3 *Euromark covered interest arbitrage. Deviations from midpoints of bid limits (January 1972 to December 1982)*

market grow? The growth must be purely determined by depositors' behaviour. As the total US money market grows, so will the Euromarket. If perceived risks of Eurodollar relative to domestic deposits diminish, there will be a rightward shift of the depositors' supply curve and the market will grow proportionately. The Eurodollar premium, however, will be unaltered. Conversely, unexpected events that increase the unique risks of Eurodollars may cause the market to shrink, but the US–Eurodollar interest differential will not rise.

The implication of the cost-of-regulation view, therefore, is that the Eurodollar premium is bank-determined, and (for a given cost differential) Eurodollar market's size is depositor determined. The Eurodollar market has grown faster than the domestic market not because of some magic multiplier, but because of greater familiarity and declining perceived risk on the part of depositors, and because when domestic rates rose in the late 1970s, the payment for bearing this risk rose in step with the greater opportunity cost of holding reserves against domestic deposits.

NOTES AND REFERENCES

1. Larry Bjorkman was the author's research assistant for this study.
2. A fuller explanation of these views can be found in Ian Giddy, 'Why Eurodollars Grow', *Columbia Journal of World Business*, Fall 1979, pp. 54–60.
3. R. B. Johnston, 'Some Aspects of the Determination of Eurocurrency Interest Rates', *Bank of England Quarterly Bulletin*, March 1979, pp. 35–46.
4. Lawrence Kreicher, 'Eurodollar Arbitrage', *Federal Reserve Bank of New York Quarterly Review*, Summer 1982, pp. 10–22.
5. Robert Z. Aliber, 'The Integration of the Offshore and Domestic Banking System', *Journal of Monetary Economics*, vol. 6, 1981, pp. 509–26.
6. Dietmar Klein, 'Wie weit passen sich Euromarktzinsen den Indlandzinsen der entspechenden Wahrungen?' Unpublished Working Paper, Deutsches Bundesbank, September 1980.

Part III

5 Eurodollars: Policy Analysis

GUIDO CARLI

INTRODUCTORY REMARKS

Mr Van Lennep calls for co-operative action to tackle debtor country problems. (5/10/82)
Mr Regan says US banks can depend on help from the Government if debtor nations default. (6/10/82)
Mr Soloman calls for co-operation among governments and central banks to deal with the international financial situation. (10/7/82)
Mr Richardson warns that it would be self-defeating for banks to quickly reduce their exposure *vis-à-vis* debtors whose creditworthiness has changed. (21/10/82)
Professor Wallich on the problem of rescheduling as seen by the supervisor and the lender of last resort. (27/10/82)
Mr Leutwiler discusses the need for debt rescheduling operations. (28/10/82)
Mr Volcker offers a plan to reduce international financial strains. (16/11/82)

These are some of the pronouncements made over a very short period on the main policy issues dealing with the Eurodollar or, better, international lending activity, a topic which has been of concern for more than ten years and which I will discuss in my presentation.[1]

The analytical framework of international lending activity is far from being settled. Existing regulatory policies, while not systematic, are basically oriented towards 'benign neglect'. Since August 1971 a new theme, the international monetary standard, has been added to other well known issues such as lack of regulation, supervision and lending of last resort. This has certainly had consequences which often need clarification on both analytical and practical grounds.[2] A brief historical survey of intervention by the authorities and their motives is appropriate, in order to clarify these issues and understand the current and prospective policies in this sector.

HISTORICAL DEVELOPMENT OF POLICY ISSUES

Decisions concerning the Eurodollar market may produce direct effects, if they are aimed specifically at regulating the market or they may bring forth indirect consequences. At the very beginning, there was the regulation of the external net position of Italian banks in the early 1960s. These regulations are, sometimes, looked upon as having triggered the expansion of Eurodollars. Indeed, they recycled official liquidity and created double counting or under certain circumstances, a process of multiplication of international means of payments.

Leaving aside some twenty years of similar interventions in the European Monetary Agreement (marks 1 and 2), we can perhaps see a decision that, while not exclusively justifiable in terms of Eurodollars, actually lays the foundations for its own *raison d'être* in that market.

The origin of the so-called Roosa bonds, which belong to the first category of decisions, can be said to lie in a deliberate intention to absorb the surplus of international liquidity. The bonds, named after Robert V. Roosa, the Treasury Undersecretary during the Kennedy administration, were introduced in October 1962 with the aim of transforming the sight dollar deposits of the industrialised countries' monetary authorities into medium-term non-negotiable securities (12 to 24 months) denominated in foreign currencies. They were issued in the currency of the country acquiring them and bore a yield equivalent to the average prevailing yield of other medium-term securities in the US market. The Roosa bonds were at first non-negotiable and unredeemable before due date; later this rigid rule was eased to meet the investment portfolio needs set by the statutes of central banks of their domestic legislations.[3]

An intervention aimed at replenishing lost liquidity rather than absorbing a surplus can be detected in the action of the central banks, operating through the BIS, designed to finance, in the London market, the losses on pound denominated deposits suffered by a number of banks, as a consequence of the crisis that hit sterling in 1967. On that occasion the BIS was prepared to use its official dollar reserves, which were kept mostly in the US.

After repeated speculative attacks leading to the revaluation of the Deutsche Mark, the BIS Standing Committee of the Eurocurrency Market was established in May 1971; this was undoubtedly a first experiment in supervision of the market. It was followed by a declaration by the central banks of the Group of 10 plus Switzerland dated 10 September 1974. The Governors agreed on the need to intensify the exchange of information about banks operating in the international market and to further tighten the regulations on foreign exchange positions. This decision was reached after a discussion on the problem of the lender of last resort in the Euromarkets. No detailed rules or procedures for the provision of temporary liquidity were established in advance; however, it was acknowledged that the necessary means were available and ready to be used.

In 1972, the German authorities had attempted for the first time to intervene directly in international credit activity that affected their credit system by imposing a compulsory reserve (Bardepot) of 50 per cent on credits obtained abroad by residents of the Federal Republic. This rule had only three exceptions: commercial credits 'for a term deemed normal in commercial practice', credits related to direct investments and purchases of bonds quoted on German stock exchanges. The measure required residents to deposit 50 per cent (changed from an initial 40 per cent) of amounts exceeding half a million Deutsche Marks (the limit was originally 2 million) in a special non-interest bearing account in Deutsche Marks at the appropriate branch of the Bundesbank.[4]

The various amendments to Regulations D and M made by the US authorities fall into the class of 'front-line' regulations. These regulations govern the compulsory reserves of member banks (Regulation D) and of foreign branches of member banks (Regulation M).

The June 1969 amendments laid down reserve ratios for US banks on Eurodollar indebtedness exceeding the level for the banks' indebtedness to their overseas branches (3 per cent for Eurodeposits up to 4 per cent of the bank's domestic deposits subject to reserve requirements, and 10 per cent for Eurodeposits above the 4 per cent level).

In 1971 the reserve ratios were raised; the method of calculating the reserve-free base was changed in order to discourage banks from repaying their Eurodollar debt (the applicable reserve ratio was raised from 10 per cent to 20 per cent). The amendments decided in the following years were all aimed at gradually tapering off the marginal reserve requirements. On 28 August 1978 the ratio was brought down to zero, in order to make it 'more attractive for member banks to borrow funds from the Eurodollar market'.[5] In 1979 and 1980 the reserve ratio was raised again, while in May 1981 International Banking Facilities (IBFs) were established and the provisions concerning their funds gave exception from any reserve requirement.

The Committee on Banking Regulations and Supervisory Practices of the Group of 10 wrote, in December 1975, a report to the Governors on the supervision of banks' establishments in which three different aspects of banking supervision were considered: liquidity, solvency, and foreign exchange operations and positions. After agreeing on the principle that each country has a duty to ensure supervision of foreign banking activity within its territory in compliance with the ideals of international co-operation, the Committee considered the extent to which the division of responsibilities for supervision could be codified. A number of general guidelines were established. In managing their liquidity, foreign banking establishments were to rely heavily on local practices and comply with local regulations, including those established for monetary policy purposes. Responsibility for supervising their liquidity had to be taken in the first place by the host authority. It was agreed that a foreign branch should be considered as a section of the institution to which it belonged as regards liquidity. Parent authorities should also be concerned in the case of foreign subsidiaries and joint ventures. In the matter of solvency controls, some sharing of responsibility for supervision between host and parent authorities was recommended, assigning a major role to the host authorities for foreign subsidiaries and joint ventures. The *dotation de capital* imposed by the host authorities in certain countries on foreign branches was above all intended to compel foreign branches, setting up business in those countries, to make a minimum investment in them, and to equalise competitive conditions between foreign branches and domestic banks. An adequate share of responsibility for foreign exchange positions was also given to the host authorities, and criteria were defined for: (a) the direct transfer of information between supervisory authorities, (b) direct inspections by parent authorities of their domestic banks' foreign establishments, (c) indirect inspections of foreign banking establishments by parent authorities through the agency of host authorities.

In April 1980, the Governors of the Group of 10 plus Switzerland agreed on the importance of ensuring the integrity of the international banking system. The Governors concluded that the system of regular indication of the economic effects produced by international banking activity, both at aggregate and national levels, had to be strengthened. They also agreed that the implementation of initiatives aimed at improving the supervision of international banking, with special reference to consolidated accounts and conrols on the procedures for country risk assessment, should be given priority. The Governors indicated the difference between regulations and official policies as one of the reasons for the expansion of the international operations of banks, and they agreed on the need to reduce these differences.

In September 1981, the IMF Committee on Banking Regulations and Supervisory Practices published a document in which criteria for country risk assessment were defined.

In closing this brief historical summary of the major policy issues, we should not overlook the decision taken by the Carter administration in November 1979 to freeze all Iran's dollar deposits with the United States banking system, following the political crisis brought about by the seizure of the American embassy in Teheran.

Without considering the detailed steps leading to changes in the composition of official reserves (IMF position, swap network and similar provisions, changes in the treatment of gold as a reserve asset, borrowing facilities in general, etc.) besides other indirect interventions on the Eurodollar, we can conclude – for the purpose of updating our analysis – with a description of the decisions taken at the recent Paris meeting.

A major increase in official international lending resources (from $75.3 to $120 billion) was approved in Paris on 18 January 1983 by the finance ministers and central bank governors of the ten leading industrial democracies.

The officials from the so-called Group of 10 agreed to almost triple their own pool of lendable funds – known as the General Arrangements to Borrow (GAB) – to 17 billion SDRs from the current 6.4 billion SDRs. A substantial increase in IMF resources was also called for, along with a 'meaningful adjustment' in the quota shares paid by member countries was negotiated at the February 1984 meeting of the IMF's policy-making Interim Committee.

These provisions are designed to relieve the strains imposed on the international financial system by the indebtedness of many developing countries, and to attenuate the unemployment problem in the world. Some commentators have seen the embryo of a lender of last resort function.

There was no discussion at the meeting, on what steps individual countries could take to help spur growth. But in contrast with the past two years, there now appears to have emerged an agreement to research for a more co-ordinated policy.

PROBLEMS IN REGULATION AND SUPERVISION

In reviewing the history of the decisions made during more than twenty years, it is clear that the issues of direct regulation at the national level and supervision at the international level have dominated the debate on the Eurodollar market and the choices of the authorities. Any sort of global indirect regulation, widely used at the domestic level in the form of control of the monetary base, definition of explicit rules for lenders of last resort and, in particular, a global approach to the problem was totally lacking.

It has to be stressed, furthermore, that the interventions implemented were prompted mostly by domestic considerations on the part of the country making them. Their impact at the international level, which led to the collapse of the Bretton Woods agreement, proved to be of secondary concern to the authorities. This is still true now, when we face the possibility of an international banking crisis. In spite of a homogeneous statistical treatment, the *set* of the balance sheet sections expressed in foreign currencies – called the Eurodollar market in Europe – has not become a *system*, i.e. a market regulated by the authorities in addition to spontaneous rules and commonly accepted uses. Some authors have explained the practical and logical absence of a system as being the result of the 'state of anarchy' arising from the benign neglect of the authorities.

The most elementary level of economic analysis tells us that if a price exists, a market, which may or may not be regulated, also exists. For example, there is no doubt that a *three-month Eurodollar deposit rate* exists, backed by a 'robust' quantity of three-month deposits in foreign currencies. There is also a term structure of Eurodollar interest rates, backed – in December 1981 according to BIS data (see Table 5.1, p. 150) – by foreign currency liabilities held by residents of the country reporting their existence (87 per cent of the total) and others not reported, for an equivalent 'gross' amount of 1778 billion US dollars; 329 billion (81 per cent reported) of the 'gross' amount, net of exchange rate effects, were accumulated during the year, mostly (89 per cent) in the form of US dollar deposits.[6]

Thus the annual 'gross' rate of increase has reached 23 per cent, compared with the almost zero real growth of world trade. It is therefore easy to draw the conclusion that the significance of this rate substantially exceeds that of any other credit or monetary indicator taken as the basis for the Western countries' policies (see Table 5.2, p. 151). However, there is considerable disagreement about the meaning of this rate and its 'net' size, leading to the corollary of the thesis on the non-existence of a market-system: neither Eurodollar nor off-shore dollar growth rates can be computed because they do not exist.

We cannot accept the non-existence of a Eurodollar problem at the aggregate level even though, from the way the authorities have dealt with it, i.e. on a purely national basis, it could be inferred that they have, in fact, adhered to this view.

The only exception consistent with belief in an aggregate 'economic reality', which is therefore common to several countries, is the surveillance activity of the BIS, in spite of 'tepid' statements by the bank itself (an understatement of solid and respectable tradition). This surveillance is also carried out by Standing Committees, the first of which dates back to May 1971, a few months before the international monetary system founded at Bretton Woods lost its standard.

At least three factors underlie the inability of the authorities to implement a system of regulation and supervision of the Eurocurrency market and, more generally, of the international credit market.

The *first* is the persistence of the ideas of the 'banking school' at the international level, after they had proved to be inefficient at the national level. According to this school, growth in the credit system is a self-regulating process, due to the saving decisions made *ex-ante* by economic agents. These ideas proved to be a dangerous fallacy, both in theory (elaborated by the 'monetary school') and in practice. Nevertheless they are supported by the poor economic quality of the existing banking regulations which aim neither at fulfilling market needs nor at guaranteeing an efficient allocation of financial resources. The abundance of direct controls – constraints on prices (interest rates) and quantities – underlines the importance of the problem examined here. There is no doubt that free credit activity is of advantage to the economy; but, following recent international experience in LDC financing, it is also true that these short-lasting advantages are coupled with serious and long-lasting damage to the stability of the monetary standard of value measure, at both national and international levels.

The *second* factor is the jealous practice of monetary sovereignty at the national level. In an economy open to multilateral trade and with international banking activity 'benignly neglected', this sovereignty can only be practised in the context of international agreements establishing a reference framework, appropriately called the 'monetary regime'.[7] The myopia of the national approach to monetary sovereignty was largely confirmed by the effects of the current vicissitudes of the dollar on the monetary policies of the countries using it for their official reserves and for their trade in goods, services and capital. The stability of the European Monetary System (marks 1 and 2) is a typical example; but the monetary sovereignty of the United States is also undermined by the double use (internal and international) of the dollar, a fact which the US sometimes fails to consider.

The *third* element is the confusion in the theory of international money and its excessive compliance with vested interests. The state of the literature is affected by US instances concurring to determine the other two factors: the misinterpretation of the meaning of the 'freedom' of international monetary and financial forces; the awareness of the fact that part of the assets involved in market activity are not monetary in nature; the wrong perception of the mainly national character of the Eurodollar problem and the wrong assessment of the scope for a disaggregate treatment. The list might be even longer, but a few examples will suffice.

The inability and the unwillingness of the authorities to proceed towards the supervision and regulation of the market is also due to the fact that, before the Eurodollar and international banking activity gained vigour, the authorities had rightly paid more attention to the completion of the international monetary system agreed upon at Bretton Woods in 1944, which gave birth to Special Drawing Rights (SDRs) in 1968. In fact, they had believed that, by concentrating their efforts on this issue, they would clear the market of the problems caused by the above mentioned issues; but the time taken to achieve the result (24 years) changed this hope into an illusion; this was confirmed by the content of the Rio de Janeiro agreement.[8]

Only later, by proposing substitution accounts, did the reformers acknowledge a changed situation. However, by that time (1978–9), the dollar was definitively the centre of the international monetary system. The attempt to create a new arrangement based on an international currency (the SDR standard) withered with the strengthening of the spontaneous system of the national currency standard, which had switched from the British pound to the US dollar. This strengthening became more 'unregulated' because of the absence of the 'barbarian', but effective and always used regulator: gold. We will come back to this later.

The supervision and regulation of the international banking system were, and still are, closely linked to the establishment of an international institutional structure that is independent of individual national currencies. This can only rest on recognition of the legitimacy of a strong US leadership which, in turn, cannot be founded on either conditions of underdevelopment and depression or a worldwide inflationary climate.

Today it is easy to forecast that progress in this direction will not be rapid. At present, in fact, interest in the problems of supervision-control and the international monetary system is obscured by concern about the effects of failing to provide solutions to them.

Today the problems of the stability (solvency) of the international banking system, which we mentioned at the beginning, its present inability to provide steady support for real growth and the resulting advance of protectionism, are paramount.

It is true that we have first to live in order to philosophise. It is not difficult to show that every problem can be solved in terms of a philosophy and that this philosophy is made impossible today by an imperfect analysis. If we wondered whether the Kronberg Summit of the 'Big 5' in December 1982 had actually overcome this obstacle, today, after the Paris meeting of the Club of Ten plus Switzerland, we have positive though not exhaustive signals.

PROBLEMS IN LENDING OF LAST RESORT

Two centuries of disputes between the 'banking school', opposed to any type of control, and the 'monetary school', conscious of the opposite need, and more than half a century of experiments have made it clear that, in order to promote growth through a monetary standard, a reliable central control institution, which can also work as lender of last resort, is necessary. At a national level, nobody believes in the magic of an 'invisible hand' in the monetary market any more.

If we look at current thinking on lending of last resort, we reach the conclusion that the choices of monetary authorities, in line with those analysed at the level of regulations and supervision problems, are influenced by the idea that either the market – through bankruptcies (Herstatt) – or the national authorities (Franklin and Privata Finanziaria) have to take care of this problem, because there is no such thing as an international banking 'system' or an international monetary regime.

Only on the 6 October 1982 did the Secretary of the US Treasury,

Regan, state that US banks could depend on help from the Government if debtor nations defaulted. But this is hardly sufficient since the qualifier 'US' should disappear and the noun 'Government' should be replaced by 'a stabilisation fund' for those banks accepting regulation and supervision by some established authority similar to the IMF. This is the procedure operating within the Federal Reserve 'system', which is well known to be based on the spontaneous adhesion of banks. The Kronberg and Paris summits do not seem to have moved towards this more appropriate view, maintaining the approach of direct lending activity plus a second line of defence for banks (the first being at the national level as Regan stated).

The troubles the world has endured because of banking systems without lenders of last resort or rules for their lending, could be experienced again in the near future. The lesson history taught, none the less, seems to have been understood at least in its principal aspects, even though others, particularly useful for today's needs, have been neglected. In this connection, knowing the philosophy and the strict monetary regime operating at the national level, the statement by Volcker that 'to reduce international financial strains can be readily justified in face of extraordinary needs . . . both a sizeable increase in basic quotas [of IMF] and a reliable stand-by borrowing arrangement' gives food for thought.[9]

More than 150 years ago a Neapolitan constructor, Francesco Fuoco, wrote an essay, under the false name of Guiseppe De Welz, a Swiss banker, in order to try to convince the Borbonic King to approve the deficit financing of some roads in the Kingdom of the Two Sicilies. I have already referred to this book when, in March 1971, I realised that the dollar-exchange standard system was collapsing under a paper pyramid, the Eurodollar.[10] I must admit that it was Joseph Alois Schumpeter in his monumental *History of Economic Analysis* who gave me a clue.[11] More than a century before Keynes, Francesco Fuoco expounded the idea of the income multiplier in unemployment. He also developed an analysis of the foundations of credit activity which Milton Friedman might well envy and which, today, might give the post-Keynesians dealing with the monetary problem and the fiscal effects of the welfare state food for thought. Credit and credibility are synonymous, according to Francesco Fuoco; with powerful insight he defined credit as 'a glass ball to be handled with care and which fogs up if one gets to close to it with one's breath', that is if one talks about it.

Another great economist, Jacques Rueff, also discussed the topic of 'gossiped money', saying that money is like a lady who, in order to remain such, does not tolerate being talked about. Rueff gave some rules in order to *établir le silence de la monnaie*, among which there is one stating that a lender of last resort has to stand behind it to 'cut the gossip short'.[12]

One wonders whether in a 'gossiped' system, in which dollars held by US banks are – at least according to what is reported – the only funds to be 'guaranteed' by a lender of last resort, is viable. In this situation, the international banking and trade systems are still more fragmentary, pushed further towards bilateralism and protectionism. Thus Paul Volcker was right when he emphasised in his 'Plan' the role of the IMF, the World Bank and the BIS, and not merely the role of the Federal Reserve System.

The IMF participants would have done better to assign all of the new facility, decided upon by the Group of 10 plus Switzerland during their meeting in Paris, to lending of last resort operations, rather than to direct loans with the choice of other forms (rescheduling of debts and intervention consortia) up to the banks, thus leaving them entirely responsible for their credit activities.

Obviously some rules, or better still an international monetary regime to refer to, should have been made explicit. We should not deceive ourselves, though: the three previously mentioned constraints which prevented systematic regulation and supervision of international money flows also hinder prompt and effective lending of last resort. When the recent growth rates of international money are observed (Tables 5.1 and 5.2), the suspicion arises, moreover, that the faults of analysis are of greater weight compared with the other two factors. As a matter of fact, the increase of the international liquidity base in the form of IMF quotas or other financial instruments was believed to be an answer to the lack of an institutional framework. This need is neither felt by the international monetary market (world money is not scarce), nor is it consistent with the recovery without inflation, that the world wishes to achieve and for which we are willing to tolerate the social costs corresponding to 33 million unemployed people in the OECD area. Banks are able to 'produce' international credit, but not to control its volume nor to absorb the impact of monetary and real changes.

If we exclude the problem of imperfect analysis, in order to make the right decision on an international monetary system, it is essential to accept the binomial 'sovereign-international money', which, the world thought, could be avoided despite its growing interdependence in the trade of goods, services and capital. If we do not accept an 'authority',

TABLE 5.1 *Estimated lending in international markets: changes in external claims of banks and international bond issues*

Lenders	*Flows excluding exchange rate effects (in billions of US dollars)* 1978	1979	1980	1981	*Stocks at end-1981*
Banks in European reporting countries	111.9	150.9	158.7	136.0	992.3
of which in foreign currency (Euro-currency market)	97.3	130.3	131.1	114.5	840.0
Banks in Canada and Japan	14.8	16.5	28.5	23.5	122.5
Banks in the United States (including IBFs)	38.0	17.1	40.7	76.5	255.4
Branches of US banks in offshore centres	15.0	21.0	13.7	31.6	171.8
Total	179.7	205.5	241.6	267.6	1542.0
minus: double-counting due to redepositing among the reporting banks	89.7	80.5	81.6	102.6	602.0
A = Net international bank lending	90.0	125.0	160.0	165.0	940.0
Euro-bond and foreign bond issues	37.5	37.3	38.0	47.8	—
minus: redemptions and repurchases	8.5	9.3	10.0	11.3	—
B = Net new international bond financing	29.0	28.0	28.0	36.5	—
A + B = Total new bank and bond financing	119.0	153.0	188.0	201.5	—
minus: double-counting	6.0	8.0	8.0	6.5	—
Total net new bank and bond financing	113.0	145.0	180.0	195.0	—
Memorandum item: non-reporting banks in offshore centres	30.0	28.0	40.0	61.0	236.0

SOURCE 1982 *BIS Annual Report*, p. 116.

the problem cannot be solved; this issue was appropriately stressed by political commentators at the conclusion of the Kronberg Summit.

THE PROBLEM OF AN INTERNATIONAL STANDARD AND SOVEREIGNTY

In December 1971, as shown by the Smithsonian Agreement, the 'dollar area' believed a fixed exchange rate system was still viable even without a strong commitment by the United States – i.e. the country supplying the medium of exchange for international trade – to defend the value of the standard. The monetary policy decided upon at the end of 1979 should have been implemented at that earlier date.

It was a typical ostrich reaction, since the declaration of non-convertibility of the dollar into gold, made just a few months before, had officially confirmed the devaluation of the dollar and the excess

TABLE 5.2 *Monetary and credit aggregates: objectives and rates of expansion*

Countries	*Monetary or credit aggregate*	*Objective (%)*				*Actual result (%)*			
		1979	*1980*	*1981*	*1982*	*1979*	*1980*	*1981*	*1982*
United States	M_1^3	3.0–6.0	4.0–6.5	3.5–8.0	2.5–5.5	5.5	6.7	2.3	10.8
	M_2^3	5.0–8.0	6.0–9.0	6.0–9.0	6.0–9.0	8.3	9.8	9.4	10.1
	M_3^3	6.0–9.0	6.5–9.5	6.5–9.5	6.5–9.5	8.1	9.9	11.3	8.9
	Total bank credit	7.5–10.5	6.0–9.0	6.0–9.0	6.0–9.0	11.0	8.0	8.8	
Japan	M_2 + CDs	11.0	8.0	7.0	10.0	11.2	7.8	10.6	10.7
Germany	Central-bank money	6.0–9.0	5.0–8.0	4.0–7.0	4.0–7.0	6.3	4.9	3.5	6.6
France	M_2	11.0	11.0	10.0	12.5–13.5	14.4	9.8	11.6	—
United Kingdom	M_1	—	—	—	8.0–12.0	14.0	8.8	8.9	6.2
	Sterling M_3	8.0–12.0	7.0–11.0	6.0–10.0	8.0–12.0	13.5	16.3	14.7	7.8
	Private sector liquidity PSL_2	—	—	—	8.0–12.0	15.0	13.0	11.7	—
Canada	M_1	6.0–10.0	5.0–9.0	4.0–8.0	4.0– 8.0	8.0	6.2	—	—
Switzerland	Adjusted central bank money	—	4.0	4.0	3.0	—	−0.6	−0.5	—
Italy	Total credit	18.5	17.5	16.0	15.5	18.4	18.4	18.7	

SOURCE 1982 *BIS Annual Report*, p.81.

supply of international money with respect to the volume of the gold-commodity standard and international trade. The market – as expected – perceived the inflationary signal implicit in the analysis which had led to that decision. Consequently it oriented its expectations in that direction. The way the problem was handled can be discussed and possibly justified. But to have fed the illusion that a standard, the dollar, controllable by the market in its basic functions, still existed, cannot be justified.

An intelligent scholar of monetary matters, Paolo Baffi, made it clear in several writings that the exchange standard system, be it the dollar or the pound, requires political and real economic strength to resist the intrinsic weakness of the currency it creates, or allows others to create (Eurodollars) in the international markets.[13] As a matter of fact, international money creation in an exchange standard system is left to liquidity deficits in the balance of payments of the country whose currency falls short; where a deficit exists there is an excess supply of one currency compared with the other. In order for the excess supply to be neutralised, there has to be a public or private operator that permanently holds it. The willingness shown by monetary authorities to hold dollars has generated official reserves in foreign currency, a prerequisite for a credible fixed exchange rate system. The same willingness shown by private and bank operators has created the Eurodollar or, more generally, the xenocurrency market (offshore currencies).

In this way the 'success' of the standard as a medium of exchange is guaranteed. If there is no regulation of the quantity of this standard, however, it cannot perform its second important function: to be a store of value. In the Bretton Woods system the regulation of the quantity of money should have been secured by the gold-convertibility of the dollar; but this convertibility assumed a dollar for international uses 'governed' at an aggregate level to prevent individual national authorities (such as the Swiss, Belgian and Netherlands authorities at the end of the Bretton Woods system) from threatening the system's survival by converting dollars into gold. Thus benign neglect allowed demand-induced dollar creation and gave practical importance to the Triffin paradox: the more dollars are created *vis-à-vis* the same quantity of gold in Fort Knox, the less credible is the promise of their convertibility at a fixed price and the less effective is the market 'regulator' of the expected system (convertibility). Expectations vanish and monetary policy can only control events in a restrictive direction.

However, we should go beyond the analysis of the mechanics of the reasoning we have developed and explain why, in the late 1960s, the Western authorities were so concerned about the lack of a regulator of the quantity of dollars for international uses. I believe that the answer is to be found in the trend of US inflation, which was moderately stable during the first period of implementation of the Bretton Woods agreement and increasing in the second period. The official authorities guaranteeing the system's stability by acquiring dollars from the official reserves saw the real value of the reserves themselves decline and US inflation affect their economies through fixed exchange rates.

In 1971, despite the solemn statements of the Smithsonian Agreement, the exchange rate regime was altered. In 1979, the US monetary system was also changed with rigorous control of the quantity of dollars created for internal uses coupled with acceptance of the impact on interest rates. This last decision brought back confidence in the dollar for international uses and re-established its function as a store of value. The trend of gold prices between 1971 and 1979 and later confirms this assessment.

But in a flexible exchange rate system, monetary restriction cannot fully restore the function of the standard. As a matter of fact, the current monetary system does not have a standard of value. The 1981 BIS report explains at length that, in order to calculate and analyse the expansion of international credit activity, it is necessary to make a two-step computation: the first to convert the nominal data (which are not exact) with constant exchange rates to obtain the 'theoretical data'; and the second to transform the theoretical *nominal* data into the twice-theoretical *real* data.

Fluctuation does not prevent the dollar from being either the reference currency for international transactions, or a store of value, but it still prevents its being a standard, i.e. a real medium of exchange. This is due to the combined effect of interest and exchange rates which deprives the dollar of its image as a pure currency (stable in value and not interest bearing) and allows a separation between the monetary economy and the 'speculative' economy. From this point of view it is understandable that some circles should have asked for a new dollar-denominated price of gold to be set in order to complete the restoration of the dollar standard's credibility. As is well known, I do not share this view; a better strategy might be to try to create an international standard requiring an equally strong political commitment and leadership than that necessary to restore and defend gold convertibility of the dollar.

In this situation, the solution to the problem of continuing international credit activity is rather irrelevant in that it is only aimed at the banking system's stability, while it overlooks the economic policy aspect of the problem, i.e. development financing. The addition of a specific purpose for monetary creation, economic strength capable of resisting an inevitably 'weak' dollar, and exchange rate stability linked to some international parameter – either gold or SDRs – would restore this characteristic. The complete absence of such a theme in the proposals by the 'Big 5' at Kronberg represents the limit of the attempts made to implement a new international monetary order after the disturbance caused by LDC insolvencies.

The question of why the return to (real or monetary) economic orthodoxy was never implemented in the leading Western country and never reached the international monetary system has to be explained.

If we could provide an answer to this practical question we could probably remove the present impasse within the international monetary system.

CURRENT PROBLEMS IN INTERNATIONAL LENDING

In the latest BIS report the current problem of the world economy is summarised as follows: policies operate on the basis of a system where the osmosis between national and international markets of goods and currencies has increased. Therefore 'there are risks in exposing countries to an extremely fast adjustment process, and there are dangers ... in postponing the adjustment process through an excessively accommodating supply of credit'.[14]

Even though the text is not clear, the risks mentioned are certainly related to the real economy, and especially unemployment, and the banking system.

Considering the risks in a real economy, there is nothing new in stating that, in the case of a successful business, debts are never repaid, even if the business is able to obtain high investment returns, since its cash flows are continuously reinvested to promote growth.

At an international level the mechanism is similar, but has further complication; credit is in fact received as money and reimbursed as goods, i.e. it is paid only if the exports of the debtor countries increase; if an increase in exports is not forseeable, any idea of reimbursement is out of place: where would the debtor country get the currency to repay? It could reduce current imports, saving an amount equal to its debt; but if imports are essential to the development of both the exporting and the importing countries, any reduction would be inconsistent with the aim of credit activity which is to promote production. This is the real risk.

The banking risk, i.e. is the possibility of insolvency of the debtor country, is often treated independently of the real risk just described, i.e. of the declared foundations of international banking. The insolvency risk of a country is thus tied to its export development prospects and is, nowadays, two-pronged. One, the extremely rapid real adjustment imposed by the United States and, two, the past laxity about credit shown by international banks and LDCs. There is a tendency to consider the second aspect as a cause of the first and not vice versa. The recent past was clearly marked by 'easy' credit in the Eurodollar and the international banking market; the analysis carried out so far should have shown that the origin of the evil lies in the absence of policies regulating international credit, rather than in international credit as such. Perhaps this judgement is also wrong, if one re-examines the final statement of the Venice Summit which assigned the international private banking system a task of recycling international surpluses of funds. This is undoubtedly a political choice.

An international monetary policy was only apparently lacking. There was a clear willingness to give the market the function of system regulator. But governing a free competitive market is, contrary to common belief, a more difficult and demanding task than governing a regulated economy. Proposals for regulating Eurodollars have often been rejected on the grounds of impracticality. However, in this way, *laissez-faire* policy creates serious problems of stability for the whole of the international banking system. The size of today's problem is probably well known (see Tables 5.3 and 5.4); but the picture is less clear for the next five years (see Table 5.5). Bearing in mind the limited validity of econometric exercises, which is none the less offset by the undoubted advantage which derives from being able to quantify 'fears' and sensations, the data supplied by the research group of Nobel prize winner Professor Klein are certainly impressive. With a sluggish recovery hypothesis, i.e. with 3.2 per cent annual world growth, the accumulated deficits in current account balances would amount to 404 billion dollars at the end of the five-year period. The LDCs are expected to account for 312 billion and the CPEs for 71 billion. At the end of 1982 the group runs an estimated debt of about 600 billion (90 of which held by the centrally planned economies); indebtedness will consequently grow at over 10 per cent per year.

Once we have seen the size of the real problem, its solution can only

TABLE 5.3 *Indebtedness and debt ratios 1973–82 (end-of-period amounts – US $ billion)*

	1973	*1978*	*1981*	*1982**
Total debt				
LDCs†	96.8	276.4	436.9	505.2
Centrally planned economy	22.0‡	58.3	80.7	92.0
Total debt as a per cent of exports of goods and services				
LDCs†	88.7	111.2	102.0	110.8
Centrally planned economy	—	170.0	140.0	144.0
Debt service ratio (per cent of exports of goods and services)				
LDCs†	14.0	17.3	21.1	23.4
Centrally planned economy	—	13.3	33.0	—
Memo item:				
6-month Eurodollar rate (London)	9.24	8.73	16.51	

* Estimates.
† Excluding short-term debts (less than 1 year).
‡ 1974.
SOURCE IMF, WEFA (from L. Dini, *Problemi finanziari dell'economia mondiale*, mimeo, November 1982).

lie in a recovery of international trade that will prevent insolvency and, consequently, an acceleration of protectionism and a return to bilateralism. This sort of concern seems to have led to the proposal to intervene in exchange rates, made by Secretary Regan at the Summit of the five major industrial countries in Kronberg and implemented by the Group of 'Eleven' in Paris. A moderate adjustment in LDC deficits would not alleviate banking risks, but would bring back the old ghosts of protectionism and the closing of national markets.

Monetary problems, in turn, can find a stop-gap solution in the form of financial engineering such as rescheduling and the re-examination of both individual guarantees (strengthening of banks' capital bases combined with a less rigorous application of the rules) and collective guarantees (interventions by governments, the IMF, the World Bank and the BIS) to restore offshore depositors' confidence.

These intermediate policies will certainly produce a more careful and prudent attitude in operators on both sides of the market. But they have to be accompanied by a more orderly organisation of the

TABLE 5.4 *LDCs Debt list for 1983 (estimated debt in billions of dollars)*

	Total at years-end 1982	*Debt service payment* for 1983*	*Payment as per cent of exports*
Brazil	$87.0†	$30.8	117
Mexico	80.1	43.1	126
Argentina	43.0†	18.4	153
S. Korea	36.0	15.7	49
Venezuela	28.0	19.9	101
Israel	26.7	15.2	126
Poland	26.0	7.8	94
USSR	23.0	12.2	25
Egypt	19.2	6.0	46
Yugoslavia	19.0	6.0	41
Philippines	16.6	7.0	79
E. Germany	14.0	6.3	83
Peru	11.5	3.9	79
Romania	9.9	5.5	61
Nigeria	9.3	4.9	28
Hungary	7.0	3.5	55
Zaire	5.1	1.2	83
Zambia	4.5	2.0	195
Bolivia	3.1	1.0	118

*Includes interest due on debt plus amortisation due in 1983.
†Time estimates.
SOURCE *Time Magazine*, 10 Jan. 1983, p. 5, based on information of the Morgan Guaranty Trust Company.

international monetary system with supernational authority exercising: (a) supervisory function, to give common directions, and (b) as a lender of the last resort, to intervene and regulate any runs on deposits.

FINAL REMARKS

The analysis of the policy issues concerning the Eurodollar and, more generally, offshore currencies has shown: (a) no substantial changes in the matters discussed and, (b) the emergence of the practical consequences of the unsolved problems raised by the rapid expansion of Eurodollar and international credit.

An international standard, not tied to either the internal or the external use of a national currency and backed by a government which

TABLE 5.5 *Current account balances (billion US $)*

	1980	*1981*	*1982*	*1983–7**
Developed countries	−71	−39	−12	−21
Europe	−59	−30	−18	−54
Non-Europe	−11	−9	6	32
US	2	4	9	27
Japan	−11	5	10	77
Developing countries	40	−14	−80	−312
Oil exporting	95	49	−18	−21
Oil importing	−55	−63	−62	−291
Centrally planned economy	−10	−12	−11	−71
Total	−42	−65	−103	−404

*Sluggish recovery hypothesis.
SOURCE 'The Wharton World Economic Outlook', *World Economic Overview*, ch. 1, p. 8, September 1982.

would secure its full and correct functions as a medium of exchange and store of value, has still to be defined. This became more serious after the gold-exchange standard changed into a dollar standard and finally collapsed, because of its consequences for expectations, when flexible exchange rates replaced fixed rates. This is not to deny the role played by flexible exchange rates in the real economy and in the adjustment process. All it means is that such a change in the absence of a 'monetary regime', i.e. a system of expectations supported by a coherent monetary policy, made the international credit system appear unmanageable with regard to both prices (interest and foreign exchange rates) and quantities.

The lack of explicit rules to control the international standard led to the inevitable return to conditions of tight domestic control of the money supply, and then to a strong dollar on international markets. The effects of this change on interest rates, and hence on the real economy, have deprived the dollar of the characteristics which made it eligible in the past as an 'orthodox' international standard.

Nowadays worldwide public opinion is aware of the defects of both an accommodating monetary policy and a non-accommodating monetary policy. The first type of policy leads to inflation and feeds inflationary expectations; the second type is characterised by a stronger concern for quantities than interest rates and shows that: (a) in the case of growing public deficits adjustment occurs in the real economy and,

(b) that equilibrium in current account balances is impaired by interest and exchange rates, when these are flexible and international credit activity is performed mostly by private operators.

Throughout the world, public opinion has realised that the defects of extreme monetary policies are also present in the two foreign exchange rate regimes (fixed and flexible). In both cases, the authorities are prevented from intervening on the foreign exchange market to regulate exchange rates according to the needs of the real economy, or to avoid abuse of speculation induced by self-generated expectations: under the fixed exchange regime because of political constraints on changing parities; under the flexible regime because of movements in expectations free from a clear political reference.

It is therefore necessary to go back to the original concept behind the Bretton Woods Agreement, not to its implementation. This philosophy is still embodied in the European Monetary System which foresees and, in fact, sees regular adjustments to exchange rates. The views expressed by the Treasury Secretaries at Kronberg in December 1982 can be interpreted as moving in this direction. The decisions taken in Paris by the Group of 10 plus Switzerland are important for the survival of the present system.

From a practical point of view as well as on the basis of theoretical analysis a flexible exchange rate regime looks quite efficient and liberal; however the likelihood that it will push economies towards protectionism cannot be overlooked. I share the concern shown by the US after the GATT meeting of last November about the dangerous trend of world trade in the direction of a suffocation of international exchanges. The interaction between the present difficulties in spontaneous international credit activities and the volatility of flexible exchange rates stems partly from such suffocation.

Any working political system is identifiable by a number of myths which countries and peoples accept as universal 'values'. The 'myth' of freedom in international trade may be the one which the Western system recognises; political co-operation could then be restored. If, on the other hand, flexible exchange rates represent an obstacle in that direction, their working can be moderated without going back to the opposite extreme of a fixed regime. This could be achieved by ensuring a more orderly performance of international credit activities and a greater presence of public institutions.

The international credit system that was centred on official sources operated efficiently until 1973; afterwards private sources replaced official sources following the directions of the responsible authorities.

The new system was also successful until it stalled; now it needs to be governed by the authorities.

At present, this means mainly that public sources should replace private sources. This substitution would revive a thrust that characterised the 1960s, when an attempt was made to replace the national exchange standard with an international standard (SDRs to be exact). The international monetary market, however, does not lack resources; instead it lacks rules of the game. The presence of public bodies should be preferred in the areas of supervision and lending of last resort, as well as of guarantees of LDC financing, which would ensure continuity in the international banking system and allow the prospect of debtors repaying their debt. The decisions taken in Paris can satisfy these needs only partially.

The return to monetary orthodoxy should not be limited to the needs of debtor countries and the necessity of guaranteeing an over-exposed banking system. Means other than monetary creation are available; I do not see why they should not be used to avoid aggravating the present over-abundant international liquidity. The idea that banks are incapable of performing their duties in assessing the credit-worthiness of their clients is wrong. But even if it were true, we would not be entitled to believe that public institutions are better qualified than banks; indeed, a number of instances of the opposite could easily be given.

The indications provided by Secretary Regan at the Kronberg Summit represent an opening through which a new light could be made to shine on the future of the international monetary system, without raising undue illusions. At any event, this attempt will widen the 'degree of common understanding', as Paul Volcker says, between public and private borrowers and lenders, which can be envisaged as a basic condition for the solution of the present crisis.

NOTES AND REFERENCES

1. A regular and complete survey of developments in international banking markets can be found in the Annual Reports of the BIS. A survey of the debate until 1972 has been edited by G. Carli *et al.* in *A Debate on the Eurodollar Market*, Quaderni di Ricerche, Ente Einaudi, no. 11, Rome, 1972.
2. An up-to-date survey on the debate can be found in the study by A. K. Swoboda for the Group of Thirty (*Credit Creation in the Euromarket: Alternative Theories and Implications for Control*, Occasional Paper, no. 2,

New York, 1980); the debate shows the limited attention given by the academic circles to the problem of the international standard envisaged by the makers of Bretton Woods.

3. See M. Fratianni and P. Savona, *La liquidita Internazionale*, Il Mulino, Bologna, 1972, p. 48.
4. See G. Carli *et al.*, *A Debate on the Eurodollar Market*, p. 34.
5. See *Federal Reserve Bulletin*, September 1978, p. 777.
6. On the logical foundation of an autonomous international system, such as the Euro- or xeno-dollar, see P. Savona (*Eurodollars*, International Banking Center, Florida International University, Occasional Paper, Miami, 1982).
7. A monetary regime – according to A. Leijonhufvud (*Notes on Rational Expectations and Economic Institutions*, mimeo 1982) – 'is a system of expectations that governs the behaviour of the public and that is sustained by the consistent behaviour of the policy-making authorities' (p. 1).
8. On the 'vicious circle' of the Rio Agreement see the mathematical analysis of M. Fratianni and P. Savona, 'Un modello esplicativo della tesaurizzazione e degli usi dei diritti speciali di prelievo', in *Economia Internazionale*, Genova, no. 1, 1974.
9. See the Address to the New England Council in Boston by Governor Volcker, 16 Nov. 1982.
10. See G. De Welz (alias F. Fuoco), *La magia del credito svelata,* Stamperia Francese, 2 vols, Naples, 1824.
11. See G. Carli, 'Eurodollars: A Paper Pyramid?', *B.N.L. Quarterly Review*, March 1971; J. A. Schumpeter *History of Economic Analysis*, Oxford University Press, New York, 1955, p. 511 states: 'it is easier to do justice to Fuoco. He was a theorist of note who does not merit oblivion ... his conception of economic equilibrium in some respects marked progress beyond Say's'.
12. J. Rueff expressed this view in many newspaper articles; the most important among them appeared in *Le Monde* (from the 15–17 May 1973) under the title 'Prolegomenes a toute reforme du systeme monetaire international'. See also G. Carli and J. Rueff, *Debat sur la Reforme du Systeme Monetaire International* (Lisbon, 1973).
13. Paolo Baffi has never presented this idea in a paper, but it lies behind his many contributions to the analysis of the behaviour of international markets (see, for example, 'Western European Inflation and Reserve Currencies', *B.N.L. Quarterly Review*, March 1968).
14. See the 1982 *BIS Annual Report*, p. 188.

COMMENT

CHARLES A. E. GOODHART

The tremendous weight of historical experience and the wide canvas of the analytical coverage of Dr Carli's paper makes it a very difficult one on which to comment. Also, while it is generally evident that Dr Carli criticises and dislikes, it was more difficult, partly because of translation problems in the first version of his paper, to identify with perfect clarity exactly what were his precise proposals for reform. Let me give an example. Dr Carli points out a number of disadvantages in having either completely fixed or completely flexible exchange rate systems. He would like to see a return towards a managed system, towards the original concept of Bretton Woods. But how could this be achieved? He says that, and I quote, 'This could only be achieved by assuring a more orderly performance in international credit activities and a greater presence of public institutions'. What exactly is meant by that? In particular, does he take the view that management of the exchange rate by the authorities is virtually impossible so long as private capital can flow unhindered through the Eurocurrency market? Or, and I would emphasise, through any other international channels? It is quite likely that he may be right in the view: but, if the solution to this problem might seem to entail some restriction on private sector capital flows, would Dr Carli actually want to propose the general introduction of exchange controls? If so, would it not be better to say so outright?

Some of Dr Carli's preferences are, however, clear enough. He claims that there is a need for a lender of last resort in the Euromarket, preferably an international body, together with a need for more regulation in the international financial markets. Dr Carli seems to believe that the current absence, and present need, of a lender of last resort in the Euromarket is almost self-evident; but is it, I wonder? If a US bank, for example, gets into difficulties, perhaps because it is stuck with a number of non-performing loans, does it actually matter whether these loans are to US companies or to foreign borrowers? The lender of last resort in either case surely remains the Federal Reserve System, in particular, and the US monetary authorities in general. And does it make a major difference to the US bank or to the US authorities, whether those non-performing loans were in dollars or in other currencies? After all, so long as there is a functioning foreign exchange market, supporting funds provided in any one currency can be transformed into any other. I know that there can be some problems here, but I would regard them as being secondary. And the same should be true for other countries, as well as, the US. Therefore, the banks of all the major nations would already be said to have a lender of last resort in the form of their own central banks. There are certainly problems; notably of the definition of a national bank in a world full of consortia, holding companies, and distant partial subsidiaries, as the Banco Ambrosiano case demonstrated. However, the need to sort out and to establish responsibility, and I would underline the word *responsibility*, would remain at least as important and as complicated, indeed, perhaps even more complicated, if there was some further international central banking or stabilisation body to be set up. Sometimes it is suggested that the Euromarket represents a kind of 'black hole', for which no one has any concern, oversight, or supervision. That is not true, Not only is there the concern of the host country, but also, in particular, there is the concern of the parental body; the US Federal Reserve for the US banks, the Bank of England for the British banks, the Bundesbank for the German banks, and so on.

Now, what exactly should be the additional rules and regulations over the Euromarkets and Eurobanks that Dr Carli apparently wants? The only clue that I can find is that of a number of favourable mentions of monetary base control. The limitations of this concept for the Euromarket had been described and discussed at some length at this conference, but I cannot refrain from adding some extra comments. The current trend of thinking on base control, evident now in the US, appears to be towards having all balances used in this country for transactions purposes, whatever the institution providing such balances might be, subject to a common reserve ratio, while all those deposits and instruments which are *not* used primarily for transactions purposes should be freed of any reserve requirements. If monetary base control would be applied analogously to the Euromarkets, it would not have very much relevance, because there would be so few transactions balances of the standard form there. Moreover, the practical problems of imposing monetary base control within a system where funds can be booked not only in any market or any financial centre, but in any currency, would be severe. Consider, for example, a reasonably stable currency which had a very low interest rate, for instance, the Swiss franc. If a reserve requirement was to be imposed, you would be surprised by the sizeable portion of reservable Euromarket balances, which would suddenly appear to be in the form of Swiss francs. Even were we to brush aside such practical considerations, the case for imposing reserve requirements on the Euromarket is dubious. Why would it improve the quality of lending, or restrain risk-taking, for example? Moreover, the imposition of a reserve requirement acts as a tax on a particular line of financial intermediation, and often directs financial flows away from reasonably well supervised channels towards those areas which are less well supervised. It is, I think, a great pity that those people who believe that Euromarkets require greater supervision do not widen their field of vision and consider other, possibly wider, alternative forms of regulation, besides an inappropriate call for some form of monetary base control.

Indeed, before we can reasonably begin to consider whether the Euromarkets do need any additional forms of regulation, we should try to review and to analyse what it is that they are being accused of. In what ways are they deficient? One of the accusations is that they are an independent source of generation of a more rapid world monetary growth and represent, therefore, an autonomous factor leading to faster world inflation. But the Euromarkets do not appear to have provided any significant check, or offset, to the present, determined policies of counter-inflation. That is not surprising, because the degree to which the Euromarkets were truly independent and autonomous was always greatly exaggerated. As Bob Aliber said in his article in this volume, the Euromarkets are closely dependent on, and interrelated with domestic markets, being an offshore version of a near-bank-financial-intermediary (NBFI). As Ian Giddy showed in his splendid diagrams in his article in this volume the interest rates in the Euromarkets are closely related with the interest rates in the wholesale markets of the relevant countries, except in those cases where there are effective exchange controls. Of course it may be asked in return, if the Euromarkets are so dependent on the wholesale national market, within such an interrelated market system, then why do they frequently exhibit such faster rates of growth? The answer here, as Bob Aliber also indicated in his above mentioned article, is that in those currencies where the Euromarkets have grown particularly fast relative to the domestic wholesale markets, you will find that the authorities have imposed on their domestic banking systems particularly burdensome regulations. Whereas, for those countries in which the authorities have not imposed severe burdens and regulations on their own domestic banking systems, there is generally much less divergence between the growth rates. Among such countries, I am glad to say is the United Kingdom, where we see no particularly faster growth in the Eurosterling market, than in the domestic sterling wholesale banking market.

Now, of course, the Euromarkets are accused of part of the responsibility of bringing about the current international indebtedness problem: I wonder whether that, too, is not exaggerated. Let us assume, counter-factually, that the OPEC surplus countries had not deposited their surplus funds in the Euromarkets, but had channelled them in other directions – would the resulting recycling, perhaps under the aegis of public bodies, have been much better designed, or controlled? After all, the authorities are now frequently accused of having encouraged the pattern of international lending that actually did occur through private markets. If the private markets had not done the recycling, then, presumably, the authorities would have tried to have achieved much the same result. Indeed, one argument now sometimes heard is that the authorities would have failed to have achieved as much recycling, but that this would have been desirable, since it would have led to earlier and more determined adjustment. Not only do I find this suggestion that official failure would have been a great success, somewhat odd, but I also believe that that argument relies more than usual on perfect hindsight. In any case, the idea that a small coterie of central bankers, or finance ministry officials, could have distributed and designed the international pattern of recycling significantly better than the private market, is an assumption that many will consider open to question, particularly in view of the political pressures that would have inevitably intruded on their deliberations.

Even so, although in several of the discussions that we have had in the last couple of days, the suggestion has been made that the bankers in the Euromarkets have been relatively faultless, close observers of the Euromarkets have, however, wondered from time to time whether these markets were not prone to certain competitive excesses. The spread over LIBOR in international lending is supposed to be, in part, a measure of relative risk. For reasons that I do not find entirely well-documented, the spreads at times during recent years appeared to narrow under the influence of banking competition to a level which, well in advance of recent events, did not appear to take sufficient account of the risks involved. Moreover, I can still think at this moment of a number of countries for which the spread over LIBOR does not seem to represent anything like a proper reward for the apparent risks involved. It may be in some cases that there are special reasons for this, because the spread over LIBOR is frequently treated as a comparative index of relative risk and relative standings: therefore some countries could be keen to have that spread artificially reduced by shifting a sizeable proportion of the return from the spread into certain introductory fees; so that it can be actually quite difficult to observe accurately what the relative overall return-to-lending in the Euromarket might be. That raises another problem, concerning the sufficiency of information. Perhaps some part of the failure to take sufficient account of risk could have been due to insufficient information, for example, on the indebtedness of various sovereign countries. Yet the BIS, and other international bodies, have been providing an increasingly comprehensive set of data on international indebtedness and bank involvement. These data have a lengthy lag in production, and anything that could be done to shorten that lag and improve the data would be desirable. Nevertheless, the data were sufficient to show the main lines of development in international indebtedness, as a letter from Alexandre Lamfalussy in the *Financial Times* stated. Nevertheless, there is certainly additional room for the better dissemination and analysis of information in this area, and the recent decision of the main commercial banks to co-operate in this respect by setting up the Institute for International Finance will be widely welcomed. But information failure was not, I would suggest, a major cause of the recent disturbances.

I had intended, at this point, to give my own attributions of the main causes of the international debt problem, but that is really not necessary, since they have been already so well described and explained by Helmut Mayer in his comments contained in this volume. I would only note that when commodity prices are going down in absolute terms and nominal interest rates are going up, the resulting real interest rates for commodity producers, whether in the LDCs or in the United States, become crippling; much more severe than might be ascertained by looking at the usual calculations of real interest rates.

I shall end by parenthetically noting that supervision and regulation are not exactly the same thing, even though in his paper Dr Carli always brackets them together. On the supervisory front, considerable progress has been made. It is *not* the case that the authorities have exhibited benign neglect to *supervision* in the Euromarkets. We have already heard quite a lot about the BIS Committee on Banking Regulations and Supervisory Practices, in which the Bank of England has taken a leading role. Perhaps one might now pose the question of whether it would be possible, or desirable, to seek to extend this framework to the point of introducing some common international agreements for the maintenance of best banking practices in the international area. One reason for trying this is that separate surveillance of their national banks by the individual national monetary authorities can result in different national standards, and this can be a ready source of disagreement and disaffection among the regulated. If a national monetary authority is trying to press its own national banks to maintain, for example, an appropriate level of capital adequacy, its own banks are quite likely to come back and say: 'But banks in country X or country Y are allowed a much lower level of capital adequacy. They are able to trade at a relative advantage, and get a larger share of the business. That is totally unfair and we should also be allowed to have more relaxed regulations'. Indeed, there will always be competitive pressures among the regulated to move towards the system with the greatest degree of laxity. That does, indeed, provide an incentive for trying to achieve greater international agreement, and understanding on what does represent good banking practice in international markets.

There are, however, severe practical complications in trying to reach international agreements and understandings of this kind, often related to the differing institutional structures of the various national banking systems. But that should not stop central banks who are individually trying to do their best to encourage in their own countries, the maintenance of good banking practices. Nor would such international agreements necessarily be more easily obtained simply by the expedient of seeking to establish yet another supra-national official body. This does not mean that central banks cannot go further in trying to analyse and assess with one another and hopefully to come to some agreement on what does represent good banking practice in international markets. I hope that progress along these lines can be achieved and taken further. But I doubt whether it can be much advanced by some simple institutional change.

COMMENT

ALEXANDER K. SWOBODA

Over the years, Governor Carli and his Italian colleagues have done much to raise the quality of debate on the Eurodollar market and on the international monetary and financial system in general. We should be grateful to George Sutija and Paolo Savona for this meeting but are also collectively indebted to the 'Italian School' (P. Baffi, G. Carli, M. Fratianni, R. Masera, R. Ossola, and P. Savona, to mention but some of its members) for providing much of the intellectual underpinnings of contemporary analysis of the Eurocurrency markets.

I find Governor Carli's rich paper somewhat difficult to discuss for two reasons. First, many remarks I should like to offer have already been made by other discussants. Second, the very richness of the paper makes any short discussion inadequate. Governor Carli's paper is wide ranging. He begins with a history of policy with respect to

Eurocurrency markets and the international monetary system; discusses regulation, supervision, and the lender of last resort; wrestles with the issues connected with alternative international standards; and concludes with an examination of some current problems of international lending and world debt. This leaves ample room for registering both agreement and disagreement on particular issues. Rather than running through, and taking issue with, individual points in the paper, I shall concentrate on three broad topics. I will take up in turn the issue of regulation, questions related to the ruling international standard, and, finally, those related to current issues and the need for a lender of last resort. The relationship between my remarks and the main themes contained in Governor Carli's stimulating paper should be readily apparent.

REGULATION

Regulation of the Eurocurrency markets is a theme that runs through not only Governor Carli's paper but through the other papers and comments as well. One school of thought seems to argue that, of course, something has to be done about the Eurodollar market and it should be regulated; another states that it is clear that the market should be left unregulated. The question I would like to ask before beginning to talk, or think, about regulation is what regulation is for or, if you prefer, why should anything, including the Eurodollar market, be regulated. There are three standard arguments for regulation of the Eurocurrency markets: on efficiency grounds, to ensure stability, and for distributional considerations.

On efficiency grounds, there is no particularly good reason why the market should be regulated unless there are externalities (market failures), the existence of which has not, to my knowledge, been demonstrated. One efficiency argument for regulation, however, can be made on second-best grounds: regulation of domestic financial markets creates distortions that can, in theory and specific cases, be somewhat mitigated by control of international financial transactions. But arguments based on such considerations need to be extremely specific, are fraught with the danger of *pro domo* and tendentious reasoning, and should not pre-empt efforts to achieve first rather than second-best solutions.

Turning to regulation for the sake of stability, four distinct, though related, arguments have been made. Eurocurrency markets are said (i) to interfere with domestic monetary control; (ii) to destabilise the world price level or rate of inflation (they are 'engines of inflation' or deflation); (iii) to be at the root of financial variability (be it of exchange rates or interest rates); and (iv) to create liquidity and solvency problems and threaten the stability of the world banking and financial system as a whole. Taking these arguments in turn, the case for regulating Eurocurrency markets to restore domestic monetary control seems a very weak one to me. This is not to deny that the high degree of capital mobility embodied in Eurocurrency markets does interfere with certain types of domestic controls; but controlling Eurocurrency markets is likely to prove rather ineffective if only because plugging one hole of a sieve will mainly increase the flow somewhere else. Further, and more important, if monetary policy aims at external balance, international capital flows will help to restore equilibrium instead of interfering with it. If domestic monetary control is aimed at internal objectives, floating exchange rates and not capital controls are the solution (a point to which I return below).

The second stability argument for control is based on the notion that the Eurodollar market is an engine of world inflation. Controlling inflation in the world economy is indeed an important question, but I am among those who believe, first, that the multiplier in the Eurodollar market is fairly small, that control of inflation has to start at home, and, third, that world inflation has more to do with the mode of organisation of the international monetary system at large than with Eurocurrency markets.[1] On that last point, I can only welcome Governor Carli's emphasis on the relationship between the nature of the international standard and the problems of worldwide inflation. On the Eurodollar multiplier, the issue is not whether it exists or not. Fritz Machlup liked to emphasise in his war on weasel words and jargon in economics, that equilibrium does not exist; it is, rather, an analytical concept. Similarly, the Eurodollar market multiplier does not exist; it is an analytical concept that is as good as the uses to which you put it. On any definition that I find useful when analysing the relationship between the Eurodollar market and world inflation, the multiplier is small. That is, attributing world inflation to the Eurocurrency market (or multiplier) is confusing symptoms with causes.

As for the instability reflected in variability of exchange rates, interest rates, and financial aggregates, and fostered by asset shifts among various sectors of the Eurocurrency markets and among the latter and other financial markets, this is indeed a serious problem. The solution, however, is not likely to be increased regulation but harmonisation towards the lowest rather than the highest common denominator of control. For, as long as a significant part of financial markets remains uncontrolled, increasing levels of regulation increase rather than reduce the incentive towards destabilising shifts among assets and liabilities in response to a changing economic environment. In the Eurocurrency market context this implies that harmonisation of reserve requirements may indeed be desirable, but towards low rather than high levels. Similarly, paying interest on required reserves is preferable to (or complementary to) trying to raise almost everybody's reserve requirements. This would contribute to reducing destabilising asset shifts at an international level, shifts that are similar to the familiar disintermediation phenomena that accompany changes in interest rates in the face of differential regulation in domestic financial markets. As for the fourth area in which Eurocurrency markets may contribute to instability, namely in fostering liquidity or solvency problems for the international banking system, this is an issue I will return to in the concluding part of this comment. Suffice it to say here that I do not think that regulation or control will solve the problem, though improved supervision is desirable on this score.

In addition to efficiency and stability considerations, control of Eurocurrency markets has also been advocated on equity, or distributional grounds. In particular, heavily regulated banking systems and small lenders, borrowers, or intermediaries appear to be at a competitive disadvantage in Eurocurrency markets. Briefly put, the case here is again for harmonisation rather than increased regulation; reduction or harmonisation of regulation is probably the most effective way of removing a number of competitive distortions and of equalising potential access to international financial markets by the banking systems of various countries. There is also a need for clarity and stability of rules, a point to which I return at the end when commenting on the need for a lender of last resort.

THE INTERNATIONAL STANDARD

A topic that figures prominently in Governor Carli's paper is the link between the nature of the international standard and the historical evolution of the international monetary system, on one hand, and the development of the Eurocurrency market and its regulation, on the other. This emphasis is to be warmly welcomed. Lack of a clearly defined international standard, or conflicts about what that standard should be, are at the root of many current problems of the world economy.

Thus, when analysing world inflation attention has to be focused on excessive credit creation, its origins, and the mechanism by which it spreads through the world economy. Such an analysis must take historical institutional realities into account; the mode of organisation of the international monetary system in the 1960s and early 1970s, essentially a form of dollar standard, is intimately connected with the generation and transmission of world inflation. I very much agree with the spirit of Governor Carli's analysis here but would emphasise that the relationship runs from lack of monetary discipline, and (implicit or explicit) disagreement as to what the international standard is or should be, to 'excessive' Eurocurrency growth rather than the other way around.

Similarly, problems of confidence and turbulence in financial markets do not have their origin in the endogenous behaviour of Eurocurrency markets. Instead, they originate, at least partly, in the lack of an agreed international standard or, more precisely, in the lack of clear rules of conduct of national monetary policies under the present system of flexible (or managed) exchange rates. That is, flexible exchange rates need rules to work properly. They are viable even without such rules; but to work properly and to achieve a certain amount of stability some degree of precommitment of national policies is needed. This implies in turn that the degree of discipline and 'co-ordination' of policies required for flexible rates to work properly may be as large as that required under a fixed rate system.[2]

The desirable exchange-rate regime is one question where I would take issue with Governor Carli's views on international monetary organisation (on the 'standard', if you wish). I am not convinced by the dismissal of either strictly fixed or purely flexible exchange rates as undesirable and/or impossible regimes; nor do I believe that an 'inbetween' system is preferable. The problem is that the middle regime is a very awkward animal that is unlikely to achieve the benefits of either system and to share the worst features of both. The notion of 'stable but adjustable parities', the slogan adopted by the Group of Twenty in its reform discussions, is, to me, a contradiction in terms. Either you commit yourself to a fixed (stable) exchange rate and you try not to adjust it; or you go to more flexibility of exchange rates, but do not pretend that you will achieve stable exchange rates. I am afraid that we are trying to go back to some form of a 'stable but adjustable parities' system which cannot, realistically, be achieved in the long run.

This is a system that is likely neither to resolve policy conflicts nor to reap the benefits from the loss of national monetary autonomy implicit in exchange-rate management.

CURRENT PROBLEMS IN INTERNATIONAL LENDING

The current problem that Governor Carli emphasises is the over-indebtedness of a number of countries and the implied threat to the stability of the international financial system. In concluding my comment, I should like to offer a few remarks on the nature, origins, and consequences of the problem, as well as on some policy implications.

Threats to the stability of the international financial system arise from the sharp rise in the volume of actually or potentially non-performing loans held by a large number of major banks. Attention has been focused on international loans to sovereign borrowers, particularly in Latin America, but it may be noted that bad domestic loans, notably in the energy-related sector, contribute significantly to current problems. Concentrating on international loans and lending flows, there has been much discussion of the origins of the current debt problem. The major sources of the problem are well-known and have already been mentioned, notably by Helmut Mayer and Charles Goodhart, in their articles contained in this volume; they are the collapse of commodity prices and its effect on developing countries' terms of trade, the sharp rise in real interest rates, the fall in rates of growth of industrial countries and worldwide recession. The problem is of course that these changes in the economic environment were by and large unexpected, at least in the late 1970s. These unexpected changes are undoubtedly responsible for turning a number of *ex ante* good loans into *ex post* bad assets. Their effect, however, has been compounded by a number of other factors.

First, the concentration of lending to a few large sovereign borrowers is a new element in bank lending. On the one hand, the capacity to service debt no longer depends on usual commercial criteria or on the return to specific projects, but on the aggregate saving propensity of the economy and on the government's capacity to tax. On the other hand, when lending is concentrated to a few large borrowers, the insurance implicit in the law of large numbers is no longer available. Nor are diversified loan portfolios easily constructed, though banks could (or perhaps should) have made much more of an effort at emphasising risk correlations in their country-risk analysis and in the structuring of their international loan portfolios.

Second, the prevalence of syndicated loans in the banks' portfolios makes it difficult to price risk efficiently and contributes to the 'feast or famine' syndrome that has recently affected lending to developing countries. As there is no proper secondary market for syndicated loans, they are carried on the banks' books either at face value or as non-performing loans (with somewhat arbitrary write-off provisions). Yet there may be a price at which the secondary market may be willing to hold the debt of a country in actual or potential difficulties. One reason some banks do not wish to see a secondary market is that they would have to write down some of their current assets. One consequence, however, is that there is little repricing of risk as perceptions and circumstances change; another is that new lending is likely to dry up since obtaining a higher risk premium on new lending is at least an implicit recognition that the value of existing loans should be written down.

A third and to my mind very important factor has contributed significantly to current debt problems. It helps explain a number of puzzles in the pattern of international lending. For instance, why has lending to a country like Mexico been so large in recent years and why did it even accelerate in 1981 when impending problems were not difficult to forecast from the statistics or, for that matter, from a reading of the gossip columns? Why did bank lending keep growing in spite of narrowing spreads deemed inadequate by most, increased perceptions of country risk, and diminishing capital/asset ratios? Why did not the banks increase their margins, issue additional capital, or refuse to engage in lending they deemed unprofitable given existing capital/asset ratios? The basic reason, I believe, is that the perceived riskiness of the loans to the banks, their stockholders and their depositors was lowered by implicit or explicit guarantees. The main forms the guarantees have taken are deposit insurance and a perception that large banks, or large borrowing countries heavily indebted to the banks, would not be allowed to fail. As the perception has been called into question over the past two years, bank lending has slowed down but the guarantee factor has played an important role in influencing the volume and pattern of international financial flows over the last decade or so.

This third factor has also created a number of important distortions in the flow of international lending. In general, depositors have been willing to lend to banks and investors have been willing to buy the stock of banks, even though they would not have been willing to acquire the portfolios of banks, because they felt that the banks benefited from a guarantee that would not have been extended to non-banks. Banks, in turn, have been willing to acquire assets at rates of return lower than the riskiness of the assets would have required had these implicit guarantees not been present. Among the resulting distortions one may mention, first, over-lending to developing countries in general. Second, implicit guarantees lead to over-exposure to individual borrowers: the more one lends to an individual large borrower, the higher the stakes in his continued solvency, the less likely that he will be allowed to default. Classic examples are that you can afford to let Yonkers or Studebaker fail, yet you cannot afford to let New York City or Chrysler do likewise. In general, large lenders and borrowers are advantaged at the expense of smaller ones. Third and related, smaller lenders have an advantage in following large lenders since they benefit from the umbrella that implies that the large over-exposed sovereign debtors to whom they have lent cannot be allowed to fail. This goes some way towards explaining the herd instinct; it does so without imputing irrationality to banks. The herd phenomenon is seen here as the rational reaction of banks that seek both to create the conditions in which guarantees will be issued to them and to exploit such guarantees once they are felt to exist.

So much for diagnosis. The next question relates to policy implications and, in particular, to the availability of and need for a lender of last resort. To speculate about proper policy to deal with international financial problems, it may be useful to list some of the objectives that are to be achieved and to ask which instruments are available and should be addressed to which objectives. The list of objectives for the international monetary and financial system might include the following: (1) proper balance-of-payments adjustment; (2) non-inflationary growth in the world economy; (3) the efficient transfer of resources from surplus to deficit areas; (4) an equitable transfer of resources from rich to poor; (5) a stable and efficient international financial and banking system that is not crisis prone (which confines money to being a veil). The question then is which institution should aim at which of these objectives and in what fashion.

As for the first of these objectives, the IMF would seem to be the institution that should help ensure effective balance-of-payments adjustment. The Fund's role should not (and under present circumstances cannot) be that of lender of last resort. As for non-inflationary growth in the world economy, the IMF's policy with respect to adjustment has a role to play, but the basic issue is the exchange-rate regime and the choice of an international standard. With freely floating rates, non-inflationary growth can only be ensured by national monetary policy; with fixed exchange rates, it will depend crucially on the choice of an international standard and the institutional mechanism that governs the supply of international reserves. Third, markets are ideally suited to effect the transfer of resources from surplus to deficit regions; distortionary incentives should, however, be removed both on efficiency and stability grounds. As for the transfer of resources from rich to poor, it can be most effectively carried out through bilateral or multilateral aid (and/or concessional loans); it should be done explicitly rather than through implicit taxes on the general public (and implicit subsidies to bank stockholders). Finally, the soundness of the international banking system should be the purview of supervisory authorities; they would be greatly helped in their task by stronger market discipline, correct pricing of risk, and the removal of distorted incentives. With respect to supervision, progress has been made, although conflicts of jurisdiction remain. Even if these were solved, absorbing the cost of past mistakes will involve socialising some of the losses; it is essential, though, to socialise them in a fashion that does not entail further distortions in the future, that is, in a way that puts higher penalties for mismanagement in the future. There is no international lender of last resort at the moment and national lenders of last resort will have to suffice at present. Provided jurisdictional conflicts are resolved, they can perform their function adequately. However, to mitigate moral hazard problems and future distortions and instability, they will also have to impose and make clear *ex ante*, adequate penalties to their customers for having recourse to the lender-of-last-resort facility.

NOTES AND REFERENCES

1. For a full development of the argument, see, for instance, A. K. Swoboda, *Credit Creation in the Euromarket: Alternative Theories and Implications for Control*, Occasional paper no. 2 (New York: Group of Thirty, 1980).
2. For development of the argument, see H. Genberg and A. K. Swoboda, 'Fixed Exchange Rates, Flexible Exchange Rates, or the Middle of the Road: a Reexamination of the Arguments in View of Recent Experience', paper presented at the 1982 Wingspread Conference on the Evolving International Financial System.

COMMENT

RICHARD C. WILLIAMS

The serious strains in the international economic and financial system have naturally given rise to the search for ameliorative actions at the national and international levels as we grope towards solutions. In this regard, Governor Carli's paper provides a useful, and appropriately comprehensive, review of shortcomings in the international monetary system as he perceives them, both in terms of the institutional framework and its workings in practice. The tone is sombre, but generally not excessively pessimistic, and the substantive conclusions bear the imprint of the practitioner, as well as of the analyst.

Although there is much in the paper that many of us could agree with, given the wide scope of the analysis and the complexity of the issues, it would be surprising if some of Dr Carli's conclusions were not subject to some challenge. In the time available to me, I would like to touch on but one theme of the paper – that the system has given rise to a serious misallocation of private capital and a possibly inescapable debt trap for the developing world, with potentially very serious systemic effects. There are considerable uncertainties about the course of the international economy and thus the global economic environment in which many of the developing economies are groping to achieve viable and sustainable external payments positions compatible with their socio-economic priorities. However, the extent of the fragility of the system and possible systemic pressures arising from the recently increasing incidence of debt reschedulings – described by the financial press as the 'house of cards' – is frequently overdrawn. Doomsday scenarios aside, there is little doubt that many of the individual borrowing countries are facing unprecedented adjustment pressures and the economic and social costs associated with them. Nevertheless, the evidence suggests that the serious strains in the world economy, particularly the precarious economic situation of many developing countries, can be overcome by a co-operative effort of all involved; the countries experiencing the problems, the donor countries, the lending banks, the bank regulatory authorities, the international agencies and the export credit insurance agencies. In this regard, it can be suggested that the worst strains have already abated as the international community has responded more vigorously to the challenge.

While there is no reason to be sanguine, it is important also not to be overwhelmed by a generalised view of the magnitude of the task. In many individual developing countries, specific ameliorative actions have been taken and there is scope for further action. The international financial community must be prepared to assist developing countries which are undertaking the efforts needed to help solve their problems. It is clear that the amount of assistance made available to countries in external difficulties is of crucial importance. As far as assistance from the Fund itself, efforts to expand significantly the amount of our available resources, including the Eighth Review of Quotas and the enlargement of the General Agreement to Borrow are at an advanced stage. These resources, provided in support of members' adjustment programmes are intended to supplement, not to supplant private capital and other sources of public capital and can provide the catalyst to help ensure stable and sustainable capital flows over time.

Where major debt servicing problems arise, co-ordinated action among the Fund, the monetary authorities of creditor countries and commercial banks can play a major role. In Latin America where the absolute size of the problem is so large as to have potentially major adverse effect on the financial system, the IMF has adopted a co-ordinating role in discussions with major countries and commercial banks. In the period ahead, the Fund undoubtedly will intensify its collaborative efforts in this area, including those with governments and banking supervisory bodies. Parallel with these specific actions, the Fund has urged the industrial countries to pursue policies conducive to a sustainable lowering of interest rates and greater stability of exchange markets in order to improve the economic environment facing the developing countries. And, as forcefully expressed by its Managing Director at the recent GATT Ministerial meeting, the Fund has argued against temptations to reduce the openness of the world trading system. A general improvement in the world economy clearly lies at the heart of the adjustment prospects for the LDCs.

Much of the current pessimism reported in the financial press relates to an assumption that the world environment automatically precludes effective adjustment measures by those countries whose current account deficits no longer appear sustainable. But the record for a large group of developing countries during the period between 1978 and 1982, when the international economic environment deteriorated considerably, suggests that some have been too pessimistic about adjustment possibilities. I am referring specifically to those countries classified as non-oil developing countries which are net importers of oil. The aggregate current account deficit of this large group of countries increased from US$31 billion in 1978 to over US$80 billion in 1981 but was reduced to US$70 billion in 1982; taking the whole period through 1982 the aggregate current deficit increased by US$39 billion. During the same period the deterioration in their oil trade balance was US$40 billion and the increase in interest payments on external debt was US$22 billion. Thus, on other current account transactions their position improved by US$23 billion. This is a positive indicator of the scope for, and success of adjustment efforts even in a difficult international economic environment. Some of these countries of course ran into payments problems and faced 'forced' adjustment and rescheduled their debts while others adjusted in time to avoid payments disruptions. Several countries in both categories undertook adjustment programmes supported by the IMF and where those programmes were implemented the 'success' rate is reasonably high.

The important thing, at this juncture is that the difficult situations which arise be worked out effectively and on a timely basis. In the cases of Mexico, Argentina and Brazil, for example, there have been co-operative efforts involving commercial banks, governments, central banks, the BIS, and the IMF to help those countries get back on a viable and sustainable path. This has required that the banks involved be willing to continue to increase their exposure – albeit on a scale much less than in the past – and their central banks and/or bank supervisory authorities do not impede this process. More broadly, it is important that the bank supervisory authorities, who rightly would like to see more transparency in the system, do not over-react and introduce new constraints in an abrupt manner. This could well disrupt financing flows further and help trigger exactly the kind of crises it is in everyone's best interest to avoid. But undoubtedly, some additional measures aimed at better prudential management of international lending are needed and will be phased in over time. Attention to appropriate provisions for sovereign loans and country risk is already well under way, for example.

An equally important question is how can these debt crises situations best be avoided in the first place. This is a subject which one could take hours discussing, and no one has all the answers, let alone the ability to implement them. But let us throw out a few ideas without elaboration or claim to originality.

The ultimate responsibility for avoiding debt servicing difficulties has and will continue to reside with the authorities of the debtor country. Aside from questions of general economic management, there should be adequate co-ordination of all external borrowing by the public sector and, ideally, reporting and recording procedures for all external debts. This information should be in the hands of the central financial authorities on a timely basis and published regularly. The international entities such as the Fund and the Bank, or perhaps the regional development banks, should provide whatever assistance is necessary to (1) help debtor countries to develop such recording systems, and (2) in collaboration with entities such as the BIS, OECD, etc., help to develop and publish debt statistics compiled by creditors on a comprehensive and timely basis.

The international institutions such as the IMF should strengthen the process of their regular consultations with their member countries and give increased attention to external debt management in that framework. If these consultations are to be successful, then the reports derived from them will have to continue to be held within official channels. However, the central banks and/or supervisory authorities or finance ministries in the creditor countries, drawing on these and other sources of information, could be prepared to have informal consultations with their major banks on country situations where they perceive the borrowing countries' situation to be changing, either for the better or for the worse. These governmental agencies could exchange views, in some forum on evolving country situations, so that in their contacts with their markets there would be some 'equity' in the distribution of official views. For the markets, of course, this would be just another source of information on which to base their own lending decisions which they should continue to make on the merits as they see them and for which they would continue to be responsible. There should also be a better basis for a dialogue between the authorities of the debtor countries and the commercial bank lenders. This might, for example, evolve through the 'Ditchley' initiative which potentially could become a forum in which debtor country representatives might outline their policies and prospects, including their external financing requirements, in much the same way as such information is made available to the Fund in its regular consultations with member countries. Again, all the participating banks would continue to make their own lending decisions based on their own commercial interests and against the background of all the information available to them.

Each bank, large or small, involved in cross border lending should have the internal capacity to make adequate judgements on country risk and to manage risk consistent with the financial health of that institution; the supervisory authorities will continue to press in this area. The 'safe' degree of 'exposure' to one country or another in relation to capital may well vary considerably from bank to bank and emphasis on a 'market share' approach probably is not the best way to proceed. For the smaller banks, whose interests in international lending may be peripheral, following the lead of major international banks, whose involvement in specific countries is substantial and who are measuring the benefits in a broad fashion and over a long time-span, may prove troublesome.

A large majority of major banks involved realise that most of the developing countries to whom they are lending should and will be net importers of capital for some time to come. When the borrowing countries have reached the stage of development where much of their capital requirements are being met from the private markets, there can be no assumption that the banks can suddenly disengage from the lending process, either individually on the assumption that other banks will necessarily take up the slack or in some aggregate sense because of perceptions that official creditors, governmental or international will fill the void. Most banks develop country lending limits designed to define the outside exposure they feel they can safely have to a specific country. No one would challenge that approach. But it is also important that exposure limits do not become targets to be attained – that is, floors rather than ceilings – and that there be a sense of continuing involvement in a country. In short, the system probably will work better if more attention is given to the speed with which country limits are used up, rather than concentrating largely on the absolute level of exposure in relation to the limits.

Banks became involved in large-scale lending to developing countries some years before the first round of oil price increases and they played a crucial role in the recycling effort subsequently. Thus, they were not dragged into this activity, which proceeded at about the same pace after the first sharp decline in the OPEC surplus. I am sure they did so because it was good business; the reported profitability and loan loss record would seem to bear this out. The decentralised process of capital allocation through international financing intermediation by and large has served the system reasonably well, but some mistakes have been made and these need to be addressed. Indeed, this process is already underway. The initiatives being taken by the interested parties, including the banks themselves, offer hope that the system of international intermediation by the banking system will provide a more effective mechanism for allocation of capital in the future.

Part IV

6 International Banking Facilities and the Eurodollar Market

HENRY S. TERRELL AND
RODNEY H. MILLS, JR[1]

The Federal Reserve Board permitted the establishment of international banking facilities (IBFs) in the United States beginning in early December 1981. The Board took this action to allow US offices of depository institutions to be more competitive in conducting banking business with non-US residents. Through IBFs, non-US residents can conduct banking transactions in the United States free of any reserve requirements or interest rate limitations, and without the costs of insurance by the Federal Deposit Insurance Corporation. In addition, various states have amended their tax structures to grant IBFs relief from locally imposed taxes.[2]

IBFs, like the conventionally defined Eurodollar market, are free of reserve requirements and interest rate limitations (so-called non-prudential regulations), and IBF transactions take place almost exclusively with non-residents.[3] IBFs differ from the conventionally defined Eurodollar market in that their assets and liabilities are denominated almost entirely in the currency of the country in which they are located; and in contrast to some Euromarket centres without exchange controls, IBFs are prohibited from conducting business with local residents.

This paper integrates IBFs into the analysis of the Eurodollar market because the volume of IBF activity has become quite important.[4] It raises several questions about whether and how international financial markets have changed since the establishment of IBFs in late 1981.

To examine these questions, IBFs should first be put into a structure perspective. Traditionally, analysts have split international banking into two parts: the Eurodollar (or, more broadly, Eurocurrency) market, defined as transactions in non-local currencies; and conventional international finance, defined as transactions with non-local residents in local currencies. Although this dichotomy has proved useful for some purposes, a more modern view is that 'Eurocurrency markets are not a phenomenon *sui generis* but merely part of a general nexus of financial relationships among open economies'.[5] We agree that international markets have become so integrated that segregating a precisely defined Euromarket is neither possible nor useful. The broader, and more useful, concept is total international banking: some part is subject to regulation, but a large and growing proportion is free of regulation. In fact, IBFs do not neatly fit the traditional definition of either the Eurodollar market or conventional international banking. Within the United States, dollar-denominated loans and deposits of non-residents are still on the non-IBF (regulated) books of banks, indicating that currency and booking location are not a clear-cut test of whether activities should be considered part of the Eurodollar market.[6]

This paper integrates IBFs into the complex of international banking as defined by the Bank for International Settlements (BIS) to include all banking transactions with non-local residents. Within that broad complex, IBFs will be considered another development in the trend towards the conduct of international banking in an environment free of reserve requirements and interest rate limitations. In particular, IBFs are simply another location where non-US residents may conduct their banking transactions in dollars and other currencies free of required reserves. Location is, of course, important because of taxation, risks associated with the country in which the transaction takes place (so-called country risk), and time zones.

Within this framework several questions arise: Has a greater proportion of international banking activity shifted to the United States since the establishment of IBFs? Have IBFs improved the competitive position of US banks? Have IBFs spurred faster growth of international banking transactions than would have otherwise happened? Have IBFs resulted in any observable change in interest rate relationships? And, finally, how have IBFs affected the character of the offshore branches of US banks? This paper deals mainly with structural issues and does not consider directly the broader question whether the Eurodollar market can independently create money and credit, an issue that has been analysed at great length elsewhere.[7]

IBFs have been in existence for only a short period, during which the international financial situation has been quite turbulent and many of their effects may not yet be discernible. Consequently, this paper asks questions and develops a framework for analysis rather than providing definite answers to any of the questions. Any conclusions, or results that are inconsistent with hypotheses, should be considered tentative and subject to further analysis.

IBFs AND THE SHIFT OF INTERNATIONAL BANKING ACTIVITY TO THE UNITED STATES

The establishment and growth of IBFs in the United States clearly can be expected to bring the United States a larger share of international banking activity and make it more competitive with other international banking centres. Banks chartered both in the United States and abroad will shift banking business to the United States because, when it is conducted with non-US residents, it will be free of any direct regulation and will offer US country risk. Some business will shift to IBFs from US offices of both groups of banks because of reduced regulation or lower taxes, but these shifts will not affect the amount or share of international banking activity conducted in the United States.

The location of the international banking intermediation carried on by banks covered by the BIS quarterly reporting system is shown in Table 6.1.[8] The corresponding percentage shares of total assets and liabilities are given in Table 6.2.[9] The data in Tables 6.1 and 6.2 are valued in US dollars. The appreciation of the dollar since September 1981 has reduced the dollar equivalents of the non-dollar assets and liabilities, almost all of which are held by banks outside the United States. In the last column in both Tables 6.1 and 6.2 the data are adjusted for exchange rate effects on non-dollar assets and liabilities between September 1981 and December 1982, an adjustment that slightly reduces the share of international banking conducted by banks in the United States.[10]

In September 1981, before the establishment of IBFs, banks located in the United States held 15.1 per cent of total international banking assets of banks reporting to the BIS, and 11.0 per cent of the liabilities. By December 1982, the share of banks in the United States in total external bank assets had risen to 21.1 per cent (after adjustment for exchange rate changes), and the share of these offices in total liabilities to 14.9 per cent. Clearly, the establishment of IBFs has resulted in an

TABLE 6.1 *External assets and liabilities of BIS reporting banks (billions of dollars)*

	1981		*1982*				
	Sept.	*Dec.*	*Mar.*	*June*	*Sept.*	*Dec.*	*Dec. adj.*
I. Assets: total	*1424*	*1550*	*1559*	*1571*	*1627*	*1687*	*1713*
A. Banks in the United States	*215*	*257*	*283*	*321*	*346*	*361*	*361*
1. US-chartered banks†	133	164	181	206	221	233	233
(IBFs)	—	30	49	54	65	71	71
(Other US offices)	132	134	132	152	156	162	162
2. Foreign banks	82	93	102	115	125	128	128
(IBFs)	—	33	43	62	68	73	73
(Other US offices)	82	60	59	53	57	55	55
B. US branches in offshore centres	*168*	*172*	*168*	*170*	*169*	*172*	*173*
C. Banks in the United Kingdom	*400*	*432*	*441*	*434*	*460*	*458* }	
D. Banks in other locations	*641*	*689*	*667*	*646*	*652*	*696* }	*1179*
II. Liabilities: total	*1414*	*1530*	*1544*	*1542*	*1581*	*1620*	*1640*
A. Banks in the United States	*155*	*177*	*203*	*230*	*240*	*245*	*245*
1. US-chartered banks†	93	111	126	134	148	142	142
(IBFs)	—	24	39	43	59	65	65
(Other US offices)	93	87	87	91	89	77	77
2. Foreign banks	62	66	77	96	92	103	103
(IBFs)	—	23	38	55	54	59	59
(Other US offices)	62	43	39	41	38	44	44
B. US branches of offshore centres	*173*	*176*	*174*	*175*	*175*	*178*	*179*
C. Banks in the United Kingdom	*412*	*447*	*430*	*456*	*484*	*482* }	
D. Banks in other locations	*674*	*730*	*706*	*681*	*682*	*715* }	*1216*

* Adjusted for changes in exchange rate since September 1981.
† Includes Edge and Agreement Corporations.
SOURCES BIS, US Treasury.

TABLE 6.2 *Shares of external assets and liabilities of BIS reporting banks (in per cent)*

	1981		*1982*				
	Sept.	*Dec.*	*Mar.*	*June*	*Sept.*	*Dec.*	*Dec. adj.*
I. Assets: total	*100*	*100*	*100*	*100*	*100*	*100*	*100*
A. Banks in the United States	*15.1*	*16.6*	*18.2*	*20.4*	*21.3*	*21.4*	*21.1*
1. US-chartered banks†	9.3	10.6	11.6	13.1	13.6	13.8	13.6
(IBFs)	—	1.9	3.1	3.4	4.0	4.2	4.1
(Other US offices)	9.3	8.7	8.5	9.7	9.6	9.6	9.5
2. Foreign banks	5.8	6.0	6.5	7.3	7.7	7.6	7.5
(IBFs)	—	2.1	2.8	3.9	4.2	4.3	4.3
(Other US offices)	5.8	3.9	3.8	3.4	3.5	3.3	3.2
B. US branches in offshore centres	*11.8*	*11.1*	*10.8*	*10.8*	*10.4*	*10.2*	*10.1*
C. Banks in the United Kingdom	*28.1*	*27.9*	*28.3*	*27.6*	*28.3*	*27.1* }	*68.8*
D. Banks in other locations	*45.0*	*44.4*	*42.7*	*41.2*	*41.1*	*41.3* }	
II. Liabilities: total	*100*	*100*	*100*	*100*	*100*	*100*	*100*
A. Banks in the United States	*11.0*	*11.6*	*13.2*	*14.9*	*15.2*	*15.1*	*14.9*
1. US-chartered banks†	6.6	7.3	8.2	8.7	9.4	8.8	8.7
(IBFs)	—	1.6	2.5	2.8	3.7	4.0	4.0
(Other US offices)	6.6	5.7	5.6	5.9	5.6	4.8	4.7
2. Foreign banks	4.4	4.3	5.0	6.2	5.8	6.4	6.3
(IBFs)	—	1.5	2.5	3.6	3.4	3.6	3.6
(Other US offices)	4.4	2.8	2.5	2.7	2.4	2.7	2.7
B. US branches of offshore centres	*12.2*	*11.5*	*11.3*	*11.3*	*11.1*	*11.0*	*10.9*
C. Banks in the United Kingdom	*29.1*	*29.2*	*29.9*	*29.6*	*30.6*	*29.8* }	*74.1*
D. Banks in other locations	*47.7*	*47.7*	*45.7*	*44.2*	*43.1*	*44.1* }	

*Adjusted for changes in exchange rate since September 1981.
†Includes Edge and Agreement Corporations.
SOURCES BIS, US Treasury.

increase in the share of international bank intermediation conducted in the United States.

The changes in shares of various types of institutions at various locations can be seen from Tables 6.1 and 6.2. IBFs currently account for 8.5 per cent of total external bank assets, and 7.6 per cent of total international bank liabilities (unadjusted for exchange rate changes). These percentages are larger than the unadjusted increases in the shares of banks in the United States in the BIS totals, because some assets and liabilities of international banks were shifted from the books of the banks' existing US offices to their IBFs and thus did not affect the share of international banking activity conducted in the United States. These data suggest that about two-thirds of the international assets and liabilities of IBFs are associated with an increase in the share of international banking activity being conducted in the United States, while the remaining one-third represents international assets and liabilities that were previously on the books of the domestic offices.

Table 6.2 shows the extent to which various centres lost shares of international banking activity as the US share rose. Despite the highly touted challenge of IBFs to the London Eurocurrency markets, the share of banks in the United Kingdom in the BIS totals for both assets and liabilities has not declined at all since the establishment of IBFs. The principal losers have been US banks in the offshore centres, most of whose eligible assets and liabilities have been shifted to their US IBFs, and banking offices in other countries that report to the BIS, whose collective shares in total international bank assets and liabilities have declined about 4 and 3½ per cent respectively since the establishment of IBFs.[11] On the assets side, the declines in share from September 1981 to December 1982 in the other principal centres were 0.4 for Japan, Canada, and Switzerland; 0.5 for Belgium and France; and 0.6 for Luxemburg. The declines in shares on the liabilities side for these countries ranged from 0.4 to 0.7 per cent, except for France whose share rose 0.1 per cent.

Tables 6.1 and 6.2 also reveal the importance of non-US banks in IBF activity. The assets and liabilities of IBFs at US agencies and branches of foreign banks are about as large as those of US-chartered banks. One reason why the IBFs of agencies and branches have become so large is their popularity with Japanese banks and to a lesser extent with Italian banks, which together account for about two-thirds of IBF activity of non-US banks. The Japanese and Italian banks have had a very limited presence in the Caribbean, and their first experience with Eurodollar banking based in the Western hemisphere has been with

IBFs. By contrast, US banks still retain their Caribbean offices, in part to accommodate both foreign and US customers that do not want a US booking of their loan or deposit transactions.

Finally, Tables 6.1 and 6.2 indicate that a considerable amount of foreign assets and liabilities of banking offices in the United States has not been shifted to IBFs, particularly for US-chartered banks. Foreign assets of US-chartered banks on their non-IBF books are two and one-quarter times their IBF foreign assets, and their non-IBF foreign liabilities also exceed their IBF liabilities. Several reasons help explain the failure to shift these transactions to IBFs. Some transactions are with US-controlled foreign entities that may be unable or unwilling to sign the required statement that these deposits or loans will not be used in the United States. Others are with foreign residents who may have decided not to shift their transactions to IBFs because they were notified that they were expected not to use these facilities for US-related business.

Other regulatory or administrative factors prevent or discourage the shift of some types of transactions to IBFs. The most important of these transactions, in terms of current dollar volume, are the operations with affiliated banking offices abroad: claims and liabilities of head offices of US-chartered banks *vis-à-vis* their foreign branches, and claims and liabilities of branches and agencies of foreign banks *vis-à-vis* their head offices or affiliated branches abroad. At the end of September 1982, claims on affiliated offices abroad amounted to about $95 billion, and the corresponding liabilities to about $60 billion. Unless a bank is using net borrowings from its offshore affiliates to fund its US activities, it has little incentive to shift such liabilities to IBFs because they are not subject to reserve requirements in any case. Moreover, regulations forestall the shift of some transactions: IBFs are not permitted to issue negotiable certificates of deposit or short-dated deposits. Consequently, foreign holders of certificates of deposit and demand deposits issued by banks in the United States – amounting to $9 billion and $4 billion respectively in September 1982 – could not shift them to IBFs.

Finally, an advance of funds by an establishing entity to its own IBF does not constitute 'eligible funding' of IBFs for purposes of New York taxation. Because some New York banks use their domestic non-IBF offices to fund their foreign portfolios, they may refrain from shifting foreign assets to their IBFs because such funding does not afford relief from local taxes.[12]

THE IMPACT OF IBFs ON THE SHARE OF INTERNATIONAL LENDING OF US-CHARTERED BANKS

Because both US-chartered and other banks have established IBFs, the share of US-chartered banks in international banking activity on a worldwide basis will not necessarily increase because IBFs have come into existence. To the extent that US banks can offer deposit facilities to customers at their home offices that are denominated in their national currency, are free of any regulatory restraints, and have easy access to the US dollar clearing systems, IBFs may offer a competitive advantage for US banks.

In this section, we attempt to determine whether IBFs have served to increase the share of US banks in overall international banking activity. Table 6.3 presents data on the amount of total external assets (and liabilities) of US-chartered banks for recent dates, and the share of US-chartered banks in claims of all banks covered by the BIS reporting system.[13]

The share of US-chartered banks in the published BIS totals for total international banking claims (excluding claims on the United States) declined initially in the fourth quarter of 1981, and then increased. These results suggest that the impact of IBFs on the share of US banks in international banking activity has probably been negligible to date. However, this conclusion must be examined in order to take into account two important developments that are known to have affected the relative shares of US and foreign banks in total international banking claims (valued in dollars) since IBFs have come into existence. (As noted earlier, variations in the exchange rate of the dollar have changed the dollar equivalents of claims denominated in non-dollar currencies.)

First, between September 1981 and December 1982, the share of US banks was raised 0.4 per cent by exchange rate changes; the adjustment for these changes is shown in Table 6.3.[14] Although it is important in principle to take account of the effects of exchange rate changes on international banking data, in this particular case, the actual impact is relatively small.

Second, account should be taken of the fact that foreign banks have shifted assets from their Caribbean branches, which are not covered by the quarterly BIS series on international banking, to IBFs, which are included in those series. Thus the coverage of the BIS data is improved.

The actual increase in the BIS totals resulting simply from expanded coverage for non-US banks cannot be estimated with precision. One

TABLE 6.3 *US-chartered banks' share of total international banking claims**

	US banks' international assets† ($ billions)	US banks' share of published BIS total (per cent)	Adjustments for: Effects of exchange rate changes‡	Adjustments for: Broader coverage of BIS total	US banks' adjusted share of BIS total
1979 – December	285	27.4	—	—	—
1980 – December	330	26.8	—	—	—
1981 – June	371	29.7	—	—	—
September	397	30.3	—	—	—
December	413	29.2	+0.2	0	29.14
1982 – March	419	29.7	−0.1	+0.1	29.17
June	435	31.0	−0.3	+0.3	31.10
September	446	30.6	−0.4	+0.4	30.16
December	453	29.9	−0.2	+0.4	30.1

* Excluding claims on the United States.
† Adjusted to a BIS basis.
‡ The observation for each date measures the adjustment needed to compensate for the cumulative effect since September 1981 of changes in dollar exchange rates.
SOURCE Data supplied by the authors.

procedure assumes that in the absence of IBFs the share of the US branches and agencies of foreign banks in total international banking claims would have remained at about the same level as in September 1981. In fact, that share – combining IBFs and non-IBF US offices – increased 1.8 per cent by December 1982. Funds were drawn from both the Caribbean centres (which do not report to the BIS) and other foreign centres (which do), but most of the funds drawn from outside the United States apparently came from the Caribbean area.

Assuming that 60 per cent of the increase in the share of agencies and branches of non-US banks in the BIS totals came from the Caribbean branches of foreign banks, by December 1982 roughly 1.1 per cent, or about $19 billion, of total international banking assets were funds drawn to IBFs of foreign banks that had not been reported to the BIS in September 1981.[15] As is shown in Table 6.3, the share of US banks in the total rose by 0.4 per cent in December 1982, and by less on earlier dates after the establishment of IBFs, when the share is adjusted for the increased coverage of the BIS data.

This second adjustment for wider reporting by non-US banks also has a negligible effect on the share of US banks in total international banking assets. Taken together, the two adjustments leave the share of US banks in total international banking assets in December 1982 (30.1 per cent), 0.2 per cent lower than it had been in September 1981, before the establishment of IBFs. Thus to date, IBFs do not appear to have had an observable impact on the share of US banks in total international lending.

IBFs AND THE GROWTH OF INTERNATIONAL BANKING ACTIVITY

The establishment of IBFs has extended the geographical scope of the Eurocurrency markets, the part of total international banking activity that is not directly regulated by monetary authorities. This extension should not be expected to increase the worldwide volume of combined international and domestic banking activity. But the expanded opportunities for unregulated international banking transactions may induce some economic entities to shift activity from the domestic sphere (where borrower and lender are located in the same country) to the international sphere (where borrowing and lending cross international boundaries). To the extent that such shifts occurred, the growth of international banking activity would be more rapid.

Table 6.4 reports a simple statistical test of that hypothesis. It compares the growth rate of international banking assets, as computed from BIS data, and the four quarters since the establishment of IBFs with the average growth rates of total international banking assets for the same calendar period for the previous three years. The data for both the pre- and post-IBF periods have been adjusted for the effects of changes in exchange rates on the dollar value of international banking assets. The data for the post-IBF period are reported both unadjusted and adjusted for the estimated impact of augmented reporting by non-US banks.

TABLE 6.4 *Average quarterly growth of international bank assets* (per cent)*

	Average quarterly growth since establishment of IBFs			
	Published IBS data	*BIS data adjusted for estimated enhanced reporting by non-US banks*	*Average quarterly growth for same quarters in three previous years*	
Q4 – 1981	7.2	7.0	8.7	Q4 1978–80
Q1 – 1982	2.3	2.0	2.3	Q1 1979–81
Q2 – 1982	2.0	1.5	5.4	Q2 1979–81
Q3 – 1982	4.4	4.1	5.7	Q3 1979–81
Q4 – 1982	3.1	3.1	7.7	Q4 1979–81
Quarterly average for the period	3.8	3.5	6.0	

*Growth rate adjusted for valuation effects of changing exchange rates.
SOURCE BIS.

Table 6.4 indicates that international banking assets tend to increase considerably in the fourth quarter of the year and then to grow more slowly in the first quarter of the following year. This pattern is repeated after the establishment of IBFs. After adjustment for changes in exchange rates and for the augmented reporting, the increase in international banking assets was in fact slower (about 3.5 per cent per quarter) in the five quarters after the establishment of IBFs than in the comparable quarters of the three previous years (about 6 per cent per quarter). These comparisons suggest that the establishment of IBFs has not raised the growth rate of international banking activity.

The comparisons in Table 6.4 are, however, quite simple and ignore factors other than the establishment of IBFs. In particular, international financial disturbances since the establishment of IBFs have affected the growth of international banking assets. Therefore, a more complete model explaining the growth of those assets is needed so that the impact of IBFs can be estimated while holding constant as many other factors as possible.

A model of this sort has been developed by the International Monetary Fund.[16] It suggests that the growth of international banking assets will be affected by the growth of world trade (measured by the total growth of world imports) and by world imbalances (measured as the sum of the absolute surpluses and deficits of 56 countries divided by world imports). The IMF model adds a dummy variable to account for the contraction in international banking assets after the Herstatt crisis and an end-of-year seasonal dummy variable.

We have modified and expanded the IMF model and estimated it through the second quarter of 1982. We have expanded the seasonal adjustment by adding a dummy variable for the first quarter to allow for the generally rapid expansion in bank assets in the last quarter of the year, in part for end-of-year window-dressing, and for some seasonal reversal in the first quarter of the next.[17] Because the BIS series is reported in dollars, we have added an exchange rate variable to estimate the impact of changes in the value of the dollar on the growth of international banking assets.[18] An increase in the value of the dollar should result in a slower increase than otherwise would be the case in the reported growth of international banking assets because there will be a decline in the value of the stock of non-dollar banking assets measured in dollars.[19] The exchange rate variable was constructed using the weights of the various currencies in the BIS aggregate data, a procedure that in particular gives more weight to the German mark and Swiss franc and less to the Japanese yen and Canadian dollar than one based on international trade shares.[20] Finally, for the quarters since the establishment of IBFs we have added a dummy variable to test for the impact of IBFs on the growth of the international assets of banks.

Table 6.5 reports the results of the regressions. The model explains about three-fourths of the variation of growth in external banking assets, and all of the variables except the dummy for IBFs were statistically significant. An increase in the exchange value of the dollar of 1 per cent (using BIS Eurocurrency weights) reduces the expected

TABLE 6.5 *Regression equations explaining quarterly percentage growth of external bank assets (per cent)*

Independent variable	*Unadjusted BIS estimate of external bank assets*	*BIS estimate of external bank assets adjusted for enhanced reporting by IBFs of non-US banks*
Constant	4.45	4.44
Percentage change of world imports	0.13 (2.11)	0.13 (2.12)
Percentage change in ratio of trade surpluses and deficits divided by world imports	0.085 (3.30)	0.085 (3.30)
Change in value of US dollar	−0.30 (4.36)	−0.30 (4.40)
Q4 dummy	5.28 (5.63)	5.29 (5.66)
Q1 dummy	−2.37 (3.06)	−2.37 (3.07)
Q3 1974 (Herstatt)	−5.56 (2.49)	−5.55 (2.49)
IBF dummy	−0.81 (0.61)	−1.35 (1.02)
R^2	0.749	0.753
Durbin-Watson	2.13	2.13
F	21.50	21.90

SOURCE Supplied by authors.

growth of external banking assets (measured in dollars) about 0.3 per centage point, a reduction that is consistent with a dollar share of about 70 per cent of all external banking assets.

The potential effects of IBFs on the growth in external banking assets have been tested in two equations: one for the growth in unadjusted BIS estimates of those assets, and one using BIS data adjusted for our estimates of augmented reporting by non-US banks. In both equations the estimated impact of IBFs on the growth of international banking assets was actually negative, but not significant statistically. The use of the adjustment to the BIS data for augmented reporting by non-US banks reduced the coefficient for the IBF dummy, as expected, and slightly, but not significantly, improved the fit of the general model.[21]

The conclusion from these findings is that, to date, IBFs have not stimulated the growth of external banking assets. The model should, of course, be tested over a longer period to determine whether the conclusion remains valid.

IBFs AND DIFFERENTIALS BETWEEN US AND EURODOLLAR INTEREST RATES

Interest rates paid on deposits at domestic offices tend to be below comparable Eurodollar rates for two reasons: first, banks in the United States are required to maintain reserves on deposits at domestic offices, and thus on a cost basis are willing to offer less interest on such deposits. Second, many US and foreign customers have been willing or required to accept a lower return on deposits at US offices than they could get on Eurodollar deposits, in order to benefit from a perceived lower country risk. The costs of reserve requirements and assessments by the Federal Deposit Insurance Corporation tend to place a lower bound on observed differentials. But at times interest rate differentials have considerably exceeded those related to pure cost considerations, because non-bank depositors wish to hold their wealth in the United States or because banks wish to expand liabilities at their non-US offices.

To induce foreign customers to shift deposits from regulated domestic accounts to IBFs, banks must pay slightly higher rates on IBF deposits than are paid on deposits at non-IBF domestic offices. Banks will have the leeway to pay higher rates on their IBF deposits because such deposits do not bear the costs of reserve requirements and FDIC insurance. At the margin, higher rates offered by IBFs on deposits may exert some slight upward pressure on interest rates at non-IBF domestic offices.

Because deposits at both offshore branches and IBFs are free of these regulatory costs, banks have little reason to encourage their customers to shift deposits from the first to the second unless the depositors are willing to accept slightly lower rates of interest on IBF deposits. Some customers are willing to do so because of the added advantage of US country risk. At the margin, relatively lower rates on IBF deposits may exert some slight downward pressure on Eurodollar interest rates. A slight upward pressure on domestic (non-IBF) deposit rates and a slight downward pressure on Eurodollar rates will be expected on balance to reduce the observed differential between these rates. These theoretical considerations suggest that by offering an intermediate deposit with some of the characteristics of both Eurodollar and domestic deposits, IBFs will further integrate international and US banking markets and will reduce potential interest rate differentials.[22]

Figure 6.1 illustrates the empirical evidence on the difference in interest rates paid on negotiable Eurodollar CDs and negotiable domestic-office CDs with a maturity of 90 days, for a sample of prime US banks in the periods before and after the establishment of IBFs. The data on interest rate differentials are presented in three ways: (1) on an unadjusted basis that reflects the return to depositors; (2) on a fully adjusted basis that takes into account the costs of domestic-office and Eurocurrency reserve requirements and FDIC insurance, and that reflects the costs to US banks of using these alternative sources of funds in their domestic-office business under the assumption that at the margin the US bank is required to maintain reserves on its Eurodollar borrowings; and (3) on a partially adjusted basis that reflects only the costs of reserve requirements and FDIC insurance at domestic offices. This third measure reflects the costs to US banks of using the alternative sources of funds for lending at their foreign offices, or at their domestic offices assuming that the Eurocurrency reserve requirement is not binding.[23]

As Figure 6.1 shows, interest rate differentials have traced an erratic pattern since the establishment of IBFs. After IBFs began operation, at a time when their balance sheets were expanding rapidly, the interest differentials actually widened on all three bases. Several factors explain that unexpected result. IBF liabilities tend to be largely intra- and interbank transactions because so far IBFs have had limited appeal to non-bank customers inasmuch as the regulations require a two-day notice for transfers and prohibit the issuance of negotiable deposits.[24] The relatively small amount of non-bank deposits suggests that existing relationships between bank and non-bank interest rates have not, as yet, been significantly affected.

In the last few weeks of 1982, the interest rate differentials between Eurodollar and domestic-office CDs narrowed substantially. This recent decline cannot easily be attributed to IBFs because the size and composition of IBF liabilities did not change significantly in this period. The timing of the narrowing of these differentials is loosely associated with a decline in the exchange value of the dollar, suggesting some simultaneous shift in investor preference, away from both dollar assets and bank deposits in the United States that may have raised the relative cost of domestic-office CDs.

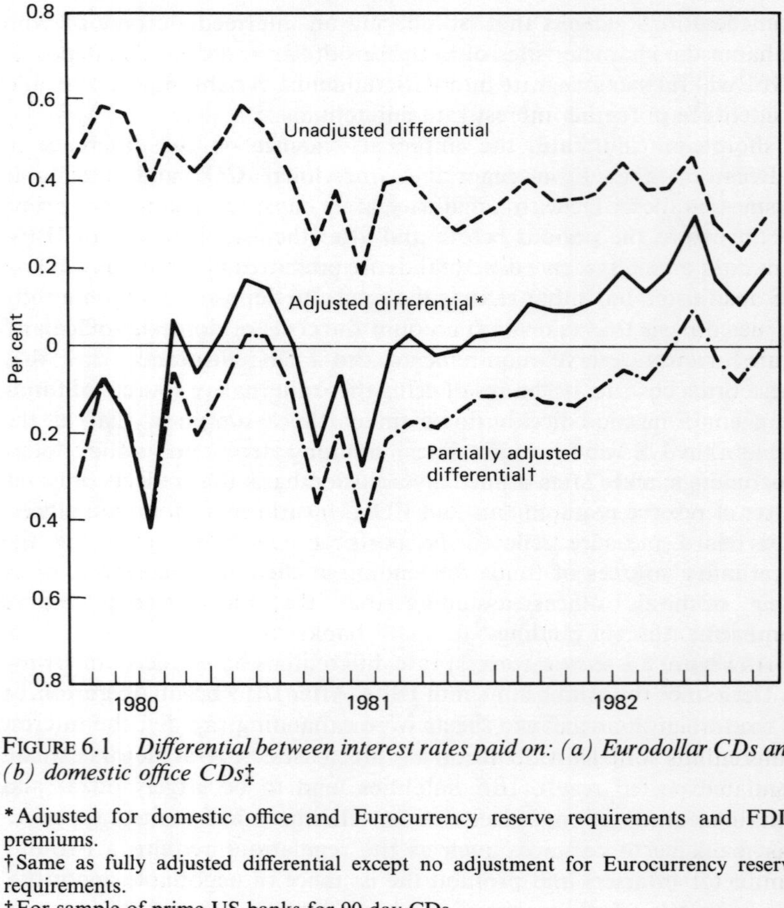

FIGURE 6.1 *Differential between interest rates paid on: (a) Eurodollar CDs and (b) domestic office CDs‡*

*Adjusted for domestic office and Eurocurrency reserve requirements and FDIC premiums.
†Same as fully adjusted differential except no adjustment for Eurocurrency reserve requirements.
‡For sample of prime US banks for 90 day CDs.

The empirical evidence of the impact of IBFs on interest rate differentials is inconclusive. In the period of fastest IBF growth, the differentials actually widened, suggesting that IBFs have had little impact. Other factors in international financial markets seem to have had a much more important impact on these differentials.

IBFs AND OFFSHORE BRANCHES OF US BANKS

As noted earlier, since the establishment of IBFs a substantial amount of international business has been shifted to those facilities from the branches of US banks in offshore banking centres, in particular the Bahamas and the Cayman Islands. The shift in business has, of course, involved transactions with non-US residents. At the same time, US residents have further intensified their activity with the branches in the offshore centres, notably with respect to deposits.

Because of these developments, a rapidly increasing share of the total business at the branches in offshore centres has been with US residents. By the end of 1982, about two-thirds of the liabilities of branches in the Bahamas and Cayman Islands *vis-à-vis* unrelated parties was owed to US residents, and more than one-fourth of the claims on unrelated parties was on US residents (Figures 6.2 and 6.3). The rapid growth of branch liabilities to US non-bank residents has reflected the ability of these branches to pay US residents higher rates of interest on deposits than could be paid by the domestic offices of US banks. Many US banks have established facilities whereby they may offer their customers market rates of interest on accounts that can be transferred into a deposit account in the United States with funds available on the next business day.[25] Although pricing practices and, in some places, local taxes make it attractive for banks to offer US residents loans at their offshire branches, the Eurocurrency reserve requirements sometimes limit incentives for US banks to book loans to US borrowers at these branches.[26]

The establishment of IBFs and the resulting change in the character of the foreign branches of US banks point up an obvious fact: banking transactions will shift to locations where they are least taxed and regulated. In an age of rapid telecommunications, the booking of banking transactions is indeed flexible. The current regulatory situation has produced a paradox: non-US residents are now encouraged to conduct their banking transactions in the United States, while US residents have incentives to book their transactions, particularly their deposit accounts, offshore.[27]

This situation, coupled with competition from money market mutual funds and other unregulated competitors with banks, has exerted pressure for further deregulation of banking in the United States. Although such deregulation is urged largely for domestic considerations, it may have implications for IBFs and other areas of international intermediation. For example, the new money market deposit account, which became effective on 14 December 1982, has very low reserve requirements (zero in some cases), earns a market rate of interest and has fairly generous limits on transfers except by cheque. Such accounts may attract some of the $16 billion that non-bank depositors now keep with IBFs, although not much relative to the

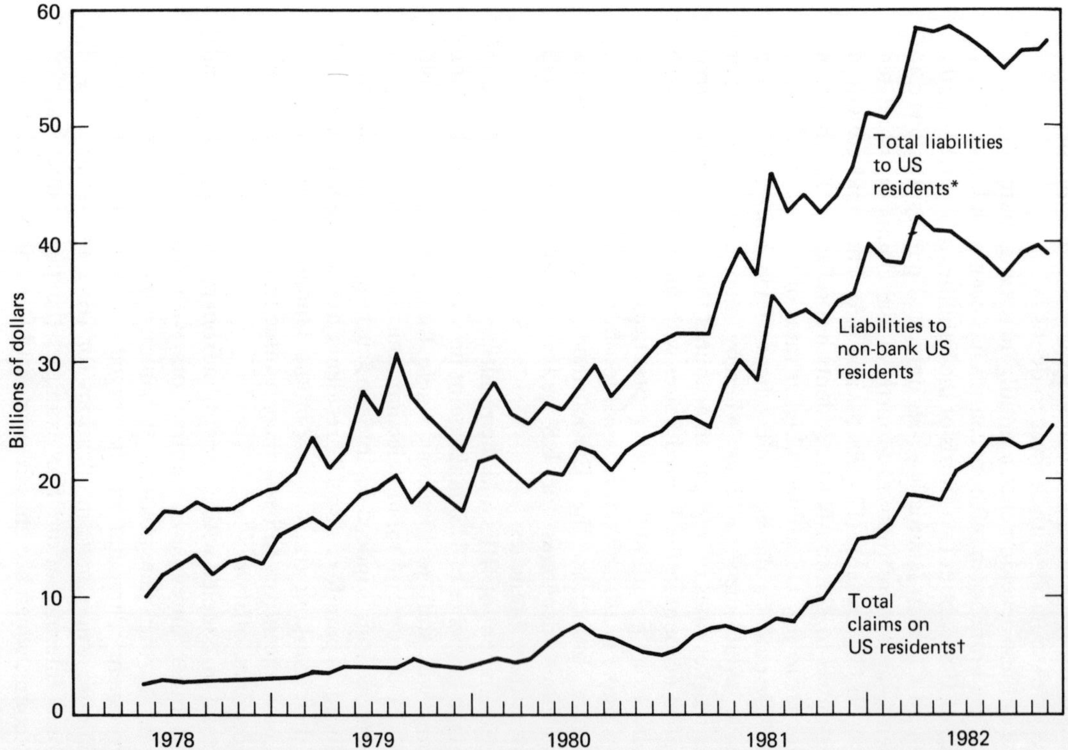

FIGURE 6.2 *Claims and liabilities of Nassau and Cayman branches of US banks with US residents*

*Includes liabilities to unrelated banking offices in the United States; excludes liabilities to related offices.

†Includes claims on unrelated banking offices in the United States; excludes claims on related offices.

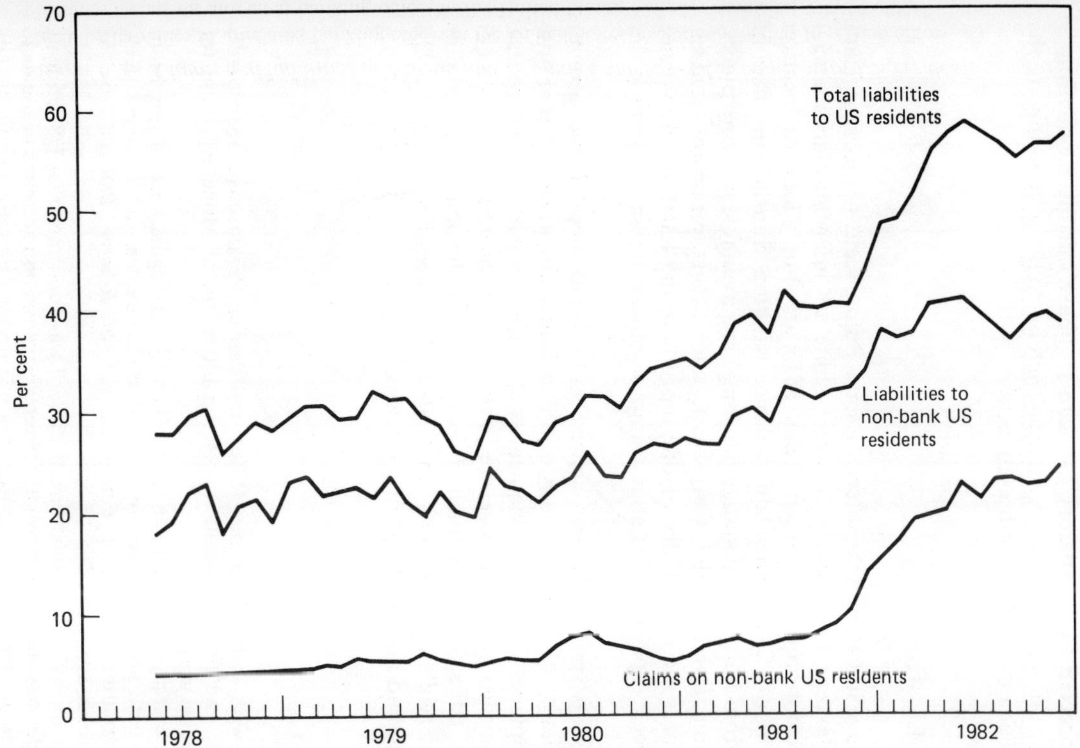

FIGURE 6.3 *Claims and liabilities with US residents as a per cent of total activity of Nassau and Cayman branches of US banks*

*Numerator and denominator exclude claims and liabilities with related entities.

aggregate balance sheet of IBFs. Perhaps more important, the Depository Institutions Deregulation and Monetary Control Act of 1980 directed the regulatory agencies to phase out the Regulation Q ceilings on interest rates by 1986, thereby making banking in the United States generally more attractive.

CONCLUSION

IBFs have not altered the international banking scene to any significant extent except by drawing a larger share of international financial intermediation to the United States. IBFs are simply another location where non-US residents can conduct banking transactions free of regulation. Such an advantage has long been available in many places, including London, the Caribbean, and other important centres. Therefore, the availability of one more booking location should not have been expected to change things significantly, and indeed, it did not.

IBFs are probably best viewed as a small step in the general deregulation of banking. Many of the measures already enacted or now contemplated for the US financial system are also part of that process. Because they owe their existence to the regulatory structure of the US market, IBFs, as well as much of the conventionally defined Eurodollar market, will be profoundly affected as the deregulation of the US banking and financial system continues.

NOTES

1. We wish to thank Sydney J. Key and Patrick Parkinson of the Board's staff, and Donald Mathieson of the International Monetary Fund for valuable assistance.
2. For a complete description of the Board's IBF regulations, of provisions for state and local taxation, and of IBF activities, see Sydney J. Key, 'International Banking Facilities', *Federal Reserve Bulletin*, vol. 68 (October 1982), pp. 565–77.

   In amending its regulations, the Board was concerned that US residents might substitute IBF accounts for certain transaction accounts or use them to circumvent reserve requirements or interest rate ceilings and thereby affect domestic monetary and credit aggregates. Consequently, the Board imposed various restrictions on IBF activities, including a minimum maturity of two business days for any transaction by non-bank customers; a minimum of $100 000 for transfers into or out of IBF accounts, except for closing an account or withdrawing accumulated interest; a prohibition against IBFs issuing negotiable instruments, which could be purchased by US residents; and a restriction on the use of IBF loans and deposits to supporting activities outside the United States.

3. 'Regulation' in this study means reserve requirements and limitations on interest rates. Prudential regulations, such as limits on loans to individual borrowers and on capital or liquidity ratios, apply to activities of banks on a consolidated (worldwide) basis, including their IBFs.

   Exceptions to the general rule of IBF-non-resident transactions are transactions with the US entity that established the IBF and those with other IBFs.
4. As of December 1982, the total assets of IBFs, excluding claims on US offices of the establishing entity, exceeded $160 billion.
5. See Ralph C. Bryant, *Money and Monetary Policy in Interdependent Nations* (Brookings Institution, 1980), pp. 100–01; and Bundesverband Deutscher Banken, *International Banking: Its New Dimensions* (Cologne: Bank Verlag GmbH, 1981). The latter reference uses the following definition: 'In a narrow sense, Eurocurrency banking consists of deposits and loans located outside the countries whose currencies are used. Often, however, total international bank lending is meant' (p. 146).
6. One can concoct fanciful examples of the way transactions affect the measured size of the Eurodollar market. For example, if IBFs are not considered part of the Eurodollar market, a shift by a non-US resident from a deposit in London to a deposit at an IBF will reduce the measured size of the Eurodollar market. By contrast, if IBFs are considered part of the Eurodollar market, then a deposit shifted from a regulated (non-IBF) banking office in the United States to an IBF will increase the measured size of the Eurodollar market.
7. A wide range of literature exists on this subject and is cited in Bryant, *Money and Monetary Policy*, p. 101. In particular, see Helmut W. Mayer, *Credit and Liquidity Creation in the International Banking Sector*, BIS Economic Papers 1 (Basle: Bank for International Settlements, 1979).

   We think that the Eurodollar market does not independently create any significant amount of monetary assets and credit and therefore IBFs will have little impact on their magnitudes.
8. The quarterly reporting system of the BIS covers banks in twelve West European countries, the United States, Canada, and Japan, as well as branches of US banks in five offshore banking centres.
9. The data in Tables 6.1 and 6.2 cover international assets and liabilities of IBFs as reported in the US balance of payments statistics of the BIS and the US Treasury. These data differ from those published in the Board's 'Weekly Report of Assets and Liabilities of International Banking Facilities' (statistical release H-14), which includes IBF transactions with eligible US residents, such as other IBFs or other US offices of the establishing entity.
10. The adjustments were made by constructing an index of the weighted average exchange rate of the dollar against the seven most important non-dollar currencies among the external assets of BIS reporting banks, based on the amounts outstanding in December 1981.

11. For a description of local tax incentives for US banks to shift funds from offshore branches to IBFs, see Key, *International Banking Facilities*, p. 568.
12. Ibid.
13. To bring the data published in the *Federal Reserve Bulletin* for US-chartered banks into conformity with the BIS series, three principal adjustments were made: (1) claims of foreign branches on local borrowers were deducted because the BIS includes only external (cross-border) claims; (2) claims of foreign branches located outside the BIS reporting area were deducted because they are not part of the BIS series; and (3) the consolidation of intrabank claims in the published data were separated again because the BIS series is on a gross basis.
14. The dollar's exchange rate, weighted by the seven leading non-dollar currencies in the external claims of BIS reporting banks, declined between the end of September and the end of December 1981, increased in the first three quarters of 1982, and declined again in the fourth quarter, so by the end of December 1982, it was 4.8 per cent above the level at the end of September 1981. But this appreciation of the dollar did not significantly increase the share of US banks in total international banking valued in dollars, even though as of December 1982, only 17 per cent of the international claims of US banks were in non-dollar currencies, compared with 36 per cent for non-US banks.
15. Key, *International Banking Facilities*, suggests a strong association between the IBF assets and liabilities of US banks and a decline in comparable balance-sheet items at these banks' Caribbean branches. We have assumed this relationship is less close for non-US banks because of the large presence of Japanese and Italian banks in total IBF activity and their limited activities in the Caribbean.
16. See Richard C. Williams and others, *International Capital Markets: Developments and Prospects, 1981*, Occasional Paper 14 (International Monetary Fund, 1982), p. 43.
17. The original IMF model had a seasonal factor only for the fourth quarter of the year.
18. The IMF model captures the exchange rate effect indirectly by using the dollar value of the GNP of six large industrial countries as an explanatory variable.
19. This model treats exchange rate changes as exogenous, with only a valuation effect.
20. An alternative specification would have been to run the regressions on the growth rates of the BIS aggregates, which themselves had been adjusted for changes in exchange rates. This approach was rejected because the IMF trade and imbalance data were computed on the basis of dollars. The alternative specification would also not necessarily have been an improvement because the composition of the non-dollar proportion of the BIS data can change between reporting dates.
21. Two other specifications, involving a more complete seasonal adjustment and dummy variables for each quarter after IBFs were established, were used to test for any impact that IBFs had on the growth of international banking assets during their phase-in. Neither of the alternative specifications altered the results of the equations reported in Table 6.5.

22. It would be useful to have a series on interest rates paid on IBF deposits to determine whether these rates tracked domestic or Eurodollar interest rates, but a published series on IBF deposit rates for similar instruments is not yet available. Market information to date suggests that such rates tend to track Eurodollar interest rates very closely. And because IBFs do not issue certificates of deposit, their impact on rates on domestic and Eurodollar CDs is somewhat indirect.
23. The Eurocurrency reserve requirement is not binding on a bank whose net advances to its foreign branches exceed the loans by its foreign branches to US residents plus any assets purchased by those branches from its domestic offices.
24. As of May 1983, IBFs held only $19 billion in liabilities to non-bank customers. In addition to the reasons given above, various requirements that banks notify customers that IBF deposits and loans are to be used only for financing activities outside the United States may also have inhibited the growth of liabilities to non-banks.
25. As of December 1982, there were about $11 billion in these deposits. The Federal Reserve includes such deposits from a sample of banks in the monetary aggregate M2.
26. US banks are permitted to net advances to their foreign offices against loans to US non-bank borrowers in computing their Eurocurrency reserve requirements.
27. The Federal Reserve only collects data on such transactions from branches of US banks. Because of the potential growth of such activities at offshore offices of non-US banks, the Federal Reserve is conducting a survey of deposits and loans to US residents from foreign offices of non-US banks.

BIBLIOGRAPHY

Ashby, David F. V., 'Will the Eurodollar Market Go Back Home?' *The Banker*, vol. 131 (February 1981) pp. 93–8.

Bennett, Robert A., 'Eurocurrency lending is a $1 trillion business that has all been going to London and island tax havens. Starting Dec. 3, banks do that business here', *New York Times*, 22 November 1981.

Board of Governors of the Federal Reserve System, 'International Banking Facilities.' Staff memoranda. Processed. Washington, 14 December 1978, and 31 October 1980.

Office of Staff Director for Monetary and Financial Policy, 'International Banking Facilities and Related Issues.' Staff memorandum. Processed. Washington, 4 June 1981.

Office of Staff Director for Monetary and Financial Policy, Federal Reserve press release on establishment of International Banking Facilities (IBFs). Processed. Washington, 18 June 1981.

Bryant, Ralph C., *Money and Monetary Policy in Interdependent Nations* (Washington: Brookings Institution, 1980).

Bundesverband Deutscher Banken, *International Banking: Its New Dimensions*. Lectures and proceedings at the 34th International Banking Summer School held at Maritim Golf- und Sporthotel, Timmendorfer, Strand/Germany, August–September 1981. (Cologne: Bank Verlag GmbH, 1981.)

Farber, Beth M., 'International Banking Facilities: Defining a Greater US Presence in the Eurodollar Market', *Law and Policy in International Business*, vol. 13 (1981) pp. 997–1046.

Johnston, R. B. 'Some Aspects of the Determination of Euro-currency Interest Rates', *Bank of England Quarterly*, vol. 19 (March 1979) pp. 35–46.

Key, Sydney J., 'Activities of International Banking Facilities: The Early Experience', in Federal Reserve Bank of Chicago, *Proceedings of a Conference on Bank Structure and Competition*, April 12–14, 1982 (Chicago: The Bank, 1982) pp. 71–87.

Key, Sydney J., 'International Banking Facilities', *Federal Reserve Bulletin*, vol. 68 (October 1982) pp. 565–77.

Key, Sydney J. and Serge Bellanger, 'International Banking Facilities: The Shape of Things to Come', *World of Banking*, vol. 1 (March–April 1982) pp. 17–23.

Kreicher, Lawrence L., 'Eurodollar Arbitrage', Federal Reserve Bank of New York, *Quarterly Review*, vol. 7 (Summer 1982) pp. 10–21.

Mayer, Helmut W., *Credit and Liquidity Creation in the International Banking Sector*. BIS Economic Papers 1 (Basle: Bank for International Settlements, 1979).

Mendelsohn, M. S., 'First Anniversary of IBFs Finds Much Ado About Little', *American Banker*, 9 December 1982, p. 2.

Mills, Rodney H., Jr, 'US Banks Are Losing Their Share of the Market', *Euromoney*, February 1980, pp. 50–8.

Mills, Rodney H., Jr and Eugenie D. Short, 'US Banks and the North American Eurocurrency Market', *Journal of Commercial Bank Lending*, vol. 61 (July 1979) pp. 27–38.

Parkinson, Patrick, 'Substitution Between Eurodollar Borrowings and Domestic CDs by Large U.S. Banks.' Processed (Washington: Board of Governors of the Federal Reserve System, 1982).

Williams, Richard C. *et al.*, *International Capital Markets: Developments and Prospects, 1982*. Occasional Paper 14 (Washington: International Monetary Fund, 1982).

COMMENT

PATRICK H. P. O'SULLIVAN

As has been previously noted, IBFs were created to encourage the repatriation to the US of control of part of the Eurodollar market with all of the attendant spin-offs that such a move would have for the financial infrastructure of cities such as New York, Miami, Houston, Chicago, etc. But, as Henry Terrell points out, despite their growth, IBFs have not had quite their anticipated impact yet. Why not?

To answer this question, we need to go back to an understanding of how the Eurodollar market grew and from that to see why the restrictions placed on IBFs by the Federal Reserve System have effectively limited their usefulness.

As has already been indicated, Eurodollars are simply dollar deposits at banks outside the United States, together with deposits in the new IBFs. Since these deposits are ultimately reflected in the reserve accounts of banks with the Federal Reserve System, one can argue that they are part of the total US money supply. Hence, the Federal Reserve System's desire, as the body charged with controlling the US money supply through changes in these reserves, to control the extent to which offshore funds are spent in the United States. Mainly because of this, severe restrictions have been placed on the uses to which dollar deposits in IBFs can be put. I will return to this point later.

The Eurodollar market has grown, as I have indicated, from a transfer of domestic deposits to branches abroad. In contrast with the highly regulated domestic market size and sophistication of Eurodollar market increased due to a lack of any regulations.

Consequently, these financial centres have attracted intermediaries to add the 'pot-pourri' of services that are commonplace to primary financial markets everywhere today.

One could, and some writers do, conclude that the ability to trade in offshore dollar deposits which IBFs have is a first step in the development of similar centres in cities such as Miami.

Let me offer some views as to why this may not necessarily be the case, and I should suggest a number of changes which will have to occur to make Miami a fully fledged financial centre in the future.

To understand this, we need to look further at the rationale for IBFs and their restrictions.

The origin of IBFs goes back to the days when New York State imposed severe taxes on banks because the authorities believed that they were partly responsible for the city's financial problems. This gave the banks an even greater incentive to trade Eurodollars in Nassau and Cayman, which are in the same time zone as New York. As indicated above, IBFs were intended to overcome this flight and to attract back onshore dollars that were booked offshore, but, nevertheless, managed in New York.

So, even though the latest figures show New York IBFs with over $100 billion of deposits, the only real switch has been a move from one set of books to another. Is this sufficient for the growth of a fully fledged financial centre? New York was already dealing in Eurodollars anyway! I would argue that, while deposits are made available in this manner, borrowers are only attracted into the market if this represents a newly available source of funds either in sufficient volume or with other attractive features attached, such as a different cost structure or availability. Neither of these conditions apply in the case of New York. Furthermore, as indicated above, the Federal Reserve System imposed restraints on IBFs to prevent them being used for domestic dollar borrowing, lending or investing. The ostensible reason used was to control the money supply; and yet, these funds, which, in any case, are freely available offshore to domestic borrowers through London, are shut off from them in the US in the belief that this will prevent onshore use of IBF funds. This restriction inhibits the growth of IBFs unnecessarily. (Specifically, IBFs may not pay interest on overnight money, cannot issue CDs, and cannot take deposits from or make loans to domestic entities.)

Therefore, given that IBFs are so restricted and are compelled to deal offshore, what is their value? As you have heard, they offer a different sovereign risk for depositors who traditionally might have deposited in London, Luxemburg, or even Singapore. But there is no other reason for other offshore depositors in London or elsewhere to move into IBFs.

Since IBFs cannot lend domestically either here or anywhere else in the US, borrowers will continue to deal with London or elsewhere offshore where the financial markets already have all the resources and skills accumulated to do so. If the restriction on domestic usage is lifted, then there would be a catalyst for further growth in the availability of a local market-place into which funds could be lent – a precondition which was present in the development of the Eurodollar market in London.

What will the IBFs do? They will continue to function as money books in offshore deposits, placing with offshore financial centres since they cannot be used to mismatch on a domestic book.

Unless, of course, offshore borrowers are attracted into these markets. How can this be achieved, given the fact that local borrowers cannot use the market directly? One way would be for the major US and foreign banks in Miami to slowly build the financial infrastructure which in itself, in due course, would attract borrowers in. Building a governmental, institutional and corporate lending activity for Latin America based in Miami would be one way to do so; and we in Bank of America have started that process. Then the deposit base in Miami's IBFs could fund Latin loan portfolios. Even then, however, for out-of-state banks the booking of international loans has to be done through their Edge Act subsidiaries, and these have a capital constraint on the size of loan per borrower which can be domiciled therein.

So, the problems are far from solved; and in my opinion, it will be some time before the world class borrowers look to the IBFs as they now do to the Eurodollar books of their major banks for an alternate source of funds, provided, of course, that deregulation or a collapse of the Western financial system does not cause a complete rethink! Of course, in the event of the latter, I do not think there will be many attractive alternatives available in any case.

COMMENT

R. RODERICK PORTER

The paper prepared by Mr Terrell and Mr Mills addresses five questions. My brief comments will reflect the somewhat different perspective of practitioners on four of those questions.

Question 1. Has a greater portion of international banking activity shifted to the US since the establishment of the IBFs? The analysis clearly shows that it has. I think that the shift is beneficial – not just for the US and the US banks – but for the international financial system in general. To the extent that activity in offshore banking centres, which exist only by virtue of the absence of regulatory constraints and taxes, shifts to centres distinguished by the underpinnings inherent in a sound financial infrastructure, we are all better off.

The shift could be accelerated by resolution of the uncertainties in the tax treatment of the IBFs which exists primarily in New York, as well as, by liberalisation with respect to IBF transactions with domestic borrowers and lenders.

Question 2. Have IBFs improved the competitive position of US banks? IBFs have marginally improved the competitive position of several major cities in the US as international banking centres. In time, that should create a halo effect which should improve the competitive position of US banks – which was already fairly good. (Parenthetically I would say that assets or liabilities are not a particularly good proxy for assessing competitiveness.) However, it is going to be some time before we can assess the long-run impact. It takes years to develop a good Eurocurrency trader or FX trader, it takes more years to develop the accounting and control systems to operate successfully and decades to create the kind of culture in which international banking can flourish. US banks have already advanced a long way down this road and IBF capability is an enhancement.

Question 3. Have IBFs resulted in a faster growth of international banking transactions than would have otherwise happened? The paper makes it clear that there is no discernible effect on growth in international lending from the IBFs. I would add that there is no reason why there should have been. And I think previous discussion (see Terrell and Mills, pp. 00–00), would support that hypothesis. IBFs only provided an alternative booking vehicle. They affected neither aggregate credit demand nor lending capability.

Question 4. Have IBFs resulted in any observable change in interest relationships? This is a very complex question. On the one hand, we would have expected IBF deposit rates to be lower than those from offshore branches in the Caribbean because of the perceived lower sovereign risk. On the other hand, a substantial portion of the money placed in the Caribbean branches emanates from domestic US sources and is ineligible funding, at least for New York IBFs.

Another point is that deposits placed by non-residents (eligible liabilities under New York law) are worth more than deposits placed by residents, by virtue of the fact that the net income which results from having them fund eligible assets receives more favourable tax treatment. We use an amended form of Mr Giddy's model to take this into account.

On balance, I would contend that the existence of IBFs has in fact resulted in subtle changes in rate relationships, but it would take more research to prove it.

COMMENT

JEFFREY R. SHAFER[1]

Henry Terrell and Rodney Mills have given us a good picture of how IBFs have and have not changed international banking in the first year of their existence. The principal change has been a shift of some international banking transactions to US locations – particularly to New York, where three-quarters of IBFs are located. Aggregate international banking patterns seem not to be significantly altered.

These results should not be surprising, given what the IBF regulations and state tax legislation provided. The authorities removed some restrictions and liberalised taxation on wholesale international banking booked in the United States. But freedom from these restrictions and a more liberal tax climate were already available abroad. Important new opportunities were not created. Therefore, one should not have expected rapid growth of jobs or other tangible benefits to be realised very quickly.

Why, if one could expect such modest results, did the New York Clearing House start the ball rolling? Why did New York State make special tax provisions for IBFs? And why did the Federal Reserve approve IBF regulation? The development of the IBF concept in New York appears to have been an effort to settle long-standing disputes between large international banks in New York and state tax authorities over what international activities should be taxable in New York. The IBF legislation attempted to resolve this conflict by providing for a phased-in exemption from New York taxes, subject to certain restrictions. But from what others have said, it is clear that the legislation has not yet put the New York tax disputes to rest.

The discussion of IBFs by the Federal Reserve Board of Governors suggests to me that their major consideration in approving IBF regulations was a general desire to reduce unnecessary regulatory burdens. Many banks and New York State authorities wanted the liberalisation, and after careful study there did not seem to be strong public policy reasons for not proceeding. The Board focused more on potential problems than on measurable benefits. They weighed closely the implications for competitive equity among different groups of banks before proceeding. From the standpoint of supervisory concerns, there was a potential advantage in having more international activities of US banks booked at home, but this was not thought to be a major consideration since US examiners can and do examine the branches of US banks abroad. The monetary control implications of IBFs had been of concern to the Board and its staff when the issue had first come before them in 1979. The restrictions that were placed on IBFs in the regulations approved in 1981 were designed largely to deal with monetary policy concerns. There was a need to keep banking that is closely related to the US economic activity out of IBFs. With the restrictions, IBFs were thought not to pose a problem for monetary policy. These assessments of benign effects seem to have been borne out so far.

In addition to the specific interests of the various players in setting up IBFs, I think even many who were sceptical of large, measurable short-run benefits were positively inclined towards the IBF proposals because they believed that the IBF initiative would create synergistic effects in the banking and financial sectors of the US economy. Even if large numbers of jobs were not to be forthcoming immediately, over a period of years New York and other US financial centres would be more dynamic and more important. This is the halo effect that Mr Porter alluded to. One year is too short a time to even begin to try to measure these effects, but IBFs have been mentioned as factors in decisions by foreign banks to develop a US presence and in decisions to add staff. One can be optimistic that the longer term hopes for IBFs will be realised.

I would like to take stock quickly of some broader trends in international banking and international bank regulations – trends that the IBFs serve to highlight. National banking markets have been faced with increasing competition from less regulated international markets. Banking offices abroad are expanding their share of deposit-taking and credit relationships with US resident customers. Now the introduction of IBFs means that a growing share of banking activity here is devoted to servicing the needs of non-residents. I agree with Robert Aliber that much of this cross-border banking is due to regulatory distortions. One can only wonder whether this process will be halted before all banking relationships are between banks in one country and customers in another country. A related trend, to which the IBF initiative is a response, has been the development of Eurocurrency banking – the taking of deposits and making of loans in currencies other than those prevailing in local use and issued by the local central bank.

Should we be concerned about these trends? They are moving us towards a less tidy world that is more mysterious to non-specialists in international finance. But these are not sufficient reasons to interfere with the trend. There may be some waste in conducting business over long distances and in arranging complex transactions to reduce the impact of regulations. Credit judgements may be less sharp when customers and their banks are so far apart geographically. But modern telecommunications, data processing and transportation keep these inefficiencies relatively small. Of greater concern are the potential problems for the conduct of monetary policy both domestically and internationally. Central banks have less control over money and money like liabilities relevant to price stability in their economy – liquid bank deposits held by their residents are denominated in their currency.

Banking regulation could move in either of two directions to counter these trends. More regulation of international banking could be undertaken, involving some degree of co-ordination among national regulatory authorities. Or domestic regulation could be reduced. I believe the best course involves some of both.

Many have suggested that an ideal world would be one with no banking regulation. But, to my knowledge, no one has produced a general equilibrium analysis that makes a convincing case for the stability of a financial system free of all regulation whatsoever. This observation does not justify all of the regulations that exist in the world, or the present extent of regulation, or the particular forms of regulation. I am convinced, however, that we will always have a need for some regulation for monetary control.

In this connection, I think we have reason to be concerned about so-called 'property rights' of central banks over currencies. A speaker in an earlier session suggested that central banks ought not think they have 'property rights' over particular currencies. Yet, what is a currency today but a unit of account defined in terms of the liabilities of a particular central bank? A dollar is simply a unit liability of the Federal Reserve System. Does this not give the Federal Reserve some proprietary stake in the dollar, as well as responsibility for it?

Innovations can change the ability to maintain and allocate property rights, but not always for the better. Money is not unique in this respect. Perhaps I can illustrate this general point with an analogy. The development of low-cost, plain-paper copiers created a situation where professors who wrote books and expected to earn royalties from them also copied one anothers books to avoid buying them and paying royalties to others. Some even carried this business further and copied books for use by their students. The new copier technology undermined property rights in books. The copyright laws and their enforcement were tightened up to contain these practices, but they have not been eliminated.

Was the exploitation of cheap copiers an example of the inexorable efficiency of the invisible hand setting appropriate rewards for academic efforts in the writing of books? Was the optimal amount of effort called forth? I think not. Some regulation of copying is better than absolutely none, although just what the optimal regulation should be is a complex issue. Similarly, the question of what banking regulation is optimal from a monetary control point is complex and open to debate, but it is extremely unlikely that an unregulated world where a central bank has no influence whatsoever over the use of its currency in banking would prove to be ideal.

Central banks do need to be concerned about the international avoidance of regulations. The problem is not urgent right now, and it will have to take a back seat for a time to the debt problems that have become more pressing. Moreover, central banks should be open to the relaxation of unnecessary regulation as in the IBF proposals. Still there is a need to bring some order to the evolution of banking regulation internationally.

A formal international rationalisation of financial regulations is not practical. National banking practices differ too widely, and national interests do not dovetail neatly. But neither do we need to think in such grand terms.

I see two general principles that could serve as guides to central banks as they make individual and joint decisions concerning regulations in the years ahead:

(1) A central bank ought not establish regulations for its banks that favour business conducted in other currencies over its own currency of issue.
(2) A central bank ought not establish regulations for its banks that favour business conducted with non-residents over business conducted with residents.

No major central bank follows these principles faithfully today, and perhaps they never will. Pressures to maintain or enhance the competitive position of their institutions and markets, and a desire to hold on to restrictions domestically and in areas where competitive pressures are weaker militate against following the principles. For example, the IBF regulations were a response to the growth of dollar banking abroad in centres where the first principle was not being followed. The IBFs themselves respect the first principle, but not the second.

We are not likely to move to a world where both principles are respected quickly or uniformly. And the principles by themselves do not assure ideal, or even uniform, regulatory structures. But giving weight to these principles will help to contain conflicts and inconsistencies in policies among central banks. Moreover, together with the competitiveness pressures operating internationally, the principles should favour the reduction of unnecessary regulation domestically.

While the IBF regulations are not in accord with one of these principles in practice, they are consistent with a longer run movement towards greater consistency. IBF regulations parallel a trend in the United States towards lower reserve requirements and elimination of interest rate restrictions on domestic deposits that are not convenient transactions vehicles. Deregulation has moved further, faster for international deposits, but favourable experience with IBFs may show the way for further movements on domestic deposit regulations.

The IBF regulations would raise more serious questions about a weakening of monetary control mechanisms internationally if one could not envision a stable domestic banking system operating under similar rules. As it is, the dual structure for regulation of foreign and domestic deposits looks like an interim step in the evolution of US monetary control regulation. A stable situation will only be reached when there is greater consistency in the rules applying to domestic and IBF deposits, and when foreign central banks have also moved towards less discriminatory regulatory structures.

NOTE

1. The views expressed are those of the author and should not be interpreted as those of the Federal Reserve Bank of New York or the Federal Reserve System.

COMMENT

GEORGE SUTIJA

Henry Terrell and Rodney Mills stated in their paper that most of the IBF funds drawn from outside the United States apparently came from the Caribbean area. Although most of these funds went to the New York banks some have been transferred to Florida. During the first months of 1982, 76 banks opened IBF offices and 13 banks were in the process of opening them, all but one are located in Miami. The total amount of IBF assets in Florida banks is rather small, only 2 per cent, or 3 billion dollars of the total of about 150 billion dollars compared with New York which has 78 per cent of IBF assets. However, the number of banking institutions that have established IBFs is about 20 per cent in Miami, whereas in New York the figure is about 50 per cent.

Miami's involvement with IBFs was unthinkable ten or fifteen years ago, because in the 1960s very few of Florida's banks had international departments and the services they offered were very limited. International banking service and the financing of trade were provided for this area by New York or London. During the late 1960s and the early 1970s this situation drastically changed and Miami, by the 1980s, had become an important international banking centre in the United States and a particularly important financial centre for the Latin American countries. In the 1960s, over half a million political immigrants arrived in Florida, mostly from Cuba, and in the 1970s tens of thousands came from Central America and other parts of the Caribbean area. The newly arrived immigrants vigorously engaged in all kinds of economic activities, particularly in foreign trade and international finance. These activities have been facilitated by strong economic and industrial development in Latin America and an influx of funds into some of these countries due to OPEC oil prices in the 1970s. The demand for goods and services in these countries as well as travel between Miami and Latin America increased tremendously. Latins looked to Miami as the place to conduct their businesses, very often in Spanish, and they used financial institutions as a haven for their capital, although they could have obtained better terms for their funds at some other places. Miami was always a tourist attraction for Latin Americans, but in the 1970s it also became a health and educational centre because of the rapid growth of educational institutions of higher learning and outstanding hospitals and other health facilities.

This growth did not go unnoticed by international banks and multinational corporations. During the decade of the 1970s over one hundred multinationals opened their offices in the Miami area to co-ordinate their operations in Latin America. At the same time, fifteen Edge Act Corporations commenced operations in Miami and several have been approved to open their offices. Florida's growing international trade with Latin America and the rest of the world benefited the economic emergence of the State of Florida. This led the State Government to promulgate banking legislation and so encouraged development of foreign banking activities in Florida. The legislation known as the international banking law was enacted in June 1977 and led a number of international banking institutions to open their agencies and representative offices in Miami. In the period 1978–80 fifteen banks received approvals to open agencies in Miami and about thirty banks were inquiring about establishing operations in Florida.

In short Miami became for Latin America what Beirut used to be for the Middle East or what Hong Kong or Singapore are for East and Southeast Asia. Whether Miami will sustain this growth will depend on the economic and political stability of Latin America and Caribbean area, particularly how major Latin countries will resolve the problems of their huge foreign debts, in which some Miami banks participated. Whether Miami will replace the Cayman Islands and the Bahamas as deposit centres for Eurodollars will depend on the advantages that IBFs in Miami banks will offer to their depositors. Banking institutions in the state are becoming more sophisticated and internationally oriented and so more competitive, thus making Miami truly a full-service international banking centre.

COMMENT

ATSUSHI WANATABE

In his presentation, Mr Terrell has come to the conclusion in his study of IBFs that they have not had a significant impact on international banking activities for the moment. I would tend to agree with his views, but to give you another perspective on the IBF, I would like to share with you some experiences of the Bank of Tokyo, New York Agency.

The Bank established an IBF on 3 December 1981. At the initial stage both assets and liabilities which had been previously booked at the agency were simply transferred to the IBF. Subsequent to these booking changes, we have endeavoured to increase the bank's activities in the market. Interestingly, if we look to the bank on the 'lending' side (in other words, cases where the bank places monies), we find that in the past year approximately 65 per cent of all funds have gone to other Japanese banks. The remainder consisting of about 18 per cent going to the European banks, 11 per cent to the American banks and others taking up 6 per cent. If we look at these banks by the location of the entity, we find 45 per cent were IBFs located in the US, 36 per cent were in Europe, and 10 per cent in the Caribbean. Now if just the IBFs were isolated, we find that 86 per cent of the funds placed were to branches and agencies of Japanese banks, only 4.8 per cent of the funds were to US Bank IBFs. It should be noted that due to market pricing, there is incentive for the lender to place with a foreign bank because of premium factors.

To look at this more equally, let us consider the 'taking' side (in other words, cases where the bank received funds). Here we find American banks providing 19 per cent of the overall volume versus 39 per cent for the Japanese banks. As for the funds received from other IBFs in the US, Japanese bank IBFs placed 70 per cent while the American bank IBFs provided 20 per cent.

While this data obviously is only one bank's experience, it has led us to believe the following:

(1) US bank IBF activity in the inter-IBF market is not too significant, to say the least, and presumably due to restrictions in taking in funds from American affiliates located abroad, in the short term, no dramatic change can be envisioned. Japanese IBFs will, however, continue to be active participants due to lack of alternative vehicles in the Caribbean.
(2) Non-IBF entities of the US banks appear to continue to maintain a functional role in the funding area, especially their Caribbean entities which seem to have a comparatively high interest in placing funds. However, no trend indicative of the situation can be determined. It would appear superficially that funding operations have been continued.
(3) Thirdly, but not lastly, the inter-IBF market continued to be a Japanese bank market. In other words, the market is basically the same as the term FF market presently consisting of mostly foreign names.

What has the IBF provided in the sense of new avenues and what can they provide us in the future?

Basically for the Japanese banks, they have been an extension of the term fed funds market providing liquidity, but at a pricing structure that forces foreign banks to pay a premium based not on the quality of the bank individually, but on just the tier for that nationality. At the same time there is a paradox in that because of the market share of the IBFs held by the Japanese, consideration would have to be given to the reliability of the market from an availability standpoint.

The IBF market would, as it now stands, 'sink or swim' on the basis of what Japan's Prime Minister has recently termed 'The Aircraft Carrier Japan'. Unless other participants join the armada, the market will not, I feel, move forward as much as had originally been hoped.

To change the status quo and to serve as the catalyst for increased participation and activity, should not the IBF be authorised to compete on an equal basis with the Euromarket, without constraints. Immediate serious discussions on the ramification, as far as monetary policy, of allowing IBFs to issue negotiable debt instruments should be conducted.

Finally, in closing, I would like to briefly comment on discussions in Japan with regard to creating an International Banking Facility in Tokyo.

In April and May 1983, the Japanese financial community sent a group of senior officers of banks and securities companies on a fact finding mission to New York, London and Singapore as well as other centres of international finance such as the Caymans, the Bahamas, Bermuda, the Isle of Man, etc. While this mission, 'The Offshore Banking Mission', as a group did not reach any definitive conclusions, the head of the mission, a former official of the Japanese Ministry of Finance, has published his personal opinions on the matter. He indicates that in consideration of the increasing importance of international business for the Japanese banking community, as seen is the fact that in the past ten years international assets and profits derived thereof have grown 12 and 8 times respectively, the time is ripe for establishment of a facility. In conceptual terms he favours in the long run a London type of market where there are no regulatory restrictions. However, in more realistic terms, he was of the opinion that an IBF type of approach would probably be more feasible, i.e. constraints would be placed on with whom a particular transaction could be conducted. Under the present framework of structured domestic interest rates, the initial move would probably be to restrict Yen transactions of the IBF and avoid any dramatic impact on the domestic market. The Bank of Tokyo is of the opinion that in the long run IBF dealings in Yen should be seriously considered. Though not necessarily directly linked to the IBF issue, the bank has also favoured the ideas of a Yen B/A market. I feel this would facilitate trade financing, in particular between Asia and Japan, as well as providing in the case of an IBF a more active role for the international banking community in Tokyo.

The establishment of a Japanese IBF should be considered within a framework of general deregulation and to ensure a smooth transition without repercussions domestically, the progress will continue to be at a moderate pace. However, in today's world the Japanese are becoming noted for being 'driven' and I am hopeful that an IBF will seriously be considered.

PERMANENT ADVISORY COMMITTEE ON EURODOLLARS (PACE)

PACE was formed during the conference on Eurodollars to promote study and research and to serve as a forum of discussion on international monetary issues combining scholarly research with practical problems of bankers. Membership is open to all those who express interest and plan to participate in PACE's activities. No membership fee is required. The promoters are all members of the panels of the conference on Eurodollars held in Miami in February 1983 and the conference on 'Strategic Planning in International Banking' held in Rome in May 1984. PACE is planning conferences on the Latin American financial crisis in Caracas, Venezuela, in 1985 and on the East European foreign debts in Dubrovnik, Yugoslavia in 1986. PACE's chairmen are professors Robert Z. Aliber of the University of Chicago and Paolo Savona of the Libera Università Internazionale per gli Studi Sociali, Rome. Secretary and programme co-ordinator is Professor George Sutija from Florida International University. PACE will have the proceedings of the conferences and other studies published by the Macmillan Press Ltd.

Name Index

Aliber, R. Z. 3–4, 5, 6, 49n32, 97, 127, 136n5, 164, 214, 220
Altman, O. 32, 34, 97, 100
Andrew, A. P. 52n66
Argy, V. 49n19
Ashby, D. F. V. 205

Baffi, P. 152, 161n13, 167
Bagehot, W. 105, 106
Baldwin, R. E. 50n35
Baschnagel, H. 48n17
Bellanger, S. 206
Bennett, R. A. 205
Bernstein, E. M. 42, 51n61
Bolton, Sir G. 53–4, 58n2
Borchard, E. 48n3
Bourguinat, H. 50n40
Brandle, A. 49n25
Bryant, R. C. 203n5, n7, 205
Butcher, W. 22

Carli, G. 7–8, 9, 10, 20, 66n6, 92, 98, 160n1, 161n4, n11, n12, 167
Cecco, M. de 40, 51n54
Ciampi, C. 65n1
Clendenning, E. W. 98
Cooke, P. 18, 24
Coombs, C. A. 41, 51n58, 52n62

Dale, R. 58n3
Dam, K. W. 51n60
Denizet, J. 35, 49n33, 50n40
De Welz, G. 148, 161n10
Dini, L. 19, 26, 48n14, 49n26, 61, 65n1
Dregasovitch 27
Dufey, G. 49n33, 51n60

Einzig, P. 22, 38, 40, 49n20, 50n36, n38, 51n46, n48, n55, 81, 98

Ellis, J. G. 114, 121
Emminger, O. 36, 39, 47, 50n42, 51n49, 52n69
Ethier, W. 92, 98

Farber, B. M. 206
Fels, G. 51n44
Ferrari, A. 50n43
Ferras, G. 50n38
Frame, A. J. 52n66
Fratianni, M. 92, 98, 109, 161n3, n8, 167
Friedman, A. 48n9, 49n23, n30
Friedman, I. S. 15, 48n4
Friedman, M. 46, 51n56, n67, 91, 98
Fuoco, F. 148, 161n10

Genberg, H. 175n2
Giddy, I. 6–7, 49n33, 51n60, 100, 121, 136n2, 210
Gilbert, M. 51n45, n61, 52n62
Goodhart, C. 8, 172
Guttentag, J. 121

Hall, W. 24, 48n7, n13
Hardy, C. O. 59n39
Harris, A. 48n6
Hawtrey, R. G. 49n23
Herring, R. 5–6, 99, 101, 105, 115, 121
Hewson, J. 55, 58n4, 92, 93, 98, 100, 116, 121
Higonnet, R. 2–3, 47n2, 50n39
Hirsch, F. 105
Holmes, A. R. 30, 49n31, 98
Howard, D. 57, 58n7

Johnson, K. 57, 58n7
Johnston, R. B. 126, 136n3, 206

Jorge, A. 47n2

Key, S. J. 202n2, 203n11, n15, 206
Keynes, J. M. 26, 27, 49n28, 103
Klein, D. 131, 136n6, 155
Klopstock, F. H. 30, 49n31, 51n59, 98, 100
Kreicher, L. 7, 121, 126–7, 128, 136n4, 206

Laffer, A. 91
Lamfalussy, A. 166
Leijonhufvud, A. 161n7
Light, J. O. 51n53
Little, J. S. 2, 3, 50n34, n37, 58n5

Machlup, F. 51n47, 98, 169
McKinnon, R. I. 98, 116, 121
McMahon, C. W. 98
Marston, R. C. 115, 121
Masera, R. 2, 3, 19, 45, 48n15, 65n2, n4, 66n5, 100, 167
Mayer, H. 2, 3, 49n19, 55, 58n6, 98, 99, 100, 116, 121, 172, 203n7, 206
Mendelsohn, M. S. 53, 58n1, 206
Mills, R. 10–11, 206
Mintz, I. 48n3
Morawetz, V. 52n66

Niehans, J. 55, 58n4, 92, 93, 98, 100, 116, 121
Nixon, R. 42
Norman, M. 35

Oppenheimer, P. 4
Ossola, R. 167
O'Sullivan, P. 11

Parkinson, P. 206
Perroux, F. 50n40
Plender, J. 48n6, n10
Pohl, K. O. 26, 49n27
Porter, R. 11
Powers, J. D. 46
Prochnow, H. V. 50n38, n42

Redlich, F. 52n66
Regan, D. 148, 156, 160
Richardson, J. D. 50n35
Rohatyn, F. 27
Roosa, R. V. 140
Rossi, E. 49n29
Rueff, J. 148–9, 161n12
Rufener, L. A. 52n68

Sakakibara, E. 92, 98
Salazar-Carillo, J. 47n2
Savona, P. 4, 5, 92, 98, 161n3, n6, n8, 167, 220
Schneider, W. M. 52n65
Schumpeter, J. A. 148, 161n11
Schwartz, A. J. 46, 51n56, 52n66, n67
Shafer, J. 11–12
Shibata, Y. 48n12
Short, E. D. 206
Shultz, G. P. 51n60
Smith, A. 27
Sutija, G. 12, 167, 220
Swoboda, A. K. 8, 9, 65n3, 81, 93, 98, 100, 160n2, 175n1, n2

Terrell, H. 10–11, 65n4
Triffin, R. 33, 50n35

Volcker, P. 149, 160

Wade, F. 46
Wallich, H. C. 21, 44–5, 48n11, 49n18, 50n33, 52n64, 68
Wellons, P. A. 25, 49n24
White, W. L. 51n53
Wilkins, M. 50n39
Williams, R. 8, 9, 65n4, 204n16, 206
Winckler, M. 48n3
Wynne, W. H. 48n3

Yeager, L. B. 36, 50n41, n44

Subject Index

airline industry (US), deregulation of 82
American Banking Association 46
arbitrage 6–7, 123–36
  cross-currency arbitrage 133–4
  domestic-offshore arbitrage 125–133
  and interbank market 116–17
'arbitrage tunnel' 127, 128, 129

Banco Ambrosiano 8, 59–60, 61, 131
Bank of England 24, 35–6, 53
Bank for International Settlements (BIS) 35, 38, 44, 166
  Standing Committee of the Eurocurrency Market 141
bank mergers 102
Banking Acts (US) 40, 47
banking school 7, 33
Banque Commerciale pour L'Europe du Nord 53
Basle Communique (1980) 64
Basle Concordat (1974) 24–5, 60
Belgium, and Eurodollar market 33
BIS *see* Bank for International Settlements
Bretton Woods agreement 42, 144, 146, 159
Bundesbank 37–8

Canada
  US removal of funds to 32
  Winnipeg agreement 57
CDs (Certificates of Deposit) 41, 54, 197
  and arbitrage 127–8
  and IBFs 197
central banks 2, 33
  disappointments with Euromarket 36–8
  information from commercial banks 21
  motives for entering Euromarket 34–9
  and regulation 12, 214
  unsound policies of 36–8
Certificates of Deposit *see* CDs
China 53
Citibank 117
Citicorp 17
commercial banks 2
  information to central banks 21–2
  and interest rate limitations 40
  supervision of 20
competition in banking 80, 82–5, 105, 165–6
Cooke Committee (Committee on Banking Regulations and Supervisory Practices) 54, 106, 143, 166

default 15–18, 104
deposit insurance 46–7
Depository Institutions Deregulation and Monetary Control Act (1980) 57, 64
deregulation 3–4, 57, 84
  of US airlines 82
  of US banks 82–3
domestic reserve base 108

Eurobanks
  deposits 31
  models of Eurobanking 62–3
  reserves 44–5, 89

Eurobusiness
consensus analysis of decisions in 106–7
need for international body 107–8
Eurocurrency market 1, 19
cross-Eurocurrency arbitrage 133–4
and interbank market 111
net Eurocurrency 20–1
see also Eurodollar market
Eurodeposits 63, 133
arbitrage between 125
Eurodollar market
characteristics of 30–4
development of 27–30, 52–3, 55–6, 78–82, 140–4
effects of growth of 83–7
Eurodollars defined 77
net size 20–1, 68–9, 99
and New York money market 39–43
policy issues 174–5
reasons for growth of 135–6
see also Eurocurrency market, regulation, supervision
exchange rates 169, 171–2
disadvantages of systems of 159, 162
impact of Eurodollar market on 35, 85–7, 95–6, 107–8
exchange risk 32

FDIC 127, 128
Federal Reserve
as lender of last resort 162
proposals of 44–5
and Regulation Q 40–1, 55
Florida, IBFs in 215–16
foreign debt *see* default, international debt
Foreign Direct Investment Requirements 56
foreign exchange, management of in interbank market 115–16

GAB (General Agreements to Borrow) 143

Germany
banks in, in 1920s 21–2
Bundesbank 37–8
and Eurodollar market 37–8
intervention in international credit activity 141
restrictions on foreign banks 27–8
Group of 10 72, 142, 143
Group of 30 111

Herrstatt collapse 128

IBFs (international banking facilities) 10–11, 12, 183–5, 206–8
as competitive advantage to US banks 190–2, 209–10
and growth of international banking 192–6, 210
and growth of US banking 185–9, 209
and interest rate relationships 196–8, 210
and offshore branches of US banks 198–202
regulations 214–15: in Florida 215–17; in Japan 217–19
restrictions on 207–8, 211
IMF *see* International Monetary Fund
inflation 19
and credit creation 171
and debt default 16
impact of Eurodollars on 21, 87–90, 107, 164, 169
interbank market 4, 5–6, 21, 99–100
abuse of 22
avoidance of tax restraints 116–17
and foreign exchange and maturity positions 115–16
functions of 100, 111–18
international role of 101, 102–3
lending in 1920s 22
lending in 1980s 22–3
and liquidity adjustment 111–15
and lowering of transaction costs 101

and non-banks 113–15
policy concerns about 118–19
interest rates 54
domestic and external relationship 124, 125
and Euromarkets 35, 80, 124–5
and interbank arbitrage 123
interest rate relationships and IBFs 196–8, 210
interest rate risk 116
and maturity transformation 25–6
in USA 16, 40, 54
international banking
assets of 193
competition in 80, 82–5, 105, 165–6
IBFs and growth of 192–6, 210
lack of information from 20
offshore banking and growth of 84–5
regulation, supervision of 43, 67
international banking facilities *see* IBFs
international debt 176–8
Euromarkets and 164–6
Latin American debt 15–18, 104
need for reform 43–4, 47
problems of 154–7, 172–5, 179–80
risks of 22–4
International Monetary Fund (IMF) 10, 102, 143
Committee on Banking Regulations and Supervisory Practices 54, 106, 143, 166
and debt-servicing 177–8, 179
and LDCs 16–17
resources of 26
role of 174–5
international monetary standard 139
international standard 158–9, 169, 170–2
and sovereignty 150–4
Italian banking 36–7

Japan
IBFs in 217–19
tax relief for banks in 18

Latin America, debt problem 15–16, 177
LDCs
IMF and 177
lending risk of 15–18, 20, 104, 154–7, 179–80
lender of last resort 143
Federal Reserve system as 162
need for 174
problems of 147–50
liquidity
adjustment of in interbank market 111–15
and central banks 34–8
creation in Euromarket 93–4
loan-loss reserves 17–18
need for 43
tax systems and 18
of US and UK banks 17–18

McFadden restrictions 57
maturity positions in interbank market 115–16
maturity transformation 25, 31–2, 54–5
Mexico 173
debt default 16
Miami, IBFs in 215–16
monetary base
control of 163–4
international monetary base 109–10
monetary policy, Eurodollars' impact on 87–90
monetary sovereignty 145–6
Moscow Narodny Bank 27
multiplier 62–3, 90–3, 107, 169
and banking stability 103, 104

New York money market 39–43
non-banks
financial services 56
and interbank market 113–15

offshore banking 3–4, 5, 31
and domestic banking 88–90, 100, 105–6

offshore banking—*continued*
growth of 80–2
and growth of banking competition 83–5, 105–6
financial incentives for entering 78–80
implications of growth of 94–7: domestic monetary implications 96; monetary implications 87–94
multiplier in 90–3
national differences in regulation of 78–9
oil prices 70
OPEC 70, 102

PACE (Permanent Advisory Committee on Eurodollars) 220

Radcliffe Report (1959) 39, 54
regulation
cost of 126, 131, 134
in domestic banking, and growth of Euromarkets 78–80, 126
of Eurodollar markets 2–4, 7, 8, 9, 16, 30–1, 44, 56–8, 72–3, 106, 162–4, 212–4
grounds for 168–70
problems of 144–7
and supervision compared 166–7
Regulation Q 40–1, 53, 55, 66
Regulations D and M 141
reserve ratios, raising of 141–2
reserve requirements 53, 55
and Euromarket control 44–5, 61–2, 64, 72, 80
risk
exchange risk 32
LDC lending risk 15–18, 20, 104, 154–7, 179–80
market-price-of-risk view 125–6
in offshore banking 79
pricing risk 173
rollover risk 32
sovereign risk 16, 23
Roosa bonds 140
Russia
Moscow Narodny Bank 27
offshore dollar deposits 53, 80–1

SDRs (Special Drawing Rights) 146
SEC (Securities and Exchange Commission) 117
Smithsonian Agreement 150, 153
sovereign risk 16, 23
Special Drawing Rights (SDRs) 146
sterling crises 35–6, 39, 53
supervision 18–19, 54

taxation
avoidance in interbank market 116–17
to cover foreign debt 26
relief to banks 18

UK
banks in, and origins of Eurodollar market 29–30
clearing banks 17
and Euromarket 35–6
sterling crises 35–6, 39, 53
USA 16, 18, 40–2, 80–1
Banking Acts 40, 47
banks: competitive advantage due to IBFs 190–2, 209–10; offshore branches of and IBFs 198–202
credit crunch 69–70
deregulation in 82–3
IBFs and growth of banking in 185–9, 209
moving of funds to Canada 32
New York money market 39–43

Voluntary Foreign Credit Restraint Program 56

Winnipeg Agreement 57

xenocurrency market 67, 152